Critical Issues in Preparing Effective Early Childhood Special Education Teachers for the 21st Century Classroom: Interdisciplinary Perspectives

A Volume in:
Contemporary Perspectives in Special Education

Series Editors
Anthony F. Rotatori
Festus E. Obiakor

Contemporary Perspectives in Special Education

Series Editors

Anthony F. Rotatori
Saint Xavier University

Festus E. Obiakor
Valdosta State University

*Multicultural Education for Learners with
Special Needs in the Twenty-First Century* (2014)
Festus E. Obiakor and Anthony F. Rotatori

*Autism Spectrum Disorders
Inclusive Community for the 21st Century* (2012)
Julie A. Deisinger, Sandra Burkhardt, Timothy J. Wahlberg,
Anthony F. Rotatori, Festus E. Obiakor

Critical Issues in Preparing Effective Early Childhood Special Education Teachers for the 21st Century Classroom: Interdisciplinary Perspectives

Edited by

Anthony F. Rotatori
Festus Obiakor

INFORMATION AGE PUBLISHING, INC.
Charlotte, NC • www.infoagepub.com

KH

Library of Congress Cataloging-in-Publication Data

Critical issues in preparing effective early childhood special education
teachers for the 21st century classroom : interdisciplinary perspectives /
edited by Anthony F. Rotatori, Festus E. Obiakor.
   pages cm. -- (Contemporary perspectives in special education)
   Includes bibliographical references and index.
   ISBN 978-1-68123-056-6 (pbk. : alk. paper) -- ISBN 978-1-68123-057-3
(hardcover : alk. paper) -- ISBN 978-1-68123-058-0 (ebook) 1. Early
childhood teachers--Training of--United States. 2. Early childhood
teachers--In-service training--United States 3. Special education
teachers--Training of--United States. 4. Special education
teachers--In-service training--United States. 5. Early childhood special
education--United States. I. Rotatori, Anthony F. II. Obiakor, Festus E.
   LB1732.3.C75 2016
   372.21--dc23
                          2015009090

Printed in the United States of America

5/9/16

CONTENTS

LIST OF CONTRIBUTORS

Lynn Adams
Associate Professor
Department of Communication Sciences and Disorders
Dewar College of Education and Human Services
Valdosta State University
Valdosta, Georgia

Bob Algozzine
Professor, Department of Educational Leadership
College of Education
University of North Carolina
Charlotte, North Carolina

Eugene F. Asola
Assistant Professor
Department of Kinesiology & Physical Education
Dewar College of Education and Human Services
Valdosta State University
Valdosta, Georgia

Tachelle Banks
Department Chair and Associate Professor of Special Education
Department of Teacher Education
College of Education and Human Services
Cleveland State University
Cleveland, Ohio

Floyd D. Beachum
Program Director for Educational Leadership
Bennett Professor of Urban School Leadership
College of Education
Lehigh University
Bethlehem, Pennsylvania

Jamie Bird
Director of Student Teaching and Field Experiences
Dewar College of Education and Human Services
Valdosta State University
Valdosta, Georgia

Patti C. Campbell
Coordinator of the Education Specialist Degree in Special Education and Professor
Department of Early Childhood and Special Education
Dewar College of Education and Human Services
Valdosta State University
Valdosta, Georgia

Gina M. Doepker
Associate Professor and Director of the Sullivan Literacy Center
Department of Early Childhood and Special Education
Dewar College of Education and Human Services
Valdosta State University
Valdosta, Georgia

Critical Issues in Preparing Effective Early Childhood Special Education Teachers for the 21st Century Classroom: Interdisciplinary Perspectives, pages vii–ix.
Copyright © 2016 by Information Age Publishing

Margaret M. Flores
Associate Professor, Special Education, Rehabilitation,
and Counseling
College of Education
Auburn University
Auburn, Alabama

Don T.D. Gala
Gala Educational Consulting
Hixson, Tennessee

María L. Gabriel
Equity and Diversity Coordinator
Poudre School District
Fort Collins, Colorado

Brian L. Gerber
Interim Dean
Dewar College of Education and Human Services
Valdosta State University
Valdosta, Georgia

Carolyn Gish
Field Experience and Clinical Practice Coordinator and
Instructor
Department of Early Childhood and Special Education
Dewar College of Education and Human Services
Valdosta State University
Valdosta, Georgia

Jessica B. Graves
Assistant Professor
Department of Early Childhood and Special Education
Dewar College of Education and Human Services
Valdosta State University
Valdosta, Georgia

Satasha L. Green
Dean and Professor
College of Education
Chicago State University
Chicago, Illinois

Vanessa Hinton
Lecturer, Special Education, Rehabilitation, and
Counseling
College of Education
Auburn University
Auburn, Alabama

Karla Hull
Professor and Coordinator
Higher Education Leadership
Dewar College of Education and Human Services
Valdosta State University
Valdosta, Georgia

Kelly A. Heckaman
Associate Professor and Coordinator
Online MAT Programs in Special Education
Department of Early Childhood and Special Education
Dewar College of Education and Human Services
Valdosta State University
Valdosta, Georgia

Florah Luseno
Chairperson
Graduate Programs in Education Department
Chicago State University
Chicago, Illinois

Deb L. Marciano, Associate Professor
Department of Early Childhood and Special Education
Dewar College of Education and Human Services
Valdosta State University
Valdosta, Georgia

James Martinez
Assistant Professor, Undergraduate and Graduate
Programs,
Middle Grades, Secondary, Reading, and Deaf
Education
Dewar College of Education and Human Services
Valdosta State University
Valdosta, Georgia

Carlos McCray
Division Chair and Associate Professor
Educational Leadership, Administration, and Policy
Graduate School of Education
Fordham University
Bronx, New York

Ewa McGrail
Associate Professor and Unit Leader, Language and
Literacy Education
Department of Middle and Secondary Education
College of Education
Georgia State University
Atlanta, Georgia

J. Patrick McGrail
Associate Professor, Department of Communication
Jacksonville State University
Jacksonville, Alabama

Sunday O. Obi
Professor, College of Professional Studies
School of Education
. Kentucky State University
Frankfort, Kentucky

Festus E. Obiakor
Department Head and Professor
Early Childhood and Special Education
Dewar College of Education and Human Services
Valdosta State University
Valdosta, Georgia

Elizabeth Omiteru
Instructional Technology Support Specialist
Dewar College of Education and Human Services
Valdosta State University
Valdosta, Georgia

Barbara J. Radcliffe
Department Head and Assistant Professor
Middle Grades, Secondary, Reading, and Deaf
Education
Dewar College of Education and Human Services
Valdosta State University
Valdosta, Georgia

Alicja Rieger
Associate Professor
Department of Early Childhood and Special Education
Dewar College of Education and Human Services
Valdosta State University
Valdosta, Georgia

Anthony F. Rotatori
Professor Emeritus
Department of Psychology
School of Arts and Sciences
St. Xavier University
Chicago, Illinois

Marty Sapp
Professor, Counseling Psychology
Department of Educational Psychology
University of Wisconsin-Milwaukee
Milwaukee, Wisconsin

Anthony Scheffler
Associate Dean and Professor
Dewar College of Education and Human Services
Valdosta State University
Valdosta, Georgia

Margaret Shippen
Associate Professor, Special Education, Rehabilitation,
and Counseling
College of Education
Auburn University
Auburn, Alabama

Shaunita D. Strozier
Assistant Professor and Program Coordinator
Department of Early Childhood and Special Education
Dewar College of Education and Human Services
Valdosta State University
Valdosta, Georgia

Stephanie Taylor
Compliance Officer
Montgomery County Public Schools
Montgomery, Alabama

Cheryl A. Utley
Director, Center on Urban Research and
Education
Graduate Programs in Education Department
Chicago State University
Chicago, Illinois

Sean Warner
Dean, School of Education
Clark Atlanta University
Atlanta, Georgia

FOREWORD

Brian Gerber

As one of the creators of Valdosta Early College Academy (VECA) at Valdosta State University (VSU), I have always been excited about innovative ways to solve educational problems of at-risk students. As a science teacher, I have always been excited about helping at-risk students to be interested in STEM (Science, Technology, Engineering, and Mathematics). Now as a teacher educator and Interim Dean of the Dewar College of Education and Human Services, I worry about how we can prepare effective educators (in this case, early childhood special education teachers) to make a difference in our complex and competitive society. While I acknowledge that what we do in Colleges/Schools of Education influence what happens in pre-K–12 programs, I do not believe we are there yet. We have not fully used interdisciplinary perspectives in tackling our general and special educational problems. We are still consumed by the blame game while our children and youth suffer. Thanks to Obiakor, Rieger, and Rotatori, we now have one of those books that will make a difference in the lives of young children with and without "special" needs. This timely book, *Critical Issues in Preparing Effective Early Childhood Special Education Teachers for the Twenty-First Century Classroom: Interdisciplinary Perspectives*, challenges all of us to make a difference, no matter how minuscule, in the lives of children and youth with and without "special" needs.

Critical Issues in Preparing Effective Early Childhood Special Education Teachers for the 21st Century Classroom: Interdisciplinary Perspectives, pages xi–xiii.
Copyright © 2016 by Information Age Publishing

This book is a must-read for teachers, teacher educators, and anyone interested in making sure effective early childhood special education teachers are in our schools. This has always been our goal at VSU. It is no surprise that most of the book's invited contributors are scholars and educators from VSU. Obiakor, Rieger, and Rotatori carefully crafted a series of compelling topics that focus on forward-thinking and innovative ideas and practices associated with early childhood special education classrooms and teachers. Ideas for the classroom or to better prepare teachers literally leap from the pages of this book screaming to be used. Specifically, Chapter 1 focuses on the "then" and "now" of teacher education; Chapter 2 discusses performance assessments of teaching and the current discourse on teacher education; Chapter 3 describes how we can dismantle deficit thinking through teacher education; Chapter 4 describes how we can prepare teachers and leaders for urban and rural special education in this age of change; and Chapter 5 examines interdisciplinary collaboration in teacher education to support students with exceptionalities. In addition, Chapter 6 addresses how to prepare teachers to maximize the potential of young students with gifts and talents; Chapter 7 explains how teachers and practitioners can be prepared to work with children with autism spectrum disorders; Chapter 8 discusses how teachers can be prepared for adaptive physical education for young children with special needs; Chapter 9 presents how teachers can be prepared to use centers such as VSU Sullivan Literacy Center to build relationships between schools, families, and communities; and Chapter 10 explains how to empower teachers to teach with comics literature in K–12 classrooms. Chapter 11 delineates how we can use technology to prepare teachers and leaders in early childhood special education; Chapter 12 examines the use of online education programs to prepare 21st century classrooms; Chapter 13 evaluates the clinical and field-based teacher preparation pedagogy and professional development of teacher educators; Chapter 14 explains how we can forge evidence-based inquiry and teaching in teacher education; and Chapter 15 discusses how we can move forward with teacher education, general education, special education, and urban education.

Critical Issues in Preparing Effective Early Childhood Special Education Teachers for the Twenty-First Century Classroom brings to life the reality that performance evaluation is an important element of teacher preparation. It also reiterates the fact that Colleges/Schools of Education are under intense pressure and scrutiny from parents, politicians, and professional accrediting agencies to produce better teachers while reducing the cost of education and the time it takes to complete a degree, all while their budgets are being slashed. Right or wrong, these are the realities. Yes, this book brings focus and clarity to key topics in the preparation of early childhood special education teachers. But it is deeper than that! The collection of insightful chapters in this book eases our fears, especially those associated with new realities in general and special education. To a large measure, it empowers readers with information that allows them to embrace change. I urge more readers to open their minds to the many new educational possibilities that are contained in this book. Finally, in my conclusion, I agree with Obiakor, Rieger, and Rotatori that this book opens more doors for "insightful scholarly discussions, creative solutions, and innovative perspectives."

Brian Gerber,
Interim Dean
Dewar College of Education and Human Services
Valdosta State University

PREFACE

Festus E. Obiakor and Alicja Rieger

Since the passage of the Education for All Handicapped Children Act of 1975, early childhood special education has changed dramatically. Services, educational intervention, assessment, and clinical practice aspects for serving young children with special needs have evolved and been modified based on research, evidenced-based practices, and technological advances. Along with these aspects, state and federal governments and professional organizations have mandated standards for teacher preparation at institutions of higher education. These mandated standards have resulted in increased accountability by those instructing future early special education teachers and clinicians as well as those teachers and clinicians who serve young children. Positively, this accountability environment has led to competency-based programs that were formulated from evidence-based research. Today, early childhood special education has transformed to meet the special needs of a diverse student population. However, early childhood special education is challenged by decreased funding and a demand for cost effectiveness. The purpose of this volume is to provide the reader with insightful scholarly discussions, creative solutions, and innovative perspectives related to providing cost-effective early childhood special education services for the 21st century classroom. This is accomplished by comprehensive chapter presentations by diverse early childhood special education professionals and other related professionals from rural, urban, and suburban areas.

Critical Issues in Preparing Effective Early Childhood Special Education Teachers for the 21st Century Classroom: Interdisciplinary Perspectives, pages xv–xvii.
Copyright © 2016 by Information Age Publishing

In this book, we address a number of educational topics that focus on teacher preparation of early childhood and special education teachers. A brief description of the chapters follows. Chapter 1 offers a discussion of a historical precedent and gives an overview of the traditional models of teacher preparation and alternative pathways to teacher certification, followed by an interdisciplinary dialogue concerned with contemporary issues, trends, and perspectives in the field of teacher preparation. Chapter 2 examines the innovative utilization and value of incorporating electronic portfolio in teacher performance evaluation. Chapter 3 delineates how students from culturally and linguistically diverse backgrounds are negatively viewed at times by educators and service providers. Embedded in the chapter are common myths heard in schools and how elements of critical race theory can be utilized to deconstruct them. Chapter 4 discusses how teachers can be best prepared to work with culturally and diverse (CLD) and urban young children and youth with special needs to transform them into valuable members of society. This is essential because traditionally there has been a disconnect between the content that CLD students are taught and the curriculum that they should be exposed to. Chapter 5 substantiates the critical educational practice of preparing educators to communicate across disciplines to enhance learner outcomes for students with exceptionalities. With this focus, the chapter examines how to develop successful working relationships and interdisciplinary supports for students with exceptionalities. Chapter 6 points out a need for national educational guidelines concerned with practices related to identifying, assessing, and instructing students with gifts and talents. This need is becoming more critical due to governmental entities that are demanding decreases in educational funding. However, world history has shown that the contributions of gifted and talented citizens is invaluable. With this in mind, this chapter provides teachers with evidence-based strategies and programs for teaching and promoting smart classroom environments for our nation's gifted and talented students. Chapter 7 points out that there is a noted increase in children identified with Autism Spectrum Disorders (ASD), which is challenging teachers, mental health providers, and parents to address their unique social, behavioral, academic, and emotional needs. This chapter focuses on how teachers and practioners can be prepared to work with children with ASD to address their special needs. Chapter 8 highlights the value of personnel development in adapted physical education which can lead to meaningful student success and positive education outcomes for students with disabilities. The chapter delineates instructional procedures for adapting or modifying developmentally appropriate physical activities for students with disabilities to enhance their motor and physical skills. Chapter 9 discusses the Valdosta State University Sullivan Literacy Center, which exemplifies a successful partnership between schools, families, and communities that leads to positive academic learning. Such partnerships become essential due to their correlation with enhanced student learning outcomes. Chapter 10 emphasizes the valuable contribution that innovative, alternative, and creative instructional practices can have on student learning of students with exceptionalities. With this focus, the chapter illustrates the potential academic value of comic and graphic media in the classroom and encourages teachers across disciplines to include these alternative media in their teaching tool box. Chapter 11 specifies that technology has become an integral part of the lesson plan in classrooms for students with exceptionalities. However, seamlessly integrating technology into an early childhood special education classroom can be challenging. This chapter discusses the practical infusion of technology into classrooms for students with early childhood special education needs. Chapter 12 relates that while most university teacher preparation is on campus, there is a growing utilization of high quality online teacher degree and certification programs. This chapter describes an online master's education degree program, which was named one of the "Best Online Special Education Degree Programs" by *BestOnlineColleges.org* in 2013. Chapter 13 points out the emphasis by professional teaching associations and accreditation organizations regarding clinical and field-based teacher preparation pedagogy and their connection to improved student learning. This chapter illustrates ways to redesign teacher observation, field and clinical experiences so that students experience a more inclusive, intense, and meaningful clinical and school-based exposure. Chapter 14 points out that teacher education today has become more evidence-based, which necessitates that teacher preparation programs prepare their students to be educational researchers. This chapter delineates ways to do this formulated from research practices from multiple disciplines. Chapter 15 presents a scholarly dialogue with faculty and researchers across several disciplines, such as general education, special education, and urban education on what teacher preparation might look like in the future.

CHAPTER 1

TEACHER EDUCATION—THEN AND NOW

Deb L. Marciano

"The U.S. Department of Education estimates that schools and departments of education produce about 220,000 certified teachers a year," Secretary of Education, Arne Duncan predicted in 2009 (U.S. Department of Education). However, not all teacher candidates are certified through Colleges of Education. "More men, more non-whites, more mature, life-experienced, educated individuals are teaching in the nation's K–12 schools as a result of a proliferation of alternative routes to teacher certification throughout the country" (National Center for Education Information, 2005, para. 1). Although alternative certifications are readily available, the vast majority of teachers have taken the traditional route to their profession, through teacher education programs situated within colleges and universities. These teacher preparation programs vary greatly, and licensing is awarded by each respective state.

Countless initiatives, research studies, grants, programs, restructurings, theories, recommendations, government regulations, and the public have repeatedly scrutinized the efficacy of the preparation of teachers to serve in elementary and secondary education schools. In this chapter, it is not my intention to politicize, rationalize, defend, or critique any policy or approach of America's sometimes repeated educational history, but rather I attempt to provide a historical frame-

Critical Issues in Preparing Effective Early Childhood Special Education Teachers for the 21st Century Classroom: Interdisciplinary Perspectives, pages 1–9.
Copyright © 2016 by Information Age Publishing

work in which to ground the subsequent chapters of this book. This is how we got here—certified educators who mostly serve the public schools of our country, for more than the past 200 years.

TEACHER EDUCATION IN THE 19TH CENTURY

Public schools in America developed as a result of President Thomas Jefferson's Virginia legislation, *Bill for the More General Diffusion of Knowledge*, in 1779 (Webb, Metha, & Jordan, 2003). This plan was intended to provide education for the masses, with basic knowledge and the goal of shaping good government, public safety, and happiness. All White children could attend free classes in reading, writing, history, and arithmetic for three years (Webb et al., 2003). In the early 1820s, President Humphrey of Amherst (MA) College said,

> It is impossible to have good schools for the want of good teachers . . . Many who offer themselves are deficient in everything; in spelling, in reading, in penmanship, in geography, in grammar, and in common arithmetic. The majority would be dismissed . . . if competent instructors could be had. (Harper, 1939, pp. 12–13)

In the early 1830s, the first Secretary of the Massachusetts State Board of Education, education reformer Horace Mann, proposed a system of free, universal, and nonsectarian schooling. Schools of this nature became known as Common Schools. The purpose of these common schools (so-called because they were to serve the common people) was to create democratic citizens, no matter their religion or social class. These schools were funded by taxes and fees paid by parents, building on Jefferson's notion of schooling for a democratic society. The period of 1830–1865 is known as the Common School Movement. Common schools offered basic curriculum and emerged as schools open to all children of different social and economic groups (Harper, 1939). During this period, women tended to be the teachers, and as the number of schools increased, an increasing need for common training in all subjects became more and more necessary. Catherine Beecher founded the Hartford Female Seminary (1828) and the Western Institute for Women (1832) in New England, both important institutions offering opportunities for females to become teachers (Webb et al., 2003). The need for teacher preparation was becoming apparent. By 1825, James G. Carter, dubbed the "Father of the American Normal School" advocated for "an institution for the education of teachers . . . which should be under the direction of the state . . . because we should thus secure at once, a uniform, intelligent and independent tribunal for decisions on the qualification of teachers" (Harper, 1939, p. 16). This marks the beginning of teacher education.

In the mid-1800s, the resulting establishment of normal schools created the curriculum and "patterns of preservice teacher preparation, and made elementary-school teaching an important career path for women" (Ornstein, Levine, Gutek, & Vocke, 2011, pp. 139–140). The normal schools "recruited a class of students who had limited opportunities for advanced education elsewhere or achievement in other professions than teaching. Such opportunities were especially meager for girls" (Borrowman, 1965, p. 22). Requirements for teaching were often merely the teacher's completion of the grade level she/he was to teach and the ability to maintain appropriate behavior in the classroom. As standards increased, expectations were that the teacher would have completed at least a year or more level of knowledge above her/his students (Labaree, 2008). Grammar school and high school graduates became elementary teachers while "college graduates frequently taught for a while until something better came along" (Labaree, 2008, p. 291). Unfortunately, it seemed that the level of societal respect for elementary teachers (those from the grammar or early childhood levels) was low from the onset of teacher education programs.

Education reformer and proponent of free, universal public education, Horace Mann, envisioned these institutions as places to prepare "a group of well-educated and professionally skilled teachers who could serve as the model for public school teachers throughout the country" (Labaree, 2008, p. 292). In a letter to his contemporary, Henry Barnard, Mann identified his goal for the normal schools to "make better teachers . . . teachers who should know more of the nature of children, of youthful developments, more of the subject to be taught, more in harmony with the natural development of the young mind" (Borrowman, 1965, p. 65).

In a 20-year span (1839–1859), 15 normal schools were established for the preparation of teachers in America. The first normal schools opened in Lexington, West Newton, Framingham, Barre, Westfield, and Bridgewater in Massachusetts. In 1844, another was established in Albany, New York, followed by New Britain, Connecticut, and then much further to the west in Ypsilanti, Michigan (1849). Three more normal schools were established back in the east: Salem, Massachusetts (1853), Providence, Rhode Island (1854), and in Trenton, New Jersey (1855). The central part of the nation was again represented in North Bloomington, Illinois, (later at Normal) and back again to the east, in Millersville, Pennsylvania, (both in 1857). Minnesota joined the normal school movement in 1858. By 1850, women who had previously been teaching in their homes, called Dame Schools, made the transition to being trained in normal schools (the first formal teacher education programs). Women were encouraged to go into teaching, especially for younger children. However, in doing so, stereotypes of the women teachers of young children began to take root.

> God seems to have made woman peculiarly suited to guide and develop the infant mind, and it seems . . . very poor policy to pay a man 20 or 22 dollars a month, for teaching children the ABCs, when a female could do the work more successfully at one third of the price. —Littleton School Committee, Littleton, Massachusetts, 1849 (Hess, 2010, p. 136)

During this time period, mention of the first schools specifically designed for children with special needs cropped up across the East. The Perkins Institution (http://www.perkins.org) and Massachusetts Asylum for the Blind was established in 1829 in Boston (where 150 years later Helen Keller was educated). The Experimental School for Teaching and Training Idiotic Children was founded in 1848, later changing its name in (1850) to the Massachusetts School for Idiotic and Feeble-Minded Youth (now the Fernald School; see Asylum Projects, 2012). This school later became a model for education in the field of educating children with mental retardation (1887–1924). A similar institution, New York State Asylum for Idiots, was authorized in 1851, followed by a private school, Pennsylvania Training School for Feeble-Minded Children, in 1853 (Sass, 2014). The Horace Mann School for the Deaf and Hard of Hearing, founded in Boston in 1869, is the oldest public day school for children for the Deaf and Hard of Hearing in the United States (Boston Public Schools, 2008). There is no mention of formal or specialized training programs of teachers for these special populations at that time.

TEACHER EDUCATION IN THE 20TH CENTURY

Until the 1900s, there is little to no mention of African Americans in teacher preparation programs. It is important to note the inception of a program devoted to the preparation of African American girls for the profession of teaching grammar school. After graduation from the Scotia Seminary for Girls in 1893 (North Carolina), Mary McCleod Bethune advocated for the education of African American children. She founded the Daytona Normal and Industrial Institute for Negro Girls in Daytona, Florida, in 1904, which later became the current Bethune-Cookman College (Bethune-Cookman University, 2013; Sass, 2014).

In constant expansion of pedagogical methods, normal schools began utilizing Maria Montessori's early childhood teachings, following the Italian scholar's first visit to the United States in 1912. This approach to early childhood education, outlined in *The Montessori Method* (Montessori, 1909), shaped beliefs and practices regarding children's development and best practice (Lillard, 1972). Private Montessori schools are still popular today in cities around the world; and practice teaching in local public schools became part of the emerging curriculum. In the1920s, a national trend of moving away from the normal school model, which was frequently viewed as offering "sub-collegiate teacher training" (Pushkin, 2001), into Teacher Colleges. In a struggle to remain true to theories of child development while striving to attain a higher level of pedagogy, methodology, and content knowledge that was offered by college-degree offering institutions, the professional path to teacher certification produced evidence of tension over where teacher education should take place. Puskin (2001) concluded that, "in essence, normal schools and four-year colleges were in direct competition rather than in cooperative relationships" (p. 2).

By becoming degree-granting institutions, the former normal schools would encourage men to enter the profession, many of whom were returning from the first World War. Male entrance into teacher education programs extended to meet the growing need for qualified high school teachers. Webb et al. (2003) described the developing perception of distinction between those teachers at the elementary level (mostly women) and those at the secondary level. Although training was similar for both levels, society placed a higher level of status for teachers who chose to teach in secondary schools. More teacher candidates opted for high school training, and in the 1920s and 1930s, junior high schools were being created to transition from elementary to high schools. These programs included extended elementary curriculum and some vocational and commercial courses, thus calling for teacher education colleges and universities to train teachers for the changing needs of America's growing population. School systems encouraged candidates to earn a degree beyond a 2-year certification, while extending incentives in pay raises for teachers earning 36 credits beyond a bachelor's degree, and slightly more for those earning a master's degree in education. By the 1940s, more than 50% of young adolescents in America were attending junior high schools (Ornstein et al., 2011).

As World War II ended in 1945, the enrollment in colleges and universities across America grew. Barriers were shattered when approximately 238,000 discharged military became teachers through the GI Bill (Labaree, 2008; Sass, 2014). It was not until the mid-1950s, however, that the majority of American teachers held a 4-year college degree (Warren, 1989). With the sweep of political and social movements, the mid-1960s onward brought radical changes to schools across the country. Teacher preparation programs quickly adapted to keep up with desegregation, compensatory education, magnet schools, open classrooms, and flexible scheduling (Cuban, 1989). Changes in the 1970s and 1980s led teacher education programs to higher academic standards and a common curriculum. Following publication of *A Nation at Risk* (National Commission on Excellence in Education, 1983), states raised graduation requirements and curriculum returned once again to more traditional studies of sciences, math, and foreign languages.

Two major reports on teaching and teacher education emerged in 1986. *Tomorrow's Teachers: A Report of the Holmes Group*, and *A Nation Prepared: Teachers for the Twenty-first Century* (recommendations from the Carnegie Forum on Education and the Economy's Task Force on Teaching as a Profession) argued that classroom teachers needed to see themselves, and be accepted by the public, as professionals (Herbst, 1989). Yet Herbst (1989) illuminated the tension evident at the beginning of the 20th century among education professionals—colleges, universities, and the normal schools; city, state, and county superintendents; professional journal editors and organization members—as to how to best improve the profession, balancing special fields as well as liberal and vocational education.

Some critical questions remain enigmatic in education. What has changed? Where are we headed as a profession? How do we best service public schools through cultural and racial population changes, technology barely imaginable a century ago, and social contextual changes that seem to have little support for teachers and the value of education, complicated by families who are struggling racially, culturally, and economically? A major area of instruction in many education programs continues to be classroom and behavior management. As school districts purchase prepackaged curriculum, adopt (or reject) varying forms of standards, and struggle to find the balance between teaching for life skills and teaching to the test, the same problems identified by scholars and educators more than a century ago still remain today.

HOW FAR HAVE WE COME? INSIDE THE NEW MILLENNIUM

Technology has taken the world of education by storm. As new technology emerges, an already overextended curriculum is expected to provide training for teachers, such as in-service training usually offered through state initiatives. Tondeur et al. (2012) found that teachers are underutilizing technology due to a gap of what pre-service teachers learn in their programs and how teachers use technology in their classrooms. Reasons include not knowing how to use technology, insufficient access to equipment in schools, lack of time, and lack of skills (Tondeur et al., 2012). Drury and Baer (2011) contended that without the ability to use technology, students will "never move beyond being consumers of products and ideas" (p. 96).

Today, high-stakes testing (i.e., No Child Left Behind), rigorous standards (i.e., Common Core), and taxpayers' dissatisfaction with teacher salaries, low achievement, and failing buildings are reflected in the news on a daily basis. Education is under scrutiny yet again! Teacher education programs rush to make adjustments, follow trends, and try to keep abreast of the newest pedagogy, technology, and theories. Puskin (2001) suggested that gaps exist because educators fail to "acknowledge the many different fabrics and flavors of the education profession" (p. 200).

A noteworthy comment by a superintendent of schools in 1882 argued that the value of teacher educators, as distinct from other faculty, was often not taken into consideration, even today: "The university professor may have his chair and from it satisfy a well-established demand, but the normal-school professor must live in his saddle in the field and on the march" (Harper, 1939, p. 116). As Harper (1939) predicted,

> The success of the teachers colleges depends not on its ability to build up courses with imposing names, nor load its catalogs with decorative Doctor's degree, nor spend annually enough money for books and equipment; but upon its ability to turn out teachers who can do the job. If it is possible to measure in some way the effectiveness of the results of the whole teacher-education process in terms of what the students can do in teaching children in public schools, then the teachers colleges can do what they have always liked to do—they can attack directly and immediately the tasks at hand . . . We may now be approaching the day when technics of qualitative measurement will be highly developed enough so that the teachers colleges will gradate students when they are able to perform intelligently and skillfully all the duties of teaching, and not after they have accumulated 130 credit hours with an average grade of not less than "C." (p. 159).

The question still remains, what has changed in the 75 years since Harper published his book in 1939? The teaching profession has taken steps toward more comprehensive education and toward higher levels of study. According to National Assessment of Educational Progress (NAEP), in 2011, some 47% of fourth graders in the nation had a teacher with a master's degree, which is higher than in 2005 and 2009 (U.S. Department of Education, 2011). Additionally, enrollment in American public schools continues to increase. In the fall of 2011, total public and private elementary and secondary U.S. school enrollment was 55 million students, representing a 5% increase since fall 1997 (U.S. Department of Education Institute of Education Sciences, 2014). Increased enrollment, however, has brought a mix of high achievers and students who do not want to be in school, different cultures and languages American teachers have not seen before, and behaviors more difficult to handle. Yet typical teacher education programs still encompass only four semesters of training and pedagogy, including a semester of in-school student teaching, carved out of a 4-year university-level program. In a sense, we keep returning to the same place. The questions seem to remain similar over two centuries: How can educators be viewed as professionals? How can education achieve higher academic status? And how can educators develop pedagogical and child developmentally appropriate content, behavior management, and engagement for our students in meaningful and lasting ways while juggling in the newest technology? Based on Buckminster Fuller's (1982) theory of the "Knowledge Doubling Curve," it is estimated that knowledge currently doubles every 12 months. This compares to a rate of knowledge doubling every 25 years following WWII, and every century until 1900 (Schilling, 2013). How can we possibly not only stay abreast of new information but process and teach it as well?

> Clearly, we continue to seek a professional identity on par with doctors, lawyers, accountants, and others with 4-year university-level degrees. The struggle continues, as everyone has an opinion on how teaching should be done, on what needs to be taught and how to manage students, since most Americans have attended school. Contemporary education reformer Diane Ravitch stated in a speech to the White House Conference on Preparing Tomorrow's Teachers that

> Education will not achieve the status that it deserves until there is a carefully constructed, validated knowledge about how to improve student learning, as well as how to measure student learning. Our universities must dissolve the historic gulf between schools of pedagogy and faculties in the arts and sciences so that those who teach are not only well-trained, but truly well educated. (U.S. Department of Education, 2003, p.3)

CONCLUSION

In over 200 years, America has moved from educating only males of wealth and status to providing a free public educational system for all citizens. What was once considered women's work, the teaching profession now includes people from all social, ethnic, and cultural groups. Teacher education programs, which started in the middle 1800s, steadily gained more status through the transformation from normal schools into teacher colleges and currently into colleges of education. Teacher education programs have continuously evolved, from providing free public education, accommodating for diversity of culture during the immigration years at the turn of the last century, and students' diverse needs over the past 200 years. Laws providing for the education of all students with disabilities resulted in the training of special educators and support staff, such as speech, physical, and occupational therapists. Further, cultural integration called for programs for students with limited English language skills. Our ever-changing society directly impacts the needs of America's students and subsequent workforce. However, public opinion has remained relatively constant: teaching lacks the professional status held by other professions, such as accountants, lawyers, and physicians. Perhaps Harper (1939) was ahead of his time when he suggested that there was a need to institute qualitative measures to judge teachers' abilities rather than merely meeting a certain number of credit hours with a passing grade. We are now seeing a move toward holistic evaluation of preservice and in-service teachers, through clinical models that integrate both content knowledge and pedagogical practice. A new chapter in teacher education has begun.

REFERENCES

Asylum Projects. (2012). *Fernald State School: The Massachusetts School for Idiotic and Feeble-Minded Youth.* Retrieved from http://www.asylumprojects.org/index. php?title= Fernald_State_School

Bethune-Cookman University. (2013). *Our founder, Mary McLeod Bethune.* Retrieved from http://www.cookman.edu/about_BCU/history/our_founder.html

Borrowman, M. L. (1965). *Teacher education in America: A documentary history.* New York, NY: Teachers College Press.

Boston Public Schools. (2008). *Horace Mann School for the Deaf and Hard of Hearing.* Retrieved from http://boston.k12.ma.us/mann

Cuban, L. (1989). The persistence of reform in American schools. In D. Warren (Ed.), *American teachers: Histories of a profession at work.* (pp. 371–392). New York, NY: Macmillan.

Drury, D., & Baer, J. (2011). *The American public school teacher: Past present & future.* Cambridge, MA: Harvard Education Press.

Fuller, B. (1982). *Critical path.* New York, NY: St. Martin's Griffin.

Harper, C. A. (1939). *A century of public teacher education: The story of the state teachers colleges and they evolved from the normal schools.* Washington, DC: National Education Association.

Herbst, J. (1989). Teacher preparation in the nineteenth century: Institutions and purposes. In D. Warren (Ed.), *American teachers: Histories of a profession at work* (pp. 213–236). New York, NY: Macmillan.

Hess, F. M. (2010). *The same thing over and over. How school reformers get stuck in yesterday's ideas.* Cambridge, MA: Harvard University Press.

Larabee, D. E. (2008). An uneasy relationship: The history of teacher education in the university. In M. Cochran-Smith, S. Feiman-Nemser, J. D. McIntyre, & K. E. Demers (Eds.), *Handbook of research on teacher education: Enduring questions in changing contexts* (3rd ed., pp. 290–306). Oxford, UK: Routledge.

Lillard, P. P. (1988). *Montessori: A modern approach.* New york, NY: Schocken Books.

Montessori, M. (1912). *The Montessori method* (A. E. George, Trans.). New York, NY: Stokes.

National Center for Education Information. (2005). *Alternative routes to teacher certification: An overview.* Retrieved from http://www.ncei.com/Alt-Teacher-Cert.htm

National Commission on Excellence in Education. (1983). *A nation at risk: The imperative for educational reform. An open letter to the American people. A report to the nation and the Secretary of Education.* Retrieved from http://files.eric.ed.gov/fulltext/ED226006.pdf

Ornstein, A. C, Levine, D. U., Gutek, G. L., & Vocke, D. E. (2011). *Foundations of education* (11th ed.). Belmont, CA: Wadsworth, Cengage Learning.

Pushkin, D. (2001). *Teacher training: A reference handbook.* Santa Barbara, CA: ABC-CLIO.

Sass, E. (2014). *American educational history: A hypertext timeline.* Retrieved from http://www.eds-resources.com/educationhistorytimeline.html

Schilling, D. R. (2013, April 19). Knowledge doubling every 12 months, soon to be every 12 hours. *Industry tap into news.* Retrieved from http:www.industrytap.com/knowledge-doubling-every-12-months-soon-to-be-every-12-hours/3950

Tondeur, J., van Braak, J., Sang, G., Voogt, J., Fisser, P., & Ottenbreit-Leftwich, A. (2012). Preparing pre-service teachers to integrate technology in education: A synthesis of qualitative evidence. *Computers & Education, 59*(1), 134–144.

U.S. Department of Education. (2003). *Diane Ravitch, PhD—A brief history of teacher professionalism.* Retrieved from http://www2.ed.gov/admins/tchrqual/learn/preparingteachersconference/ravitch.html

U.S. Department of Education. (2009). *Teacher preparation: Reforming the uncertain profession: Remarks of Secretary Arne Duncan at Teachers College, Columbia University.* Retrieved from http://www.ed.gov/news/speeches/teacher-preparation-reforming-uncertain-profession

U.S. Department of Education. (2011). *Classroom context: Teachers' highest degree.* National Assessment of Educational Progress, National Center for Education Statistics. National Assessment Governing Board, Institute of Education Sciences.

U.S. Department of Education Institute of Education Sciences. National Center for Education Statistics. (2014). *Projections of education statistics to 2022.* Retrieved from http://nces.ed.gov/pubsearch/pubsinfo.asp?pubid=2014051

Warren, D. (Ed.). (1989). *American teachers: Histories of a profession at work.* New York, NY: Macmillan.

Webb, L. D., Metha, A., & Jordan, K. F. (2003). *Foundations of American education* (4th ed.). Upper Saddle River, NJ: Merrill/Prentice Hall.

CHAPTER 2

PERFORMANCE ASSESSMENTS OF TEACHING AND THE CURRENT DISCOURSE ON TEACHER EDUCATION

Jessica B. Graves, Barbara J. Radcliffe, and Karla Hull

There is an increasing national recognition of what is at stake in the field of teacher education (Cochran-Smith, Piazza, & Power, 2013). Every teacher candidate who is credentialed and enters a P–12 classroom has the potential to positively or adversely influence the lives and academic achievement of children. The impact of having an effective teacher in P–12 classrooms is well documented (Kane, Rockoff, & Staiger, 2006; Sanders & Rivers, 1996). It is estimated that students could attain as much as 50 percentile points higher on beginning mathematics scores if they were assigned to highly effective teachers 3 years in a row (Sanders & Rivers, 1996). With so much on the line, accrediting agencies are seeking assessments that provide valid and reliable measures of teacher candidate performance and teacher preparation program effectiveness (Chung, 2008).

Historically, teacher candidates have been evaluated for credentialing using standardized measures to assess the ability to recall and apply knowledge to particular situations. Examples of these standardized assessments include the PRAX-

Critical Issues in Preparing Effective Early Childhood Special Education Teachers for the 21st Century Classroom: Interdisciplinary Perspectives, pages 11–23.
Copyright © 2016 by Information Age Publishing

IS Series and the Georgia Assessment for the Certification of Educators (GACE). While the intent of these assessments is to capture the content knowledge of candidates, it could easily be questioned how this knowledge may transfer into the authentic nature of the classroom where particular variables cannot be manipulated or controlled. Ultimately, it must be determined whether candidates are capable of having a positive impact on P–12 student learning through application of content and content pedagogy within a variety of unique classroom environments. Federal policies are reflecting this concept as well. In the "Our Future, Our Teachers" report (U.S. Department of Education, 2011) released by the Obama Administration, a call was issued for teacher educator programs to begin analyzing data on program effectiveness through the lens of effect on student learning.

Teacher performance assessments, collections of evidence, and reflection that document an educator's teaching effectiveness are not new; but they have gained prominence in the current education reform movement related to teacher preparation, national standards for teaching, and accountability for teacher effectiveness. The practice of setting national standards in teacher education dates back to 1922 with the development of the American Association of Teachers Colleges, which later became the American Association of Colleges for Teacher Education (AACTE) in 1948 (Kraft, 2001). In 1954, the National Council of Accreditation of Teacher Education (NCATE) was established and served as a voluntary accrediting organization. While a focus on national standards for teacher education never disappeared, the publication of *A Nation at Risk* and the subsequent reports following its publication influenced both the standards movement as well as the performance assessment model (Kraft, 2001). In response to *A Nation at Risk* (National Commission on Excellence in Education, 1983), the field of education saw the birth of the Interstate New Teacher Assessment and Support Council (INTASC), as well as the National Board of Professional Teaching Standards (NBPTS). The arrival of INTASC and NBTPS, along with the National Council for Accreditation of Teacher Education (NCATE), resulted in the development of procedures for accreditation (NCATE), teacher licensure (INTASC), and advanced certification (NBPTS). In 1997, the Teacher Education Accreditation Council (TEAC) was founded, adding a second voluntary teacher education accrediting body. Noting the overlap and inefficiencies of having two different accrediting bodies in the field of educator preparation along with the goal to have one voice in educator preparation, NCATE and INTASC merged in 2013 to create the Council for the Accreditation of Educator Preparation (CAEP). Now the sole accreditor for educator preparation in the United States, CAEP is dedicated to raising "the stature of the entire profession by raising the standards for the evidence the field relies on to support its claims of quality" and showing "the value we add to quality assurance, accountability and the overall performance of the profession" (Cibulka & Murray, 2011, p. 2–3).

One optional assessment used to document quality assurance is the National Board Certification assessment. Several researchers (Bond, Smith, Baker, & Hattie, 2000; Cavaluzzo, 2004; Vandevoort, Amrein-Beardsly, & Berliner, 2004) concluded that the National Board Certification assessment process identified teachers who were more effective at improving student achievement from those who were less effective. Similar results have been noted (Darling-Hammond, Newton, & Wei, 2012; Newton, 2010) when using Connecticut's Beginning Educator Support and Training (BEST) teacher assessment (Wilson & Hallum, 2006), and California's Performance Assessment for California Teachers (PACT). In 2011, the "Gearing Up: Creating a Systematic Approach to Teacher Effectiveness" report was issued by a task force of the National Association of State Boards of Education. This report included recommendations for (a) common statewide standards for teaching, (b) performance-based assessments, (c) local evaluation systems aligned to the same standards, (d) support structures for training evaluators and mentoring teachers, and (e) professional development opportunities aligned with assessments and standards.

Amidst the flood of policy reports and decisions being released, the National Council on Teacher Quality (NCTQ), an advocacy group with the goal of advancing the accountability measures of teacher educator programs, raised the bar even further by charging teacher preparation programs with giving candidates an adequate return on their investment in a program (Greenberg, McKee, & Walsh, 2013). In other words, candidates must receive the curriculum and associated experiences that prepare them to provide quality instruction to the diverse population of students represented in America's classrooms. NCTQ has developed a rating system to determine the extent to which teacher preparation programs are effectively training teacher candidates, thereby raising the stakes and providing an incentive for programs to reevaluate and improve. Although the data collection and analysis methods associated with the NCTQ rating system have been called into question, the underlying intent—to provide a national look at the quality of teacher preparation programs—is still valid. With increasing accountability measures, many are beginning to ask, "Will the teacher performance assessment provide the quality data needed to determine the extent to which candidates are being prepared to provide quality instruction to P–12 learners?"

TEACHER PERFORMANCE ASSESSMENTS: PROS AND CONS

Teacher performance assessments not only impact an individual's professional development, but they also have the potential to inform and influence program improvement (Darling-Hammond, 2006; Pecheone & Chung, 2006). These assessments provide a variety of products reflecting candidates' performance that can be examined to identify strengths and gaps in teacher preparation programs (Darling-Hammond et al., 2012). Researchers have looked at the impact of performance assessments on program improvement. One study considered how faculty used the performance assessment from an inquiry stance. Researchers noted that faculty used the data to improve the alignment of program elements to connect practices and to use common language across their courses. While use of the teacher performance assessment was mandated, faculty still moved from a reactive stance to a proactive stance, thus allowing them opportunities to reconceptualize their program. Ultimately, the perceived autonomy to make programmatic changes based on data, increased faculty motivation and led to significant improvements in both coursework and field experience across the program (Peck, Galluci, & Sloane, 2010). Additionally, for educator preparation programs with varied program components and multiple course instructors, the experience of completing a teacher performance assessment was shown to provide a more standard set of teacher preparation experiences across a program (Chung, 2008).

For example, the portfolio used for National Board Certification is the longest-standing and most utilized teacher performance assessment for practicing teachers (Darling-Hammond et al., 2012). In order to earn National Board Certification, teachers must successfully develop a portfolio that documents their pedagogical and content knowledge, shows evidence of best practices in instructional delivery, and demonstrates engagement in professional activities (Cavaluzzo, 2004). There are copious group comparison studies of teachers who were or were not successful or who did or did not attempt the rigorous National Board Certification assessment, and the findings across studies vary greatly. Some researchers reported finding significant differences (Clotfelter, Ladd, & Vigdor, 2006; Goldhaber & Anthony, 2007) among the groups in terms of teacher effectiveness and student learning outcomes; others reported no statistical significance (Harris & Sass, 2007), while others reported finding mixed results, depending on the comparisons being made (Cantrell, Fullerton, Kane, & Staiger, 2008). Although there are discrepancies across comparison studies, self-report studies for in-service and preservice teachers participating in teacher performance assessments are more promising even though critics cite inherent issues in the use of self-reporting. A survey of more than 5,600 National Board candidates found that 92% believe the National Board Certification process helped them become a more effective teacher (NBPTS, 2001). National Board certified teachers attributed their increased teaching effectiveness to the process of analyzing both their students' work and their own instructional practice. Additionally, National Board certified teachers reported improvements in their content knowledge, pedagogical knowledge, classroom management, and assessment practices (Sato, Chung Wei, & Darling-Hammond, 2008).

The push for greater quality assurance and accountability in teacher preparation programs is evident in the current movement to develop and use teacher performance assessments to inform teacher licensure, recruitment, induction, retention, and recognition (Darling-Hammond, 2010). Supporters have suggested that directly linking teacher performance assessment scores to teacher candidates' eligibility for an initial teaching license or to beginning teachers' eligibility for an upgrade from a temporary license to a professional license will move teacher education toward a national standard of practice and advance the teacher education professionalization movement (Darling-Hammond, 2010). Teacher performance assessments have garnered immense support from many in the field as a way of documenting a move toward greater quality assurance and accountability in teacher preparation. Advocates have used the teacher performance assessment in a summative fashion to evaluate the way that candidates use their knowledge, skills, and dispositions in teaching and learning contexts for licensure purposes. Additionally, portions of the assessment have also been used as a formative tool to further candidates' professional development and improve educator preparation programs. Still, the use of teacher performance assessments as a means to demonstrate mastery of standards and effective instructional performance has spurred a heated debate.

As it appears, the value of teacher performance assessments is often contrasted with the traditional, pencil-and-paper licensure exam. Although 41 states reported using passing rates on state credentialing exams for teacher licensure in 2011 (USDOE, 2013), such tests are considered limited. Traditional licensure exams are constructed to measure basic skills as well as general, content-specific, and teaching strategy knowledge, but are not constructed to test all competencies teachers must possess to be effective (Mitchell, Robinson, Plake, & Knowles, 2001). While credit is given for establishing academic standards, many suggest current credentialing exams measure only what teachers know but fail to directly measure what teachers do in the classroom. Critics note teacher licensure tests "are not constructed to predict the degree of teaching success a beginning teacher will demonstrate," (Crowe, 2010, p.7) and assert that the scores on traditional exams fall short in demonstrating a significant relationship to student learning gains in the classroom (Wilson, Hallam, Pecheone, & Moss, 2007). An additional criticism of traditional certification exams focuses on the scoring and the inability to differentiate between moderately qualified and highly qualified teacher candidates (Mitchell et al., 2001).

While candidates take high-stakes certification exams in order to gain licensure in their states, the field relies on a variety of performance-based assessments to determine whether or not teacher candidates evidence the necessary skills, knowledge, and dispositions to successfully complete an educator preparation program. Proponents of the teacher performance assessment advocate for assessments that are not only tied to professional teaching standards but also reflect a high degree of consensus about what constitutes effective teaching. Instead of licensing beginning teachers on the basis of coursework completion and their possession of knowledge and skills, supporters promote assessments that consider the way in which candidates use their knowledge, skills, and dispositions in teaching and learning contexts (Darling-Hammond & Snyder, 2000; Mitchell et al., 2001; Pecheone & Chung, 2006). In contrast to traditional paper-and-pencil exams, teacher performance assessments measure the ability of candidates to plan, implement, and assess instruction by including artifacts such as lesson plans, curriculum maps, video clips capturing instructional delivery and student engagement, student work samples with evaluative comments, and reflective commentaries regarding instructional decision-making based on student needs and curricular goals (Darling-Hammond et al., 2012; Pecheone & Chung, 2006; Peck et al., 2010).

Clearly, the ability to learn from one's own practice is a critical element of effective teaching (NBPTS, 1999). Teacher performance assessments are grounded in this developmental view of teaching. Although teacher performance assessments serve a summative function, they can also support teachers and candidates in their professional development (Bunch, Aguirre, & Tellez, 2009; Darling-Hammond & Snyder, 2000). When used as a formative assessment, completed performance assessment tasks can be used as learning tools to enhance the teacher preparation experience in ways that lead to more learner-centered, assessment-driven instruction (Chung, 2008; Darling-Hammond et al., 2012).

Although there are many recognized benefits of teacher performance assessment, researchers have also raised many concerns. To summarize, criticisms have largely focused on the multiple functions this assessment serves, the potential for curriculum reduction, the impact on resources, and issues related to field experience. Critics of the teacher performance assessment have cited competing demands in terms of using the assessment for multiple functionality including high-stakes credentialing decisions, accreditation determination, professional development promotion, and program improvement. The major concern is the degree to which one measure is considered more significant than another (Chung, 2008; Snyder, 2009).

The development of teacher performance assessments has been largely based on the National Board Certification portfolio that was designed for evaluation of in-service teachers. The application of these same performance assessment procedures with the preservice teacher population causes some to call into question whether strategies used to assess practicing teachers are as relevant or informative for evaluating preservice teachers. Those challenging the appropriateness of performance assessment use with preservice teachers cited complications with distinguishing the impact of the assessment from the multiple sources of preservice teacher learning, including coursework, clinical experiences, and mentorship (Chung, 2008). With this in mind, while critics agree that performance assessments are more beneficial when compared to traditional evaluations, they still recognize challenges of ensuring their performance measures are valid, reliable, and fair (Sandholtz & Shea, 2012). While many educators acknowledge the positive impact of teacher performance assessment on program improvement, others challenge this notion citing the potential for curriculum reduction in educator preparation programs as an unintended consequence. Critics of standards-based assessment systems argue that relevant knowledge, skills, and dispositions not present in the standards are also not included in the evaluation of candidates. One such example is the inadequate attention given to culturally relevant teaching (Zeichner, 2003). Such perceived deficiencies lead to teacher educators viewing performance assessments as limiting the richness of their programs and negatively impacting practices they see as essential for learning (Snyder, 2009).

Teacher performance assessments receive criticism in terms of their relationship to both financial and human resources. Financially, performance assessments require several hundreds to thousands of dollars per candidate for the scoring and processing of assessments (Guaglianone, Payne, Kinsey, & Chiero, 2009; Snyder, 2009). However, the toll on human resources is far greater. Time is perhaps one of the most limited resources, and yet in the realm of completing a teacher performance assessment, it is the most taxed. The literature is rife with discussions regarding the negative impact these assessments have on human resources for both practicing teachers as well as preservice teachers. Concerns regarding the negative impact on students' achievement and candidates' dissatisfaction with their level of performance on coursework and in student teaching are attributed to the extensive time devoted to completing the performance assessment (Goldhaber & Anthony, 2007; Okhremtchouk et al., 2009). Researchers have suggested that these negative consequences are the result of teachers and candidates shifting their focus from teaching and learning to completing demanding and time-intensive requirements for the performance assessment (Goldhaber & Anthony, 2007).

One final criticism of teacher performance assessment is the degree to which candidates' field placements, a decision beyond their control, can impact their success on the assessment. In the area of field or clinical placements, researchers found several challenges such as limited supervisor and cooperating teacher support and constraints placed on teacher candidate practice in student teaching placements (Chung, 2008). In a study of factors impacting teacher candidates' success on the PACT, Okhremtchouk et al. (2009) identified and underscored the critical nature of what they referred to as "the local factor;" a term representing the actual clinical experience placement. Inherent in the local factor is the mentor teacher's depth of knowledge about the PACT assessment. They found that mentor teachers' understanding of the teacher performance assessment influenced their ability to support the teacher candidate.

On the whole, in light of the many advantages and disadvantages attributed to teacher performance assessment, the need for dialogue and further research is clear. While use of teacher performance assessments for initial and professional licensing can support more rigorous evaluation and provide a more consistent approach to determining teacher licensure (Darling-Hammond, 2010), the need to evaluate the validity and reliability of such assessments is absolutely critical (Darling-Hammond et al., 2012; Sandholtz & Shea, 2012).

THE EDTPA: A NATIONAL TOOL FOR TEACHER PERFORMANCE ASSESSMENT

It has been recognized that the field of education may, at times, be driven by policy written by policymakers detached from authentic experiences of the classroom. In the state of California, a group of educators sought to challenge the status quo, introducing the notion of teacher performance assessments as an important addition to teacher credentialing via standardized, paper-and-pencil measures (Pecheone

& Chung, 2006). In response to this policy-driven decision, this group of educators launched an initiative that would resonate with other teacher educators across the country. This assessment has been refined over the years based on substantive advice from teacher educators and classroom teachers. After launching several pilots across the nation, faculty and staff at the Stanford Center for Assessment, Learning, and Equity (SCALE) developed edTPA, formerly the Teacher Performance Assessment (TPA). Experience gained at Stanford from over 25 years of developing performance-based assessments of teaching, including the National Board for Professional Teaching Standards (NBPTS), the Interstate Teacher Assessment and Support Consortium (InTASC) Standards portfolio, and the Performance Assessment for California Teachers (PACT) provided the knowledge and research that informs the edTPA. The design and review teams were composed of more than 100 university faculty, national subject-matter organization representatives (e.g., NCTM, NCTE, and NSTA), and K–12 teachers.

Not only is edTPA predictive, providing evidence-based insight into how a teacher candidate might perform as a classroom teacher, it is also educative, illuminating what is and what is not working within preparation programs. In essence, edTPA captures a professional consensus on what the standards should be for beginning teacher practice, while shining light on how well programs are preparing their teacher candidates. The edTPA includes three tasks to be completed by candidates with the goal of providing evidence of their ability related to planning, instruction, and assessment. In task one, candidates think critically about the backgrounds of the students in their classrooms as they plan a sequence of lessons that should drive all learners toward success in achievement of an identified central focus for learning. For task two, candidates are prompted to evaluate through analysis and reflection of video clips of their teaching, the quality of the instruction they provided. This task is unique in that candidates must go beyond describing what they can do. Instead, candidates must substantiate their claims about their teaching abilities with video evidence. Finally, in task three, candidates examine the qualitative and quantitative data they collected on student learning to identify patterns of learning and plan for future instruction. Ultimately, a completed edTPA should result in a portfolio that demonstrates the ability of a candidate to move through all stages of the instructional process while engaging in consistent reflective practice.

INSIGHTS ON IMPLEMENTATION OF EDTPA

In 2013, after participating in a national pilot of the TPA, our university (Valdosta State University) began the implementation and integration of the edTPA. Multiple departments and programs were represented in this initial phase of the process. Ultimately, this pilot achieved two key goals: Faculty and teacher candidates were introduced to edTPA as an assessment measure; and data were collected on candidate ability to successfully complete the assessment. Findings from this study revealed that simply requiring students to participate in a teacher performance assessment would not be enough. Instead, adopting edTPA required a transformative experience that would impact multiple facets of the teacher preparation program, including faculty roles, philosophical shifts, pedagogy, and curriculum. The edTPA offered candidates unique opportunities to apply the required knowledge of master teachers within the authentic context of a given classroom. Additionally, edTPA did not ask teacher candidates to redesign their existing context. Instead, the prompts were designed in such a way that candidates only had to respond transparently about how particular components were translated within their classrooms. This resonated with mentor teachers who (rightly so) were against adjusting their classrooms in response to university requirements. In evaluating portfolios, the need for candidates to receive strategic preparation in designing assessments aligned with clearly articulated evaluative criteria became evident. Candidates also needed to be prepared to offer extensive feedback to students and other stakeholders as well as to effectively use feedback to guide future instructional decisions. We learned that developing formative experiences for teacher candidates in earlier semesters was essential for the development of proficiencies required by edTPA and representative of effective teaching practices.

The ability of faculty to undergo a philosophical shift directly contributed to the likelihood that the process of edTPA integration would occur in meaningful ways. This shift involved realizing the value that edTPA brought to developing teacher candidates. Results of the edTPA pilot supported the notion that faculty needed to make some curricular and pedagogical changes. As faculty recognized the value in the edTPA experience for teacher candidates, dynamic shifts occurred in curricular experiences, increasing alignment and relevance to teacher candidates in their field experiences as well as to articulated goals of the assessment. Faculty had to exhibit a willingness to consistently and deliberately adjust the curriculum and resultant experiences provided in particular courses. Adjusting the curriculum and streamlining curricular tasks made the tasks more meaningful rather than having a series of disconnected and isolated assignments. Ultimately, the process of curricular revision on the part of faculty was linked to the notion that "the more support provided to candidates by program faculty . . . the more likely candidates are to have positive learning experiences and by extension, stronger performances" on the teacher performance assessment (Pecheone & Chung, 2006, p. 32). Faculty realized that successful performances on edTPA were directly linked to improved teaching effectiveness. Collaboration across faculty was essential as content-area expertise and experience played a tremendous role in the success of edTPA planning and implementation.

As a result of collaborative interactions, consistency of language/terminology was addressed during curricular revisions to align with the language used in the edTPA. Development of a common language ensured that candidates would be exposed repeatedly to similar terms across courses. Formative experiences were embedded in classes to enable teacher candidates to have opportunities for guided practice with relevant knowledge and skills. The edTPA experience provided the context for richer and deeper levels of reflection. For example, one teacher candidate acknowledged that she spoke of reflective practice while in the program, but she never fully understood what the expression meant until she completed the edTPA process. Noting the importance of authentic reflective practice, faculty members continue to embed reflective opportunities into field-based experiences so candidates can engage in connecting theory to practice in meaningful ways. As the current education reform movement questions what it means to be an effective teacher, educator preparation programs must redefine, reenvision, and redesign their curriculum and pedagogy in a way that allows them to not only prepare candidates for success but also allows them to document their candidates' professional growth and effectiveness.

CONCLUSION

Undoubtedly, in the field of education, with any newly implemented process or procedure, both critics and advocates will have to work alongside one another. However, with this effort, it is largely recognized that this important work influences the lives of P–12 learners (Duncan, 2011). As research continues on best practices with regard to teacher performance assessment, Pecheone and Chung (2006) acknowledge that "beyond accountability purposes, a well-designed performance assessment system has the potential to be a powerful tool in providing meaningful feedback to individual candidates and to evaluate the impact of teacher education programs" (p. 33). The ultimate goal is for educator preparation programs to understand that what they do and the way they do what they do impacts young children, with and without special needs. With collaboration and consultative efforts among stakeholders (e.g., students, parents, general and special educators, school leaders, community leaders, accreditation bodies, and government agencies), it has become finally clear that there must be shifts in how we evaluate, prepare, and develop the needed skillsets for new and experienced teachers.

REFERENCES

Bond, L., Smith, T., Baker, W. K., & Hattie. J. (2000). *The certification system of the National Board for Professional Teaching Standards: A construct and consequential validity study.* Greensboro, NC: Center for Educational Research and Evaluation, University of North Carolina.

Bunch, G. C., Aguirre, J. M., & Tellez, K. (2009). Beyond the scores: Using candidate responses on high stakes performance assessment to inform teacher preparation for English learners. *Issues in Teacher Education, 18*(1), 103–128.

Cantrell, S., Fullerton, J., Kane, T., & Staiger, D. (2008). National Board Certification and teacher effectiveness: Evidence from a random assignment experiment. *NBER Working Paper 14608.*

Cavaluzzo, L. (2004). *Is National Board Certification an effective signal of teacher quality?* National Science Foundation No. REC-0107014. Alexandria, VA: CNA.

Chung, R. R. (2008). Beyond assessment: Performance assessments in teacher education. *Teacher Education Quarterly, 35*(1), 7–28.

Cibulka, J., & Murray, F. (2011, February 17). Statement by James Cibulka and Frank Murray on NCTQ ratings and CAEP accreditation. *NCATE.* Retrieved from http://www.ohio.edu/education/about/ncate/loader.cfm?csModule=security/getfile&pageid=2159930

Clotfelter, C., Ladd, H., & Vigdor, J. (2006). *Teacher credentials and student achievement.* NBER working paper 11936. Washington, DC: National Bureau of Economic Research.

Cochran-Smith, M., Piazza, P., & Power, C. (2013). The politics of accountability: Assessing teacher education in the United States. *The Educational Forum, 77*(1), 6–27. doi:10.1080/00131725.2013.739015

Crowe, E. (2010). *Measuring what matters: A stronger accountability model for teacher education.* Washington DC: Center for American Progress.

Darling-Hammond, L. (2006). Assessing teacher education: The usefulness of multiple measures for assessing program outcomes. *Journal of Teacher Education, 57*(2), 120–138.

Darling-Hammond, L. (2010). *Evaluating teacher effectiveness: How teacher performance assessments can measure and improve teaching.* Washington DC: Center for American Progress.

Darling-Hammond, L., Newton, S., & Wei, R. (2012). *Developing and assessing beginning teacher effectiveness: The potential of performance assessments.* Retrieved from http://edtpa.aacte.org/wp-content/uploads/2012/07/Developing-and-Assessing-Beginning-Teacher-Effectiveness.pdf

Darling-Hammond, L., & Snyder, J. (2000). Authentic assessment of teaching in context. *Teaching and Teacher Education, 16*(5/6), 523–545.

Duncan, A. (2011, October 3). *A new approach to teacher education reform and improvement. U.S. Department of Education.* Retrieved from http://www.ed.gov/news/speeches/new-approach-teacher-education-reform-and-improvement

Goldhaber, D., & Anthony, E. (2007). Can teacher quality be effectively assessed? National board certification as a signal of effective teaching. *The Review of Economics and Statistics, 89*(1), 134–150.

Greenberg, J., McKee, A., & Walsh, K. (2013). Teacher prep review: A review of the nation's teacher preparation programs. *National Council on Teacher Quality.* Retrieved from http://www.nctq.org/dmsView/Teacher_Prep_Review_2013_Report

Guaglianone, C. L., Payne, M., Kinsey, G. W., & Chiero, R. (2009). Teaching performance assessment: A comparative study of implementation and impact among California State University campuses. *Issues in Teacher Education, 18*(1), 129–148.

Harris, D. N., & Sass, T. R. (2009). The effects of NBPTS-certified teachers on student achievement. *Journal of Policy Analysis and Management, 28*(1), 55–80.

Kane, T. J., Rockoff, J. E., & Staiger, D. O. (2008). What does certification tell us about teacher effectiveness? Evidence from New York City. *Economics of Education Review, 27*, 615–631. doi:10.1016/j.econedurev.2007.05.005

Kraft, N. (2001, April 10–14). *Standards in teacher education: A critical analysis of NCATE, INTASC, and NBPTS.* Paper presented at the annual meeting of the American Educational Research Association. Seattle, WA. Retrieved from http://files.eric.ed.gov/fulltext/ED462378.pdf

Mitchell, K. J., Robinson, D. Z., Plake, B. S., & Knowles, K. T. (2001). *Testing teacher candidates: The role of licensure tests in improving teacher quality.* Washington, DC: National Academy Press.

National Association of State Boards of Education (NASBE). (2011). *Gearing up: Creating a systemic approach to teacher effectiveness.* Arlington, VA: Author.

National Board for Professional Teaching Standards (NBPTS). (1999). *What teachers should know and be able to do.* Arlington, VA: Author.

National Board for Professional Teaching Standards (NBPTS). (2001). *I am a better teacher: What candidates for National Board Certification say about the assessment process.* Arlington, VA: Author.

National Commission on Excellence in Education. (1983). *A nation at risk: The imperative for educational reform. An open letter to the American people. A report to the nation and the Secretary of Education.* Retrieved from http://files.eric.ed.gov/fulltext/ED226006.pdf

Okhremtchouk, I., Seiki, S., Gilliland, B., Atch, C., Wallace, M., & Kato, A. (2009). Voices of pre-service teachers: Perspectives on the Performance Assessment for California Teachers (PACT). *Issues in Teacher Education, 18*(1), 39–62.

Pecheone, R. L., & Chung, R. R. (2006). Evidence in teacher education: The performance assessment for California teachers. *Journal of Teacher Education, 57*(1), 22–36.

Peck, C., Galluci, C., & Sloan, T. (2010). Negotiating implementation of high-stakes performance assessment policies in teacher education: From compliance to inquiry. *Journal of Teacher Education, 61*(5), 451–463.

Sanders, W. L., & Rivers, J. C. (1996). *Cumulative and residual effects of teachers on future student academic achievement.* Knoxville, TN: University of Tennessee Value Added Research and Assessment Center. Retrieved March 10, 2015, from http://www.cgp.upenn.edu/pdf/Sanders_Rivers-TVASS_teacher%20effects.pdf

Sandholtz, J., & Shea, L. (2012). Predicting performance: A comparison of university supervisors' predictions and teacher candidates' scores on a teaching performance assessment. *Journal of Teacher Education, 63*(1), 39–50.

Sato, M., Chung Wei, R., & Darling-Hammond, L. (2008). Improving teachers' assessment practices through professional development: The case of National Board Certification. *American Educational Research Journal, 45*(3), 669–700.

Snyder, J. (2009). Taking stock of performance assessments in teaching. *Issues in Teacher Education, 18*(1), 7–11.

U.S. Department of Education. (2011, September). *Our future, our teachers: The Obama administration's plan for teacher education reform and improvement.* Washington, DC: U.S. DOE. Retrieved March 10, 2015 from http://www.ed.gov/sites/default/files/our-future-our-teachers.pdf

U.S. Department of Education, Office of Postsecondary Education (2013). *Preparing and credentialing the nation's teachers: The Secretary's ninth report on teacher quality.* Washington, DC: U.S. Department of Education.

Vandevoort, L. G., Amrein-Beardsley, A. & Berliner, D. C. (2004, September 8). National board certified teachers and their students' achievement. *Education Policy Analysis Archives, 12*(46). Retrieved [March 10, 2015] from http://epaa.asu.edu/ojs/article/view/201

Wilson, M., Hallam, P. J., Pecheone, R., & Moss, P. (2007). *Using student achievement test scores as evidence of external validity for indicators of teacher quality: Connecti-*

cut's *Beginning Educator Support and Training program.* Berkeley, CA: Berkeley Evaluation and Research Center.

Zeichner, K. M. (2003). The adequacies and inadequacies of three current strategies to recruit, prepare, and retain the best teachers for all students. *Teachers College Record, 105*(3). 490–519.

CHAPTER 3

DISMANTLING DEFICIT THINKING THROUGH TEACHER EDUCATION

María L. Gabriel, James Martínez, and Festus Obiakor

Teacher preparation programs have struggled on issues of providing equitable educational practices for *all* learners. Arguably, they seem to lack the wherewithal in instituting reflective learning experiences that could challenge current retrogressive ideas. To a large measure, reflective learning experiences dismantle colonized thinking and help to galvanize communities that (a) value critical consciousness (Obiakor, 2014), (b) acknowledge structural inequality (Obiakor, 2012), (c) dislocate levels of oppression inherent in schooling (Scheurich & Young, 1997; Villenas & Foley, 2011), (d) address intersectionality (Crenshaw, 1991; Delgado & Stefancic, 2001; Solórzano & Yosso, 2001), (e) counter deficit thinking (Gorski, 2008; Valencia, 1997, 2010), and (f) discuss how all the aforementioned variables impact teaching, learning, and schooling of *all* students (Obiakor, 2014). In this chapter, we discredit information that negatively influences how students, especially those who come from culturally and linguistically diverse (CLD) backgrounds, are viewed by educators and service providers. Embedded in our discussion are common myths heard in schools and how elements of critical race theory can be utilized to deconstruct them.

Critical Issues in Preparing Effective Early Childhood Special Education Teachers for the 21st Century Classroom: Interdisciplinary Perspectives, pages 25–36.
Copyright © 2016 by Information Age Publishing

ENDEMIC MYTHS AND TRADITIONAL EDUCATION

Teachers are answerable for more than being empathetic, considerate, and sensitive but also to address the needs of diverse students who differ by race, ethnicity, gender, sexual orientation, language, ability, or socioeconomic status (Banks, 2006; Irvine, & Armento, 2001; Martinez, Tost, Hilgert, & Woodard-Meyers, 2013; McLaren, 2007; Zamudio & Rios, 2006). To investigate the education myths about CLD students, we employed a systematic analysis by simultaneously verifying a shared body of literature, research policy briefs, current policy reports, and other identified references (e.g., Gabriel, 2013; Martinez, Unterriener, Aragon, & Kellerman, in press).

The two prevailing educational myths are

Myth 1: "CLD students lack background knowledge when they enter preschool and therefore will never catch up."

Myth 2: "The disparities in achievement for students are not really about race. It's just about poverty."

MYTH 1

Myth 1 is a frequently heard statement by educators, practitioners, and administrators who frequently correlate the number of words students know at an early age with their parents' educational attainment (Heath, 1983; Jensen, 2009). These professionals make links between poverty and background knowledge (Heath, 1983; Jensen, 2009; Payne, 1996). More often than not, teachers who may unpurposely endorse Myth 1 are not familiar with the cultural context of the CLD students being taught. Viadero (1996) referred to this phenomenon as a "culture clash," which arises when individuals within school systems adopt its "deficit theory" (Valencia, 1997). What is missing is when schools fail to examine the structural inequality that persists within systems and how individuals contribute to the inequities that exist between CLD students and their White and Asian American peers (Gabriel, 2013; Gorski, 2013; Heath, 1983; Valencia, 2010).

Researchers have focused on the cultural discontinuity of White teachers in diverse classrooms (Davis, 2007; Hawley & Nieto 2010; Howard, 2006; Hughes & Willink, 2013; Landsman & Lewis, 2006). Although the demographics of students are shifting in classrooms, teachers in U.S. schools have remained largely White (Cammarota, 2008; National Collaborative, 2004; Paris, 2012; Redeaux, 2011; Shim, 2014), creating a cultural gap between teachers and students. Leadership within schools, specifically the school principal role, too has also been well documented with similar findings. For example, since 2010, approximately 1 in 4 kindergartners were Latino (El Nasser & Overberg, 2010), yet in 2003–2004, some 4.8% of public and private school principals in the United States were Latino (NCES, n.d.). This phenomenon, "culture clash" (Viadero, 1996), exists when schools fail to be in alignment with the cultures of students in attendance.

With culture defined as being inclusive of material elements, observable patterns of behavior and customs, and "'ideational' elements: ideas, beliefs, knowledge, and ways of acquiring knowledge and passing it on" (Trumbull, Rothstein-Fisch, Greenfield, & Quiroz, 2001, p. 1), the need for conversations about culture and race in classrooms and surrounding communities is magnified, "Even without our being consciously aware of it, culture determines how we think, believe, and behave, and these, in turn, affect how we teach and learn" (Gay, 2000, p. 9; Scheurich & Young, 1997). A cultural mismatch suggests "the classroom culture or the teacher's culture is at odds with the culture of ethnic minority students" (Gregory, Skiba, & Noguera, 2010, p. 63). Yet culture is often the way the classroom setting is created and maintained. The culture mismatch has been shown to lead to discipline and achievement disparities between CLD students and White peers (Alexander, 2012; Bell, 1992; Curtis, 2014; Elias & Buzelli, 2013, Martinez et al., 2013); school leaders, teachers, and the inherent structure of schools have continued to model a racial paradigm. Further examples of culture clash are shown in the assumptions White teachers make about Black students who may not respond to questioning in the classroom related to time-telling. Viadero (1996) explained that "in the African American children's families such questions were posed only when someone genuinely needed to know the answer" (p. 39). Additionally, educators rely on assumptions and continue to respond to the situation with discipline that further complicates the culture clash. When the culture of schools and the ethnic backgrounds of students who attend are not in alignment, the cultural gaps that exist impact academic achievement (Gay, 2000, 2002; Gregory et al., 2010; Martinez et al., in press; Nieto & Bode, 2008). A deeper focus on the concept of the culture clash includes a deeper look at the levels of oppression (Scheurich & Young, 1997). "School culture is relatively consistent across the United States and reflects the individualistic values of the dominant, European American culture" (Rothstein-Fisch & Trumbull, 2008, p. xiii). It is no wonder that many students who enter the school doors have felt like a "guest" (Hughes & North, 2012; Lewis, 2003; Spann, 1990; Valencia, 2010) who do not fully belong, thereby creating a "chilly climate" (hooks, 1997). Students in this situation give up part of who they are to participate (Howard, 2006; Suinn, 2006).

Many years ago, Brophy and Good (1974) demonstrated that teachers' perceptions were based on personal social values, and therefore perceptions of students' abilities and efforts are often inaccurate. The cultural assumptions that White teachers have about CLD students have contributed to negative educational responses and outcomes (Bell, 1992; Delgado & Stefancic, 2001; Hill Collins, 2003; Shim, 2014). Encapsulated in these is deficit thinking. The six characteristics of deficit thinking, according to Valencia (2010), are (a) blaming the victim, (b) oppression, (c) pseudoscience, (d) temporal changes, (e) educability, and (f) heterodoxy. Often manifested in and within classroom interaction between teachers and students, these common assertions of deficits all lead to deficit thinking, blaming the victims for the shortcomings of the education system's failure to provide appropriate education for all students, particularly CLD students and low socioeconomic status, rather than considering such categories as assets or strengths. Instead of examining the structure or functions of schools, school leadership often points the proverbial finger at students and/or the families' internal deficiencies for educational failure (Valencia, 1997, 2010). Furthermore, the deficit perspective is one in which educators are "defining students by their weaknesses rather than their strengths" (Gorski, 2008, p. 34) and becomes a way of understanding students. Deficit theory has two strategies for reinforcing this worldview: building on stereotypes; and overlooking systemic and perpetuated inequities (Gorski, 2008). Often this manifests as teachers perceptions' of inherent student deficits such as cultural inadequacies, lack of motivation, poor behavior, poverty, language, and families and communities (Cammarota, 2008; Diaz Soto, 2007; Griffin, Martinez, & Martin, 2014; McKenzie & Scheurich, 2004).

MYTH 2

Myth 2 is a frequently heard statement by educators, practitioners, and/or administrators. These professionals demonstrate a limited, narrow, and deficit perspective that requires further interrogation to include sociopolitical and sociohistorical contexts to deconstruct the myth. Focusing on interest convergence to further understand why this type of thinking has been sustained is critical.

Throughout the 1800s and much of the 1900s, public schools in the United States were set up for reasons that included socializing immigrant populations (Moe & Chubb, 2009). Earlier, Viadero (1996) noted that, "from at least the start of the 20th century, one job of schools was to help assimilate the large numbers of immigrants flocking to the nation's shores." Teaching, curriculum, and instructional practices have continued to support the assimilationist perspective (Anyon, 1980; Gorski, 2012; Lindsey, Nuri Robins, & Terrell, 2009). Taylor's (2009) historical analysis of the U.S. educational system indicated that race had an unwavering impact on the current system. Additionally, a more comprehensive examination of the history of schooling includes the fact that property rights in the United States were rooted in racial domination (Harris, 1995), which impacted the schooling experience for CLD students. While the privileges owned by Whites are often "invisible, unearned, and not consciously acknowledged," McIntosh (1988) and later Picower (2009) argued "these privileges, ideologies and stereotypes reinforce institutional hierarchies and larger systems of White supremacy" (p. 198). Sleeter (2000) used a personal family example to help create understanding about White privilege and property rights:

> My grandfather was a painter and wallpaper hanger who did fairly well in his life by buying property, renovating it, and then selling it. I grew up with the family story that he only had a second-grade education and look how well he did. Yet he was buying property at a time which property ownership was much easier for white people. As a part of New Deal legislation, Franklin Delano Roosevelt made a deal

with southern senators that the money for low-cost federal subsidized housing loans would be made available to white families and not to families of color, because the southern senators wanted to keep African Americans working as sharecroppers. Part of that New Deal legislation was specifically crafted so that people like my grandfather could buy property. I have inherited then, the benefits of that piece of systemic, historic white racism. Even today, I can walk into a real estate office and will more likely be shown places in "better" neighborhoods. I am also more likely to be given a better mortgage deal. (p. 1)

Uncovering White dominance and property rights supports learning "how the lives of our students have been scripted by their membership in groups differing in degrees of social dominance and marginality" (Howard, 2006, p. 34), and how CLD students have been treated as outsiders and learning needs have been unmet.

Milner (2008) presented an example of how educational decisions in K–12 schools are made to benefit White students. A school district began bussing immigrant students into a high-achieving school in the district. While those students learning English benefited from the bussing, the White students had the opportunity to become bi- and trilingual. The benefit to White students was the main and final reason to bus immigrant students to the high-achieving school. According to Milner,

The district and school were willing to negotiate and provide the resources necessary for the "non-English speakers" to "learn English" because the majority White students would, of course, benefit from the various racial, ethnic, cultural, and linguistic backgrounds that would be present and represented in the school. (p. 333)

While most CLD Americans have felt racism on almost a daily basis, most White Americans have not felt racism or acknowledged it as a significant social issue (Jones, 2008). Therefore, overt racism, the intended act by of a person(s) from one race to hurt or damage a person(s) of another race is easier to identify than covert racism, which is not explicitly public (Scheurich & Young, 1997). Racism's complexity and depth exists almost everywhere, "therefore, the strategy of those who fight for social justice is one of unmasking and exposing racism in its various permutations" (Ladson-Billings, 1999, p. 213).

Scholars who are critical race theorists have focused on racial discourse, and more recently the central tenet of the intersection of race with class, gender, ability, and sexuality (Delgado & Stefancic, 2001; Solórzano & Yosso, 2001; Zamudio, Russell, Rios, & Bridgeman, 2011). The intersectionality framework supports the idea that "women have multiple and layered identities [sic] derived from biological inheritance, social relations, political struggles, economic status, and societal power structure" (Lockhart & Mitchell, 2010, p. 17). Social and cultural patterns of oppression intersect in race, gender, socioeconomic status, and ethnicity to the experiences related to each identity that shapes existence (Crenshaw, 1991; Hill Collins, 1998). This inclusive lens is useful because of the very "limitation of race or gender-only frameworks" as "intersectional approaches contextualized in lived experience belie the us/them thinking that constructs race and gender as parallel and different systems where men dominate women, whites oppress people of colour, and oppressors victimize the oppressed" (Hill Collins, 1998, pp. 935–936). Attention to intersectionality provides a deeper and wider understanding of the many identifiers expressed in the experiences of discrimination and oppression by CLD youth in schools and communities.

BEYOND THE MYTHS

When determining best practices for moving forward, adequately preparing to support CLD students in school settings is needed (Gabriel, 2013; Gorski, 2013; Martin-Paulk, Martinez, & Lambeth (in press). It is important to develop a critical consciousness (Hill Collins, 2003; Hughes & North, 2012) to examine power, privilege, and positionality. Also important is the examination of languages and behaviors used to describe CLD students and their needs to develop a form of cultural proficiency (Griffin et al., 2014; Lindsey et. al, 2009). Because privilege and penalty are experienced simultaneously, it is crucial to demand a vision of justice beyond the rhetoric of abstract liberalism and provide a unique opportunity to engage in meaningful dialogue placed in the context of useful teaching tools such as the Matrix of Oppression/Opportunity (Hill Collins, 2003; Zamudio & Rios, 2006). Furthermore, the Compass Matrix (Hughes & North, 2012) allows one the opportunity to "see" the uneven social landscape (positionality) and the ways people often experience oppression and privilege simultaneously. Moving within and beyond one's race, ethnicity, gender, age, sexual orientation, and ability helps to uncover access, opportunity, and privilege in educational settings (Gabriel, 2013; Zamudio et al., 2011). More recently, social justice advocates have encouraged educators to move beyond cultural proficiency, which can be stagnant, to practicing "equity literacy" (Gorski, 2013) by learning how to uncover inequitable practices anyplace.

The framing of conversations about changing demographics, integrated communities, or achievement and opportunity gaps (Carter, Welner, & Ladson-Billings, 2013; Gabriel, 2013; Gorski, 2013) becomes as important as the ways we seek solutions to the present barriers to educating all U.S. students. Engaging in critical conversations related to the myths heard about the students served in integrated schools and communities is important as a first step. School district administrators, principals, assistant principals, school staff, and other school leaders can address the deficit model in a variety of ways, yet a strong start is to engage faculty and staff in conversations about beliefs and perceptions of their diverse students; for example, basic questions in anonymous surveys, such as "Do you have achievement gaps in your school? If so, what do you attribute to those gaps?" Answers and discussions to such questions can then help school leaders deconstruct and reconstruct a place of learning that is inclusive and based on high expectations for all students (Gabriel, 2013).

Achievement gaps in K–12 education, such as student grades, standardized test scores, dropout rates, and high school graduation rates have become focal points of education reform efforts (Engel, 2009; Gorski, 2013; Martinez, et al., 2013, 2014) and are often deemed a socially acceptable way of problematizing demographic groups. Created and maintained by educational systems that separate the skilled from the unskilled (Valencia, 2010; Vollmer, 2010), these gaps must be framed as "educational debt" (Ladson-Billings, 2006) to provide solutions to the problem in a responsive and critical way. While there is not a single strategy or an easy solution to the dismantling of settler ideologies that guide the actions of colonized minds, there are substantial steps that may be taken—yet not as a recipe or agenda for critical education—to resituate diversity in a U.S. and global context (Smith, 1999; Villenas, 1996). Dismantling hierarchies is not a step-by-step-process, but a perspective in which teaching and learning are committed to expanding rather than restricting the opportunities for CLD students to be social, political, and economic agents (Giroux, 2012; Smith, 1999). Such critical practice must be honestly and systematically tested in a principled manner, especially when it pertains to issues of critical consciousness in defeating deficit pedagogy. Clearly, the traditional curriculum taught in K–12 public schools reproduces a predominant mindset that embraces and sustains the common history, theory, and practice of public schools. When teachers are guided in examining positions of power, they may critically reflect on the deficit model and dismantle the common myths that pervade a capitalistic school system's effect on public education.

CONCLUSION

In this chapter, we counter the deficit thinking of two common myths and how they impact teaching, learning, and schooling of *all* students. In addition, we argue for equitable educational practices instituted through reflective learning experiences. We know that these learning experiences dismantle colonized thinking and build communities grounded in critical consciousness that acknowledges structural inequality and levels of oppression inherent in U.S. schooling. We believe more professional learning opportunities for critical reflection are necessary to expose and counter ineffective traditional models and levels of multicultural education that sustain current ineffective educational structures. In addition, we prescribe culturally sensitive intervention models for teacher preparation programs. These models must examine power, positionality, privilege, and access that go beyond pretentious color-blindness, blaming the victim, practicing fraudulent multiculturalism, and engaging in phony equitable practices (Alexander, 2012; Lewis, 2001). In the end, it is necessary that teacher preparation programs and teacher-leaders focus on equity literacy to produce more well-rounded learners (Carter et al., 2013; Hughes & Willink, 2013). The old framework of assimilating CLD students through deficit orientation has failed; and to move forward, our paradigm must be shifted.

REFERENCES

Alexander, M. (2012). *The new Jim Crow: Mass incarceration in the age of colorblindness.* New York, NY: New Press.

Anyon, J. (1980). Social class and the hidden curriculum of work. *Journal of Education, 162*(1), 67–92.

Banks, J. A. (2006). *Cultural diversity and education: Foundations, curriculum, and teaching* (5th ed.). Boston, MA: Pearson Education.

Bell, D. (1992). *Faces at the bottom of the well.* New York, NY: Basic.

Brophy, J., & Good, T. (1974). *Teacher-student relationships: Causes and consequences.* New York, NY: Holt, Rinehart and Winston.

Cammarota, J. (2008). *Sueños Americanos: Barrio youth negotiating social and cultural identities.* Tucson: University of Arizona Press.

Carter, P. L., Welner, K., & Ladson-Billings, G. (2013). *Closing the opportunity gap: What America must do to give every child an even chance.* New York, NY: Oxford University Press.

Crenshaw, K. W. (1991). Mapping the margins: Intersectionality, identity politics, and violence against women of color. *Stanford Law Review, 43*(6), 1241–1299.

Curtis, A. J. (2014). Tracing the school-to-prison pipeline from zero-tolerance policies to juvenile justice dispositions. *Georgetown Law Journal, 102*(4), 1251–1277.

Davis, B. M. (2007). *How to teach students who don't look like you: Culturally relevant teaching strategies.* Thousand Oaks, CA: Corwin.

Delgado, R., & Stefancic, J. (2001). *Critical race theory: An introduction.* New York: New York University Press.

Diaz Soto, L. (Ed.). (2007). *The Praeger handbook of Latino education in the U.S.: Vol.1.* Westport, CT: Praeger.

Elias, M., & Buzelli, C. (2013, Spring). The school-to-prison pipeline. *Teaching Tolerance.* Retrieved from http://www.tolerance.org/magazine/number-43-spring-2013/school-to-prison

El Nasser, H., & Overberg, P. (2010, August 27). Kindergartners see more Hispanic, Asian students. *USA Today.* Retrieved October 6, 2010, from http://www.usatoday.com/news/nation/census/2010-08-27-1Akindergarten27_ST_N.htm

Engel, A. (2009). *Seeds of tomorrow.* Boulder, CO: Paradigm.

Gabriel, M. L. (2013). A practical and hope-filled tool to address the "achievement gap." In J. Brooks & N. Witherspoon-Arnold (Eds.), *Anti-racist school leadership: Toward equity in education for America's students* (pp. 93–111). Charlotte, NC: Information Age.

Gay, G. (2000). *Culturally responsive teaching: Theory, research, & practice.* New York, NY: Teachers College Press.

Gay, G. (2002). Preparing for culturally responsive teaching. *Journal of Teacher Education, 53*(2), 106–116.

Giroux, H. A. (2012). *Education and the crisis of public values: Challenging the assault on teachers, students, & public education.* New York, NY: Lang.

Gorski, P. (2008). Peddling poverty for profit: Elements of oppression in Ruby Payne's framework. *Equity & Excellence in Education, 41*(1), 130–148.

Gorski, P. (2012): Perceiving the problem of poverty and schooling: Deconstructing the class stereotypes that mis-shape education practice and policy. *Equity & Excellence in Education, 45*(2), 302–319.

Gorski, P. (2013). *Reaching and teaching students in poverty: Strategies for erasing the opportunity gap.* New York, NY: Teachers College Press.

Gregory, A., Skiba, R. J., & Noguera, P. A. (2010). The achievement gap and the discipline gap: Two sides of the same coin? *Educational Researcher, 39*(59), 59–68.

Griffin, R., Martinez, J., & Martin, E. (2014). Rosetta Stone and language proficiency of international secondary school English language learners. Engaging cultures & voices. *The Journal of English Learning through Media, 6*(2), 36–73.

Harris, C. I. (1995). Whiteness as property. In K. Crenshaw, N. Gotanda, G. Peller, & K. Thomas (Eds.), *Critical race theory: The key writings that formed the movement* (pp. 276–291). New York, NY: New Press.

Hawley, W., & Nieto, S. (2010). Another inconvenient truth: Race and ethnicity matter. *Educational Leadership, 68*(3), 66–71.

Heath, S. (1983). *Ways with words: Language, life, and work in communities and classrooms.* New York, NY: Cambridge University Press.

Hill Collins, P. (1998). The tie that binds: Race, gender and US violence. *Ethnic and Racial Studies, 21*(5), 917–938.

Hill Collins, P. (2003). The politics of Black feminist thought. In C. R. McCann & K. Seung-Kyung (Eds.), *Feminist theory reader: Local and global perspectives* (pp. 318–33). New York, NY: Routledge.

hooks, b. (1997). *Wounds of passion: A writing life.* New York, NY: Henry Holt.

Howard, G. R. (2006). *We can't teach what we don't know: White teachers, multiracial schools* (2nd ed.). New York, NY: Teachers College Press, Columbia University.

Hughes, S. A., & North, C. E. (2012). Beyond popular cultural and structural arguments: Imagining a compass to guide burgeoning urban achievement gap scholars. *Educationand Urban Society, 44*(3), 74–293.

Hughes, S. A., & Willink, K. (2013). Engaging co-reflexive critical dialogues when entering and leaving the "field": Toward informing collaborative research methods at the color line and beyond. In K. Luschen & J. F. Carmona (Eds.), *Crafting critical stories: Toward pedagogies and methodologies of collaboration, inclusion, and voice* (pp. 423–449). New York, NY: Peter Lang.

Irvine, J. J., & Armento, B. J. (2001). *Culturally responsive teaching: Lesson planning for elementary and middle grades.* San Francisco, CA: McGraw-Hill.

Jensen, E. (2009). *Teaching with poverty in mind: What being poor does to kids' brains and what schools can do about it.* Alexandria, VA: ASCD.

Jones, J. M. (2008, August 4). *Majority of Americans say racism against Blacks widespread. Americas.* Retrieved January 5, 2011, from http://www.gallup.com/poll/109258/majority-americans-say-racism-against-Blacks-widespread.aspx

Ladson-Billings, G. J. (1999). Preparing teachers of diverse student populations: A critical race theory perspective. *Review of Research in Education, 24,* 211–247.

Ladson-Billings, G. (2006). From the achievement gap to the education debt: Understanding achievement in U.S. schools. *Educational Researcher, 35*(7), 3–12.

Landsman, J., & Lewis, C. W. (Eds.) (2006). *White teachers, diverse classrooms: A guide to building inclusive schools, promoting expectations, and eliminating racism.* Sterling, VA: Stylus.

Lewis, A. (2001). There is no "race" in the schoolyard: Color-blind ideology in an (almost) all-White school. *American Educational Research Journal. 38*(4), 781–811.

Lewis, C. W. (2003). From a minority to a majority teaching environment: Lessons learned and transferable. In W. M. Timpson, S. S. Canetto, & E. Borrayo (Eds.), *Teaching diversity: Challenges and complexities, identities and integrity* (pp. 35–42). Madison, WI: Atwood.

Lindsey, R., Nuri Robins, K., & Terrell, R. D. (2009). *Cultural proficiency: A manual for school leaders* (3rd ed.). Thousand Oaks, CA: Corwin.

Lockhart, L. L., & Mitchell, J. (2010). Cultural competence and intersectionality: Emerging frameworks and practical approaches. In L. L. Lockhart & F. S. Danis (Eds.), *Domestic violence: Intersectionality and culturally competent practice* (pp. 1–28). New York, NY: Columbia University Press.

Martin-Paulk, S., Martinez, J., & Lambeth, D. (in press). Effects of culturally relevant teaching on seventh grade African American students. *Middle Level Education in Texas.*

Martinez, J., Tost, J., Hilgert, L., & Woodard-Myers, T. (2013). Gang membership risk factors for eighth-grade students. *Nonpartisan Education Review, 9*(1), 1–31.

Martinez, J., Unterreiner, A., Aragon, A., & Kellerman, P. (in press). Demystifying mythologies about Latina/o students: Immigration reform and education. *Multicultural Teaching and Learning.*

McIntosh, P. (1988). *White privilege and male privilege: A personal account of coming to see correspondences through work in women's studies.* Working paper no. 189. Wellesley, MA: Wellesley College Center for Research on Women.

McKenzie, K. B., & Scheurich, J. J. (2004). Equity traps: A useful construct for preparing principals to lead schools that are successful with racially diverse students. *Educational Administration Quarterly, 40*(5), 601–632.

McLaren, P. (2007). *Life in schools: An introduction to critical pedagogy in the foundations of Education* (5th ed.). Boston, MA: Allyn & Bacon.

Milner, H. R., IV (2008). Critical race theory and interest convergence as analytic tools inteacher education policies and practices. *Journal of Teacher Education, 59*(4), 332–346.

Moe, T. M., & Chubb, J. E. (2009). *Liberating learning: Technology, politics, and the future of American education.* San Francisco, CA: Jossey-Bass.

National Center for Education Statistics (NCES). (n.d.). School and staffing survey: Percentage distribution of school principals by race/ethnicity, percentage minority, school type, and selected school characteristics: 2003–2004. *Institute of Education Sciences.* Retrieved from http://nces.ed.gov/surveys/sass/tables/sass_2004_27.asp

National Collaborative on Diversity in the Teaching Force. (2004, October). *Assessment of diversity in America's teaching force: A call to action.* Washington, DC: Retrieved from http://www.ate1.org/pubs/uploads/diversityreport.pdf

Nieto, S., & Bode, P. (2008). *Affirming diversity: The sociopolitical context of multicultural education* (5th ed.). San Francisco, CA: Pearson Education.

Obiakor, F. E. (2012). Culturally responsive teaching and special education. In J. Banks (Ed.), *Encyclopedia of diversity in education* (pp. 552–556). Thousand Oaks, CA: Sage.

Obiakor, F. E. (2014). Multicultural education: The mismeasured but important phenomenon. In J. Holliman (Ed.), *The Routledge international companion to educational psychology* (pp. 181–190). Abingdon, UK: Routledge.

Obiakor, F. E., & McCollin, M. J. (2011). Using the comprehensive support model to work with culturally and linguistically diverse students with learning disabilities. *Learning Disabilities: A Contemporary Journal, 9*(1), 19–32.

Paris, D. (2012). Culturally sustaining pedagogy: A needed change in stance, terminology, and practice. *Educational Researcher, 41*(3), 93–97.

Picower, B. (2009). The unexamined Whiteness of teaching: How White teachers maintain and enact dominant racial ideologies. *Race Ethnicity and Education, 12*(2), 197–215.

Redeaux, M. (2011). The culture of poverty reloaded. *Monthly Review: An Independent Socialist Magazine, 63*(3), 96–102.

Rothstein-Fisch, C., & Trumbull, E. (2008). *Managing diverse classrooms: How to build on students' cultural strengths.* Alexandria, VA: Association for Supervision and Curriculum Development.

Scheurich, J., & Young, M. D. (1997). Coloring epistemologies: Are our research epistemologies racially biased? *Educational Researcher, 26*(4), 4–16.

Shim, J. M. (2014). Multicultural education as an emotional situation: Practice encountering the unexpected in teacher education. *Journal Of Curriculum Studies, 46*(1), 116–137.

Sleeter, C. (2000). Interview: Diversity vs. White privilege. *Rethinking Schools, 15*(2), 45–49.

Solórzano, D. G., & Yosso, T. J. (2001). Critical race and LatCrit theory and method: Counter-storytelling: Chicana and Chicano graduate school experiences. *Qualitative Studies in Education, 14*(4), 471–495.

Smith, D. (1999). Outlaw women writers, (un)popular culture, and critical pedagogy. In J. Weaver & T. Dastip (Eds.), *Critical pedagogy, popular culture, and the creation of Meaning* (pp. 151–168). New York, NY: Garland.

Spann, J. (1990). *Retaining and promoting minority faculty members: Problems and possibilities.* Madison: University of Wisconsin System.

Suinn, R. M. (2006). Teaching culturally diverse students. In W. McKeachie & M. Svinicki (Ed.), *Teaching tips: Strategies, research, and theory for college and university teachers* (12th ed., pp. 151–171). Boston, MA: Houghton Mifflin.

Taylor, E. (2009). The foundations of critical race theory in education: An introduction. In E. Taylor, D. Gillborn & G. Ladson-Billings (Eds.), *Foundations of critical race theory in education* (pp. 1–13). New York, NY: Routledge/Taylor & Francis.

Trumbull, E., Rothstein-Fisch, C., Greenfield, P. M., & Quiroz, B. (2001). *Bridging cultures between home and school: A guide for teachers with a special focus on immigrant Latino families.* Mahwah, NJ: Erlbaum.

Valencia, R. R. (Ed.). (1997). *The evolution of deficit thinking: Educational thought and practice.* Washington, DC: Falmer.

Valencia, R. R. (2010). *Dismantling contemporary deficit thinking: Educational thought and practice.* New York, NY: Routledge.

Viadero, D. (1996, April 10). Culture clash. *Education Week, 15*(29), 39–42.

Villenas, S. (1996). The colonizer/colonized Chicana ethnographer: Identity, marginalization, and co-optation in the field. *Harvard Educational Review, 66*(4), 711–731.

Villenas, S. & Foley, D. (2011). Critical ethnographies of education in the Latino/a diaspora. In R. Valencia (Ed.), *Chicano school failure and success: Past, present and future* (3rd ed., pp. 175–196). New York, NY: Routledge/Taylor & Francis.

Zamudio, M., & Rios, F. (2006). From traditional to liberal racism: Living racism in the every day. *Sociological Perspectives, 49*(4), 483–501.

Zamudio, M., Russell, C., Rios, F., & Bridgeman, J. L. (2011). *Critical race theory matters: Education and ideology*. New York, NY: Routledge.

CHAPTER 4

PREPARING TEACHERS AND LEADERS FOR URBAN AND RURAL SPECIAL EDUCATION IN THIS AGE OF CHANGE

Tachelle Banks, Festus E. Obiakor, Floyd Beachum,
Bob Algozzine, and Sean Warner

The majority of teachers and school leaders in the United States are of a different race, ethnicity, class, gender, and linguistic dominance from that of their students (Banks, Zionts, & Sanchez-Fowler, 2011; McCray & Beachum, 2014;Gay, 2003; Tillman, 2003). Special education teachers are specifically challenged by a variety of racial and ethnic issues as they enter their classrooms (Artiles, Rueda, Salazar, & Higareda, 2000; Obiakor, 2006, 2007). In an age plagued with the overrepresentation of culturally and linguistically diverse (CLD) students in special education programs, it is important that teacher preparation programs within the field of special education devote attention to the devastating effects of deficit thinking. Retrogressive deficit thinking exists when teachers and service providers hold stereotypical or prejudicial views and engage in illusory generalizations that change their interactions with and expectations of CLD students (Obiakor, 1999, 2001, 2006, 2007, 2008). Similarly, leadership preparation programs have

Critical Issues in Preparing Effective Early Childhood Special Education Teachers for the 21st Century Classroom: Interdisciplinary Perspectives, pages 37–58.
Copyright © 2016 by Information Age Publishing

had a long tradition of silencing the voices of CLD people as well as not providing a vast array of course offerings to help administrators work with racially and ethnically diverse communities (Dantley, 2005, Karpinski & Lugg, 2006). Clearly, such thinking, policies, and actions exacerbate difficulties that plague urban and rural schools and the students they serve (Obiakor & Beachum, 2005).

The current focus on the achievement gap and poor graduation rates has highlighted the challenges facing urban and rural schools in our nation. In response to these challenges, many colleges and universities have established programs designed specifically to prepare teachers for work in high-needs schools. These programs seek to address concerns about the (a) large numbers of unqualified teachers in urban schools (Zeichner, 2003), (b) poor or ill-prepared teachers to meet the needs of diverse learners (Delpit, 2002; Hilliard, 2002; Ladson-Billings, 2000; Obiakor, 2006, 2007; Tidwell & Thompson, 2009; Zygmunt-Fillwalk & Leitze, 2006), (c) lack of understanding the social context of urban and rural education (Giroux & McLaren, 1996; Hilliard, 2002; Kincheloe, 2004; Liston & Zeichner, 1991; Weiner, 1993), and (d) inability to bridge the cultural divide between many teachers and their students (Beachum & McCray, 2011; Obiakor, 2007; Sleeter, 2001; Zeichner, 2003). As it appears, problems and issues pertinent to urban areas are also visible in rural communities. This chapter discusses how teachers and leaders can be prepared to work with urban children and youth with and without special needs.

TEACHER AND LEADERSHIP PREPARATION FOR HIGH-NEEDS AREAS

Preparing teachers and administrators to work in urban and rural public schools— and to remain there—is a daunting challenge. Urban schools are some of the most challenged, underresourced schools in the nation (Obiakor & Beachum, 2005; Payzant, 2011). These students are entangled with (a) high proportion of students from low-income families, (b) high proportion of CLD students, (c) high proportion of students who are limited English proficient, and (d) state or national designation as "high needs," "hard to staff," or "underresourced." It is important to note that students in high-poverty and high-minority schools are more likely to have teachers who are not content specialists in their respective subject matter (Peske & Haycock, 2006). Specifically, classes in high-poverty and high-minority secondary schools are more likely to be taught by "out-of-field teachers," those without a major or minor in the subject they teach. This statement is especially true when we consider highly qualified teacher (HQT) standards for special education teachers. Research indicates that students in high-poverty schools are twice as likely (20% versus 11%) to have inexperienced teachers, those with three or fewer years of teaching, or those who are uncertified (Au & Blake, 2003; NCTAF, 2003). In high-poverty secondary schools, approximately 33% of core academic classes are taught by out-of-field teachers, compared to approximately 20% of classes in low-poverty schools (Peske & Haycock, 2006). The pattern persists when we consider CLD students in major cities in the United States. In secondary schools, 33% of classes are taught by an out-of-field teacher compared to about 20% in low-minority schools (Peske & Haycock, 2006).

The United States continues to become more ethnically and racially diverse, especially with regard to the student population. This is juxtaposed with a very homogeneous teaching and administrative core. The Bureau of Labor Statistics (2010) revealed that 72.5% of all preschool and kindergarten teachers are White females. Hancock (2006) stated,

> The reality that White women are on the front lines of urban education is clearly evident. While we continue to recruit and retain minority teachers, it is critical that we also focus our attention on helping to educate White women teachers about the realities of teaching students who may hold a different sociopolitical, sociocultural, and socioeconomic perspective. (p. 97)

Similarly, most school administrators are White males (Tillman, 2003). They too must be supported as they lead schools in the midst of demographic flux. When educators are unaware or unconcerned about the cultures and realities of their students, the higher chances there are of "cultural insensitivity, lack-luster teaching, and apathetic leadership" (McCray & Beachum, 2014, p. 92). This underscores the point that attitudes, perspectives, and expectations are critical to teaching and leading. We recognize that teachers and administrators from culturally and linguistically diverse (CLD) backgrounds can also underserve students from CLD backgrounds (Kunjufu, 2002). And we realize that currently, there are not enough CLD teachers and administrators to educate the rapidly changing population. Therefore, White educators have a large role to play in the educational success of most vulnerable students. Challenges also cripple service delivery for students who attend rural schools.

Rural school districts face many challenges in meeting the needs of all their students, including students with disabilities. Research indicates that very small districts, those with 200–300 students, spend more per pupil than larger districts. This occurs because a school board, superintendent, principal, faculty, and equipment are needed no matter how small the district, and because low enrollment districts are likely to occur in sparsely populated areas that require more costly transportation (Hicks, 1994). These costly administrative expenditures increase the per-pupil cost while simultaneously reducing the funds available for education and educational services, such as an expanded curriculum or specialized teachers. Rural location and small size have negative effects on education because of

- Isolation imposed by terrain and distance;
- Declining economies in many rural areas (including high rates of poverty and unemployment);
- The financial burden of federal and state-mandated but underfunded or unfunded programs;

- Reduced community value placed on formal education; and
- Inappropriate and/or poor fiscal management practices (McIntosh, 1986, 1989).

In fact, the most troubling issue is providing programs and services for students with disabilities living in rural areas. Other issues are the rural district's inability to compete in the teacher job market; limited opportunities for in-service training or preservice training specifically designed for special educators in rural areas; crime, violence, and drug abuse; and limited curricular offerings due to small district size (Hicks, 1994). The geographic isolation common to rural districts can impede every aspect of the special education process—identification and assessment, service delivery, and availability of adequate personnel. In addition, geographic isolation common to rural areas may affect delivery of special education and related services through factors such as placement, personnel, and parental involvement. For example, service delivery may be difficult in rural communities in which the population fluctuates in response to a local industry such as mining (Helge, 1981, 1987). Moreover, the alignment of NCLB and IDEA 2004 requires special education teachers to be content specialists in subject-matter areas that they will be responsible for teaching. Over 12% of teachers employed to provide special education services to children ages 6–21 are not fully certified compared to 10.5% of teachers in general education (Boe & Cook, 2006; U.S. Department of Education, n.d.). High percentages of uncertified educators staffing special education programs enter teaching each year (Billingsley, Fall, & Williams, 2006). Evidence suggests that these uncertified teachers are less likely to stay in their positions (Miller, Brownell, & Smith, 1999); and attrition rates among beginning teachers with minimal preparation are twice as high compared to those with more extensive preparation (Boe, Cook, & Sunderland, 2006). Related situations make it difficult to maximize the potential of children and youth who live and attend schools in urban and rural areas with and without special needs.

TEACHER QUALITY, HIGH-NEEDS SCHOOLS, AND SPECIAL EDUCATION

Special education teachers remain at or near the top of the list for state and national teacher shortage (Prater, 2005). Apart from personnel shortages, other factors are compounding the challenge of preparing appropriately qualified special education personnel to serve the needs of students with mild to moderate disabilities (e.g., NCLB requirements of content area expertise as well as the expectation for special educators to be subject-matter specialists in every content area that they teach and for which they are the teacher of record). This data highlights the need for enhanced teacher preparation programs in special education to assist with meeting the demand to produce highly qualified teachers. It is important to note that special education teaching is not like subject-matter instruction, and training models based on the subject-matter model do not fit special education well. Special education teachers require extensive training in pedagogy, instructional accommodations, behavior support, and communication skills that complement verbal ability and subject knowledge expertise. A highly qualified teacher is one of the most important factors in improving student achievement (Darling-Hammond, 2000; Darling-Hammond, Chung, & Frelow, 2002; Gerstner, 2005; Laczko-Kerr & Berliner, 2003; Zientek, 2007). However, an increasing number of teachers are entering the education field without teaching credentials or sufficient preparation to teach a diverse and urban student population (Darling-Hammond, 2002; NCES, 2006; Rubin, 2007). The shortage of qualified and effective teachers is particularly a concern in urban and rural areas where teachers are working with students faced with the greatest challenges as learners—those from CLD backgrounds, those at risk for school failure, those living in impoverished conditions, those living in isolated areas, and those with unique and special needs. To a large measure, teachers indicate that they are unprepared for the challenges they face in urban schools, with only 20% reporting that they feel confident in working with students from diverse backgrounds or those with disabilities (Darling-Hammond, 2006a, 2006b; Gándara, Maxwell-Jolly, & Driscoll, 2005; Gay, 2005; National Collaborative on Diversity in the Teaching Force, 2004; U.S. Department of Education, 1999; Zumwalt & Craig, 2005). Moreover, although the student population is becoming increasingly diverse, the majority of teachers are White, with few CLD teachers entering the field (Banks et al., 2011; NCES, 2006). As a result, most teachers are from backgrounds that are different from those of their students, and most have little experience or knowledge about their students.

It is common knowledge that teachers who are underprepared leave their jobs at much higher rates than those teachers who are fully certified (Darling-Hammond, 2003; Zumwalt & Craig, 2005). However, given the teacher shortage, the number of underprepared teachers entering the teaching field has increased. The large and increasing percentage of untrained teachers not only results in inadequate services for students but also increases the likelihood that these teachers, who work with the most demanding students, will leave the profession (Darling-Hammond, 2006a; Darling-Hammond & Sykes, 2003). More than one fifth of classroom teachers leave their positions within the first 3 years of teaching (Fideler, 2000); in urban schools, up to one half of all new teachers leave teaching within the first 5 years (Claycomb, 2000). Moreover, 35% of emergency credentialed teachers leave within the first year of teaching, and more than 60% never receive a credential; however, 70% of prepared teachers remain after 5 years of teaching (Darling-Hammond, 2002).

The retention of teachers is critical to providing high quality education. Students with teachers who stay in their classrooms for more than 5 years have higher achievement levels than do students of teachers with less than 3 years of experience (Fideler, 2000). Clearly, educators, researchers, and policymakers recognize that teacher preparation needs to be restructured to provide qualified teachers (Levine, 2006; McFadden & Sheerer, 2006; Whitcomb, Borko, & Liston, 2007).

Common concerns regarding teacher preparation include an emphasis on theory over practice, weak linkages between coursework and fieldwork, poor quality of student teaching experiences, and limited early clinical experiences (Allsopp, DeMarie, Alvarez-McHatton, & Doone, 2006; Beck & Kosnik, 2002; Bullough, Clark, Wentworth, & Hansen, 2001; California Alliance of Pre K–18 Partnerships, 2004; Dean, Lauer, & Urquhart, 2005). These concerns are particularly critical for high-needs schools in urban and rural areas.

SCHOOL LEADERSHIP PREPARATION FOR THE 21ST CENTURY

Educational leadership, like many other fields, has looked to business and industry to inform its approach to leadership. Dantley (2002) stated that educational leadership "has borrowed idioms and syntax from economics and the business world all in an effort to legitimate itself as a valid field" (p. 336). While this has its benefits, it must also be balanced with the very human side of what happens in schools. Schools are still places where students learn, teachers inspire, and leaders guide and direct. Beachum and McCray (2014) cautioned against the overreliance on business models when they wrote, "These ideas should not be used as a way to ignore the difficult issues of race/ethnicity, gender, class, etc." (pp. 93–94). Unfortunately, such perspectives can place processes ahead of people, policy in front of practices, and rhetoric before reality. In other words, it is easier for an administrator to emphasize efforts to increase standardized test scores as opposed to trying to close the achievement gap. The latter could require fearless, open, honest, and difficult discussions with teachers and service providers about their real perceptions and actual teaching practices (Singleton & Linton, 2006).

School leadership preparation must continue to change with the times in order to best serve students. It cannot be guided by the same leadership models decade after decade. Bryant and Jones (1993) asserted that "it is idealistic to think that contemporary school administrators can set things straight simply by directing teachers and students in a manner that may have worked a few decades ago" (p. 14). New ideas, approaches, frameworks, and theories must be allowed into the knowledge base and into preparation programs (Theoharis, 2009). If not, the result could be "transactional management by school leaders when it comes to the teaching and learning process instead of progressive transformational leadership—leadership designed to critique, interrogate, and unearth potential inequities within the school climate and culture that prohibits learning among all students" (McCray & Beachum, 2011, p. 491). And this is the problem in school leadership preparation—far too many programs are narrowly focused on management, not emphasizing issues of diversity or inclusion, and do not have CLD staff (English, 2008; Tillman, 2003).

PREPARING HIGH QUALITY SPECIAL EDUCATION TEACHERS

Currently, the U.S. teaching force is significantly less diverse than the student population; as indicated, the majority of teachers are White (Gay & Howard, 2000; Villegas & Davis, 2007). The chance of the diverse array of students enrolled in urban and rural public schools having a teacher who shares a similar background to themselves is remote indeed (Banks et al., 2011). As a result, preparing special education teachers to appreciate the divergence of students with disabilities is prominent. Most teacher preparation programs report promoting cultural diversity to prepare preservice interns for diverse teaching experiences. Scholars have reported that some programs have used immersion and/or field experiences to prepare prospective teachers for diverse classroom settings (Blasi, 2002; Causey, Thomas, & Armento, 2000; Olson & Jimenez-Silva, 2008; Wilkins & Brand, 2005). However, many universities' curriculum reform is simply to incorporate one culturally diverse course into the curriculum, as mandated by national standards. However, helping prospective teachers develop competencies necessary to meet the needs of diverse learners has been a difficult, complex, yet critical task for teacher educators: it is clearly beyond the scope of one class. Various studies have confirmed that preservice teachers have negative beliefs and low outcome expectancies for CLD students even after successfully completing multicultural coursework (Easter, Shultz, Neyhart, & Reck, 1999; Garmon, 1996, 2004; Obiakor, 1999), indicating that courses alone are inadequate in providing prospective teachers with the skills, knowledge, and dispositions to transform attitudes (Case & Hemmings, 2005; Hill-Jackson, 2007; Milner, 2005; Sorrells, Schaller, & Yang, 2004).

Clearly, teacher preparation programs have been challenged to expose and refine preservice teachers' attitudes toward diverse student populations (Case & Hemmings, 2005; Gay, 2000; Milner, 2005). Given this reality, these programs are researching and sampling tactics to better prepare culturally responsive teachers. These strategies include (a) infusing cultural diversity into courses, (b) requiring urban and rural field experiences, (c) assigning students cultural shadowing partners, and (d) mandating urban and rural community visits (Gay, 2000; Irvine, 2003; Krei, 1998; Ladson-Billings, 1994; Ukpokodu, 2004; Villegas & Lucas, 2002). Universities must restructure the entire preparation program (all courses) to aid preservice teachers in bridging subject matter, pedagogical expertise, and cultural diversity (Gay, 2000; Ladson-Billings, 1994; Milner, 2005). Following is a section that fully discusses ways to modify traditional teacher preparation programs.

MODIFYING TRADITIONAL
MODELS OF TEACHER PREPARATION

The call for teacher preparation programs to confront the challenge of preparing a cadre of predominantly White, middle-class, and female prospective teachers to successfully work with an increasingly diverse population of students from both urban and rural areas resonates across the country (Darling-Hammond, 2002, 2006b; Galman, Pica-Smith, & Rosenberger, 2010; Ladson-Billings, 1999; Mc-Fadden & Sheerer, 2006; Risko, 2006; Sleeter, 2008; Villegas, 2007). The constant criticisms of schools, colleges, and education departments (McFadden & Sheerer, 2006; Risko, 2006; Villegas, 2007) have resulted in U.S. Secretary of Education, Arne Duncan, accusing teacher education programs of doing a mediocre job at best in preparing teachers for the realities of the 21st century classroom (Duncan, 2009). Teachers are entering the profession at a time when teacher education is "under severe if not outright vicious attack" (Villegas, 2007, p. 370). Currently, a major issue confronting America's schools is the lack of teachers capable of successfully teaching in diverse settings (Villegas, 2007; Weisman & Hansen, 2008). Earlier, Ladson-Billings (2001) urged teacher education programs to begin to examine ways to align their preparation with social and political changes taking place in K–12 institutions.

Researchers have constructively criticized traditional teacher education programs, describing them as limited in their ability to produce high quality teachers. Some years ago, Haberman (1995) stated that the traditional model of teacher education is actually counterproductive for many teachers, including those working in impoverished areas or diverse settings. Blackwell (2003) and Risko (2006) criticized colleges of education for failure to demonstrate conclusively that certified teachers are more successful in the classroom than noncertified teachers (Blackwell, 2003; Risko, 2006). Researchers have also noted the role of the educator as critical in the development of high quality teachers. Howard (2007) argued that "change has to start with educators" (p. 18). The reason why some teacher preparation programs are resistant to change is because "what they do is what they have always done" (Ladson-Billings, 2001, p. 7). As the NCES (1999) noted, approximately 80% of teachers who teach ethnically diverse students suggested feeling unprepared to meet their needs. Farkas, Johnson, and Foleno (2000) explained that the majority of new teachers need additional preparation to confront challenges of the "real" classroom, supporting other accusations in the literature that only a small number of teacher preparation programs train teachers to be successful in diverse settings (Ladson-Billings, 2001; Villegas, 2007; Weisman & Hansen, 2008). In sum, teacher educators fear being ostracized by their peers and therefore accept a monocultural curriculum (Blackwell, 2003). As a result, teacher education programs fail to meet challenging standards that adequately prepare teachers for the 21st century classroom (Blackwell, 2003; Duncan, 2009; McFadden & Sheerer, 2006; Risko, 2006; Villegas, 2007).

Researchers are suggesting that program coherence may be critical to teacher preparation, as defined by a program's conceptual and structural features (Darling-Hammond, 2006a; Grossman, Hammerness, McDonald, & Ronfeldt, 2008). Generally, there are critical components implicit in the guiding principles and structure of high-needs educational programming that may inform teacher preparation program practices in urban and rural areas. These include the following:

- Resources provided to facilitate school-university collaboration, with school and university faculty meeting on an ongoing basis to implement and evaluate the program.
- Program coordination, with faculty meeting on a regular basis to discuss the connections between courses and field experiences and to monitor candidates' progress in the program.
- An emphasis on addressing the diverse needs of an urban student population, with candidates completing course assignments and field experiences in urban schools.
- Supportive learning environment with ongoing advisement and mentoring by coordinators, faculty, and university supervisors.
- Collaborative community, with supportive and personable instructors and collegiality among students and faculty.
- Ongoing and coordinated field experiences throughout a program, with experienced cooperating teachers selected by university supervisors in collaboration with school administrators, with cooperating teachers oriented to the program and working closely with university supervisors, and with courses that provide structured assignments requiring direct application to the classroom.
- Data-driven model that informs program practices.

To be effectively prepared for high-needs schools, prospective candidates will need to

- Actively learn about the ways schools and communities are socially, economically, politically, culturally, historically, and geographically situated and related.
- Have rich, sustained, firsthand opportunities throughout their program to work with racially/ethnically, economically, and linguistically diverse children in urban and rural schools and neighborhoods.
- Learn that good teaching always begins with seeing each child, fully and fairly, as a multidimensional being, an individual with a unique history, hopes, and dreams—a child of promise and possibility.
- Understand the importance of valuing students' cultures and lived experiences—and making space for them in the classroom—while espousing the crucial importance of subject-area content as well.
- Rigorously question stereotypical views of city and rural children, families, and neighborhoods, and learn to see the assets of the communities rather than the deficits.
- Examine the ways their own racial, cultural, and class identities have shaped their perspectives; and if they have economic and social privilege to

analyze the advantages they have enjoyed that may have previously gone unrecognized.

- Examine and critique the sources of economic, racial, gender, and linguistic inequity within schools and communities, and understand how these factors influence students' lived experiences within and outside of the classroom.
- Explore together whether and how educators can and should be part of social movements that seek to overcome racial, economic, and linguistic barriers.
- Focus on urban schools but with interest in collaborating with others who attend to the related needs of rural, small town, and suburban schools.

Further, Collins (1999) suggested schools use "grow your own" strategies. He went on to acknowledge that most rural teachers came from the area so it made sense to have programs to assist local residents in their goal to become educators. Rural special education teachers can be prepared to meet the challenges of teaching in a rural district through the effective implementation of programs by colleges and universities. Colleges can educate their students not only in teaching practices but also in meeting challenges of working in a rural setting. For instance, it may be necessary to develop specific courses to help teacher candidates better understand the distinctive nature of the rural lifestyle, the unique aspects of rural schools, and the myth of socioeconomic dissonance (i.e., the idea that poverty is the cause of all educational problems confronting rural students). Courses that involve the study of specific regional cultures, religions, and history would be appropriate to offer in colleges and universities. To this end, unique strategies can be implemented to recruit, train, and support future teacher candidates.

FUTURE PERSPECTIVES

A well-articulated program is needed whereby issues of cultural, linguistic, and socioeconomic diversities are examined throughout the entire teacher and leadership preparation curriculum instead of in specialized courses (Villegas, 2007; Villegas & Lucas, 2002; Zeichner & Hoeft, 1996). This should be complemented with a commitment to follow-up programs for graduates, which would offer the best hope for moving preservice teachers and school leaders toward greater cultural, linguistic, and socioeconomic sensitivities (Pohan, 1996; Tillman, 2003). More importantly, teacher educators must examine how their experiences "reflect, confirm, or trouble their understanding of their practices and beliefs" (Galman et al., 2010, p. 226). Research shows that teachers are unprepared to meet the needs of diverse students; the teachers (in-service and preservice) themselves have consistently reported feeling unprepared to teach in culturally diverse settings (Ladson-Billings, 2000; NCES, 1999; Rushton, 2000, 2001). Knoblauch and Woolfolk Hoy (2008) confirmed that teachers need more than content knowledge to be affirmed in their practice of teaching students in high-needs schools. With-

out a comprehensive understanding of rural and urban communities, deficit thinking could emerge. As Villegas and Lucas (2002) elaborated,

> Teachers [and school leaders] looking through the deficit lens believe that the domi-
> nant culture is inherently superior to the cultures of marginalized groups in society.
> Within this framework, such perceived superiority makes the cultural norms of the
> dominant group the legitimate standard for the United States and its institutions.
> Cultures that are different from the dominant norm are believed to be inferior . . .
> Such perceptions inevitably lead teachers to emphasize what students who are poor
> and of color cannot do rather than what they already do well. (p. 37)

This can also extend to students with disabilities creating a situation where able-
bodied people are consciously or unconsciously preferred, valued more, or privi-
leged (Theoharis, 2009). Conversely, when dealing with students, any of them
who does not fit into what we call "general education" are "defaulted to another
group of students loosely labeled as non-general education students who do not
meet the criteria of academic, physical, emotional, social, or behavioral success of
the normed dominant group, the general education students" (Frattura & Topinka,
2006, p. 327). These nongeneral education students are also known as students
with special needs when teachers and school leaders are not well informed about
diversity, assumptions, and stereotypes; they could fall into the trap of always
comparing students with special needs against their nondisabled peers.

We believe developing educators for rapidly transitioning schools requires a
reexamination of the current models of teacher and leadership preparation because "continuing with business as usual will mean failure or mediocrity" (Howard, 2007, p. 17) for the nation's K–12 population as the data related to racial
and cultural achievement gaps illustrate (Howard, 2007; NCES, 2005). As efforts
to best prepare tomorrow's teachers for diversity are examined, there is general
agreement that a culturally competent and responsive pedagogy is a useful approach (Gay, 2000; Irvine & Armento, 2001; Ladson-Billings, 1994; Obiakor,
2001, 2006, 2008; Siwatu, 2006, 2007; Villegas, 2007; Villegas & Lucas, 2002).
Preparing culturally responsive teachers and service providers involves

1. Transforming preservice teachers' multicultural attitudes (Banks, 2001;
    Gay, 2000; Obiakor, 2001, 2006, 2008; Pang & Sablan, 1998; Phuntsog,
    2001; Villegas & Lucas, 2002, 2007).
2. Increasing their cultural competencies (Barry & Lechner, 1995; Hilliard,
    1998; Obiakor, 2001, 2006, 2008).
3. Providing efficacy building opportunities for interns to gain confidence
    with teaching diverse students (Obiakor, 2006, 2008; Siwatu, 2006,
    2007).
4. Helping interns believe in the positive outcomes associated with cultur-
    ally responsive teaching (Obiakor, 2006, 2008; Siwatu, 2006).

5. Arming them with the abilities necessary to successfully educate cultur-
    ally diverse students (Leavell, Cowart, & Wilhelm, 1999; Obiakor, 2006,
    2008).

Ladson-Billings (2001) credited teacher preparation programs for acknowledging the necessity of reform. These programs must be a rigorous, research-
based curriculum that requires interns to understand differences in student learning across disciplines instead of relying on one "disconnected course, which often
serves as the only exposure pre-service teachers have to witness how students
learn" (Blackwell, 2003, p. 363). The difficulties of changing teacher education,
however, should not be mistaken with impossibilities (Ladson-Billings, 2001). It
is possible for teachers with backgrounds different from their students to provide
effective classroom instruction if they approach teaching in a way that is responsive to cultural and linguistic diversities of their students (Gay, 2000). Consequently, it is crucial for teacher preparation programs to challenge not only the
teaching of academic skills necessary to increase students' learning, but also the
provision of multiple experiences requiring preservice teachers to critically examine issues of culture, linguistic diversity, poverty, and social justice (Darling-
Hammond, French, & Garcia-Lopez, 2002; Obiakor, Grant, & Obi, 2010). This
type of reform offers the best hope for creating special education teacher preparation programs.

As we look at educational leadership, there has been a movement in the field
toward more diverse perspectives and approaches (Bogotch, Beachum, Blount,
Brooks, & English, 2008; English, 2008; McCray & Beachum, 2011; Shoho,
Merchant, & Lugg, 2005; Singleton & Linton, 2006). A more recent framework
for school leaders interested in understanding themselves and diversity is culturally relevant leadership (Beachum, 2011; McCray & Beachum, 2011, 2014).
Culturally relevant leadership is composed of three tenets: liberatory consciousness, pluralistic insight, and reflexive practice. Liberatory consciousness encourages administrators to raise their own consciousness levels. This can be done by
reading diversity-related literature, attending seminars and conferences, engaging
diverse communities, starting a book club on a diversity-related topic, to name
a few. By doing this, they start to liberate their minds from the confining effects
of the status quo and unawareness. Next, pluralistic insight deals with the educators' attitudes toward students. This notion supports an affirming and positive
image of all students that acknowledges the uniqueness of their experiences and
their rich diversity. This includes both urban and rural communities. According to
Obiakor, Harris-Obiakor, Garza-Nelson, and Randall (2005), "We must begin to
understand that traditional educational programs are loaded with discriminatory
practices, unrealistic expectations, disproportionate representations, and illusory
conclusions. It is important that we shift our paradigms and powers as we look
for innovative ways to solve urban problems" (p. 29). Finally, reflexive practice
highlights "leadership actions, skills, and practice" (McCray & Beachum, 2014,

p. 106). Thus, "the work of the educator is not viewed as strictly objective, but rather educators' work is connected to the surrounding community of the school and the external society at large" (Beachum, 2011, p. 33).

When preparing culturally relevant leaders, they should be trained to do the following (see Beachum & McCray, 2012, pp. 241–242):

1. *Encourage and support diverse teaching methods*: Teachers should be allowed to explore multiple ways of teaching and learning.
2. *Create thoughtful learning communities that focus on student learning*: The notion of teachers sharing teaching strategies, having collaborative planning time, and collectively looking at student data is a relatively new phenomenon. School leaders should work to create the time and space for teachers to collaborate as well as organize professional development activities around student learning (Hord & Sommers, 2008).
3. *Share leadership opportunities and value multiple voices*: The culturally relevant leader should look for opportunities to build leadership capacity among teachers. More specifically, this means identifying and encouraging others to take on more responsibilities, speak to broader audiences, and think beyond their immediate classrooms. Similarly, it is important that school leaders value the voices of all in the organization.
4. Connect the school with the community: Schools are often intricately connected to the communities in which they reside. Thus, educational leaders must support efforts to involve the community at-large in the life of the school. "Schools can never divorce themselves from the communities where they exist" (Swaminathan, 2005, p. 195). Educational leaders should create opportunities for dialogue, invite speakers, host events, and build coalitions with the external community.

CONCLUSION

One of the most pressing issues in **urban and rural education** is the number of vacancies that go unfilled each year and the number of **teachers** assigned to teach in areas where they lack certification. State Departments of **Education** throughout the nation are partnering with **teacher preparation** programs to produce a cadre of certified **teachers** to meet the demand and satisfy the requirements of NCLB legislation. Much has been written about the strengths of traditional teacher **education** programs, especially those that serve traditional in-service **teachers** (Darling-Hammond, 2003; Darling-Hammond & Youngs, 2002). Research in this field clearly indicates that **urban** and rural areas suffer the most from **teacher** shortage, **teacher** under**preparation**, limited resources, state takeovers, and high **teacher** turnover (Anyon, 1997; Kozol, 1991; Yeo, 1997). It is clear, however, that producing more certified **teachers** under traditional teacher education program models will not necessarily address the issue of **teacher** shortage in high-needs **urban** and rural **school** districts.

In educational leadership, one of the greatest problems is the status quo. This is the idea that what we see in everyday educational practice is normal and that there is little that we can do. So the achievement gap, overrepresentation of urban/rural students in special education, high drop-out rates, teacher apathy, low parental involvement, high numbers of office referrals, have all become commonplace. A question that we must ask is, would we allow what happens in urban and rural communities to also happen in suburban communities? If the answer is no (and it is), then we must gather up the collective will to alter our leadership perspective, attitude, and approach to truly save our most vulnerable students.

Finally, thinking differently about teacher and leadership preparation is incongruent with monolithic programming and relying on single-course options to equip prospective teachers with the dispositions necessary for successful teaching in high-needs diverse urban and rural settings. Research has identified traditional teacher preparation programs at the forefront of the problem for failing to provide the type of transformative experiences critical to developing a cadre of teachers and administrators confidently and effectively prepared to work in urban and rural educational settings. High-needs schools require the best, the brightest, and the most committed educators. To that end, all teacher and leadership preparation programs must increase efforts to attract high quality candidates who truly care about all children.

REFERENCES

Allsopp, D. H., DeMarie, D., Alvarez-McHatton, P., & Doone, E. (2006). Partnerships, data collection, and teacher preparation: Does an on-site course-practicum delivery model enhance early preservice teacher preparation? *Teacher Education Quarterly, 33*(1), 19–35.

Anyon, J. (1997). *Ghetto schooling: A political economy of urban educational reform.* New York, NY: Teachers College Press.

Artiles, A. J., Rueda, R., Salazar, I., & Higareda, I. (2000). *Factors associated with English learner representation in special education: Emerging evidence from urban school districts in California.* Paper presented at the conference on Minority Issues in Special Education in the Public Schools, Harvard University, Cambridge, MA.

Au, K. H., & Blake, K. M. (2003). Cultural identity and learning to teach in a diverse community. *Journal of Teacher Education, 54*(3), 192–205.

Banks, J. A. (2001). *Cultural diversity and education: Foundations, curriculum and teaching* (4th ed.). Boston, MA: Allyn & Bacon.

Banks, T., Zionts, P., & Sanchez-Fowler, L. (2011). Knowledge, skills and dispositions for culturally competent and interculturally sensitive leaders in education. In E. D. McCray, P. Alvarez McHatton, & C. L. Beverly (Ed.), *Initial commitment to the profession of teaching: Examining intentions of teachers of color to remain in the field* (pp. 221–243). Lexington, KY: TED Diversity Caucus.

Barry, N. H., & Lechner, J. V. (1995). Pre-service teachers' attitudes about and awareness of multicultural teaching and learning. *Teaching and Teacher Education, 11*(2), 149–161.

Beachum, F. D. (2011). Culturally relevant leadership for complex 21st century school contexts. In F. W. English (Ed.), *Sage encyclopedia of educational leadership and administration* (2nd ed., pp. 26–35). Thousand Oaks, CA: Sage.

Beachum, F. D., & McCray, C. R. (2011). *Cultural collision and collusion: Reflections on hip-hop culture, values, and schools.* New York, NY: Lang.

Beachum, F. D., & McCray, C. R. (2012). The fast and the serious: Exploring the notion of culturally relevant leadership. In J. Moore & C. W. Lewis (Eds.), *Urban school contexts for African American students: Crisis and prospects for improvement* (pp. 231–247). New York, NY: Lang.

Bureau of Labor Statistics. (2010). *FY 2010 Congressional budget justification.* Retrieved from http://www.dol.gov/dol/budget/2010/PDF/CBJ-2010-V3-01.pdf

Beck, C., & Kosnik, C. (2002). Components of a good practicum placement: Student teacher perceptions. *Teacher Education Quarterly, 29*(2), 81–98.

Billingsley, B. S., Fall, A., & Williams, T. O. (2006). Who is teaching students with emotional and behavioral disorders?: A profile and comparison to other special educators. *Behavioral Disorders, 31*(3), 252–264.

Blackwell, J. (2003). Three steps forward: Adopt a teacher. *Childhood Education, 80*(1), 28.

Blasi, M. J. (2002). An asset model: Preparing preservice teachers to work with children and families "of promise." *Journal of Research on Teacher Education, 153*(1), 106–121.

Boe, E., & Cook, L. H. (2006). The chronic and increasing shortage of fully certified teachers in special and general education. *Exceptional Children, 72*(4), 443–460.

Boe, E. E., Cook, L. H., & Sunderland, R. J. (2006). *Attrition of beginning teachers: Does teacher preparation matter?* (Research Rep. 2006-TSDQ2). Philadelphia: University of Pennsylvania, Graduate School of Education, Center for Research and Evaluation in Social Policy.

Bogotch, I., Beachum, F. D., Blount, J., Brooks, J., & English, F. (2008). *Radicalizing educational leadership: Dimensions of social justice.* Rotterdam, The Netherlands: Sense.

Bryant, B., & Jones, A. (1993). *Seeking effective schools for African American children.* San Francisco, CA: Caddo Gap Press.

Bullough, R. V., Clark, D. C., Wentworth, N., & Hansen, J. M. (2001). Student cohorts, schoolrhythms, and teacher education. *Teacher Education Quarterly, 28*(2), 97–110.

California Alliance of Pre K–18 Partnerships. (2004, January). *Raising student achievement through effective education partnerships: Policy and practice.* Retrieved June 25, 2012, from http://www.calstate.edu/capp/publications/Alliance_for_Pre_K-18_Partnerships.pdf

Case, K. A., & Hemmings, A. (2005). Distancing strategies: White women preservice teachers and antiracist curriculum. *Urban Education, 40*(6), 606–626.

Causey, V. E., Thomas, C. D., & Armento, B. J. (2000). Cultural diversity is basically a foreign term to me: The challenges of diversity for pre-service teacher education. *Teaching and Teacher Education, 16*(1), 33–45.

Claycomb, C. (2000). High-quality urban school teachers: What they need to enter and to remain in hard-to-staff schools. *The State Education Standard, 1*(1), 17–20.

Collins, T. (1999). *Attracting and retaining teachers in rural areas.* Charleston, WV: ERIC Clearinghouse on Rural Education and Small Schools. (ERIC Document Reproduction Service No. ED438152)

Dantley, M. E. (2002). Uprooting and replacing positivism, the melting pot, multiculturalism, and other impotent notions in educational leadership through an African American perspective. *Education and Urban Society, 34*(3), 334–352.

Dantley, M. E. (2005). African American spirituality and Cornel West's notions of prophetic pragmatism: Restructuring educational leadership in American urban schools. *Educational Administration Quarterly, 41*(4), 651–674.

Darling-Hammond, L. (2000). Teacher quality and student achievement: A review of state policy evidence. *Education Policy Analysis Archives, 8*(1). Darling-Hammond, L. (2002). *Access to quality teaching: An analysis of inequality in California's public schools.* Stanford, CA: Stanford University Press.

Darling-Hammond, L. (2003). Keeping good teachers: Why it matters, what leaders can do. *Educational Leadership, 60*(8), 6–13.

Darling-Hammond, L. (2006a). Assessing teacher education: The usefulness of multiple measures for assessing program outcomes. *Journal of Teacher Education, 57*(2), 120–138.

Darling-Hammond, L. (2006b). Constructing 21st century teacher education. *Journal of Teacher Education, 57*(3), 300–314.

Darling-Hammond, L., Chung, R., & Frelow, F. (2002). Variation in teacher preparation: How well do different pathways prepare teachers to teach? *Journal of Teacher Education, 53*(4), 286–302.

Darling-Hammond, L., French, J., & Garcia-Lopez, S. P. (2002). *Learning to teach for social justice.* New York, NY: Teachers College Press.

Darling-Hammond, L., & Sykes, G. (2003). Wanted, a national teacher supply policy for education: The right way to meet the "highly qualified teacher" challenge. *Educational Policy Analysis Archives, 11*(33). Retrieved from http://epaa.asu.edu/ojs/article/view/261

Darling-Hammond, L., & Youngs, P. (2002). Defining "highly qualified teachers:" What does "scientifically-based research" actually tell us? *Educational Researcher, 31*(9), 13–25.

Dean, C., Lauer, P., & Urquhart, V. (2005). Outstanding teacher education programs: What do they have that the others don't? *Phi Delta Kappan, 87*(4), 285–289.

Delpit, L. (2002). No kinda sense. In L. Delpit & J. K. Dowdy (Eds.), *The skin that we speak: Thoughts on language and culture in the classroom* (pp. 31–48). New York, NY: New Press.

Duncan, A. (2009, October 22). Teacher preparation: Reforming the uncertain profession. *U.S. Department of Education.* Retrieved from http://www.ed.gov/news/speeches/teacher-preparation-reforming-uncertain-profession

Easter, L. M., Shultz, E. L., Neyhart, T., & Reck, U. (1999). Weighty perceptions: A study of the attitudes and beliefs of preservice teacher education students regarding diversity and urban education. *Urban Review, 31*(2), 205–220.

English, F. W. (2008). *The art of educational leadership: Balancing performance and accountability.* Thousand Oaks, CA: Sage.

Farkas, S., Johnson, J., & Foleno, T. (2000). *A sense of calling: Who teaches and why.* New York, NY: Public Agenda.

Fideler, E. F. (2000). State-initiated induction programs: Supporting, assisting, training, assessing, and keeping teachers. *The State Education Standard, 1*(1), 12–16.

Frattura, E. M., & Topinka, C. (2006). Theoretical underpinnings of separate educational programs the social justice challenge continues. *Education and Urban Society, 38*(3), 327–344.

Galman, S.A., Pica-Smith, C., & Rosenberger, C. (2010). Aggressive and tender navigations: Teacher educators confront Whiteness in their practice. *Journal of Teacher Education, 61*(3), 225–236.

Gándara, P., Maxwell-Jolly, J., & Driscoll, A. (2005). *Listening to teachers of English learners.* Santa Cruz, CA: Center for the Future of Teaching and Learning.

Garmon, M. A. (1996). Missed messages: How prospective teachers' racial attitudes mediate what they learn from a course on diversity. (Doctoral dissertation, Michigan State University). *Dissertation Abstracts International, 57*(9), 3896A.

Garmon, M. A. (2004). Changing preservice teachers' attitudes/beliefs about diversity: What are the critical factors? *Journal of Teacher Education, 55*(3), 201–213.

Gay, G. (2000). *Culturally responsive teaching: Theory, research, and practice.* New York, NY: Teachers College Press.

Gay, G. (2003). The importance of multicultural education. *Educational Leadership, 61*(4), 30–35.

Gay, G. (2005). Politics of multicultural teacher education. *Journal of Teacher Education, 56*(3), 221–228.

Gay, G., & Howard, T. C. (2000). Multicultural teacher education for the 21st century. *The Teacher Educator, 36*(1), 1–16.

Gerstner, L. V. (2005). An education reform agenda for the next four years—and beyond. *Education Week, 24*(16), 60.

Giroux, H. A., & McLaren, P. (1996). Teacher education and the politics of engagement: The case for democratic schooling. In P. Leistyna, A. Woodrum, & S. A. Sherblom (Eds.), *Breaking free: The transformative power of critical pedagogy* (pp. 301–331). Cambridge, MA: Harvard Educational Review.

Grossman, P., Hammerness, K., McDonald, M., & Ronfeldt, M. (2008). Constructing coherence: Structural predictors of perceptions of coherence in NYC teacher education programs. *Journal of Teacher Education, 59*(4), 273–287.

Haberman, M. (1995). *Star teachers of children in poverty.* Indianapolis, IN: Kappa Delta Pi.

Hancock, S. (2006). White women's work: On the front lines in urban education. In J. Landsman & C. Lewis (Eds.), *White teachers/diverse classrooms: A guide to building inclusive schools, promoting higher expectations, and eliminating racism* (pp. 93–109). Sterling, VA: Stylus.

Helge, D. I. (1981). Problems in implementing comprehensive special education programming in rural areas. *Exceptional Children, 47,* 514–520.

Helge, D. I. (1987). Strategies for improving rural special education program evaluation. *Remedial and Special Education, 8*(4), 53–60.

Hicks, J. (1994). *Special education in rural areas: Validation of critical issues by selected state directors of special education: Final report.* Alexandria, VA: National Association of State Directors of Special Education.

Hilliard, A. (1998). *SBA: The reawakening of the African mind.* Gainesville, FL: Makare.

Hilliard, A. G., III (2002). Language, culture, and the assessment of African American children. In L. Delpit & J. K. Dowdy (Eds.), *The skin that we speak: Thoughts on language and culture in the classroom* (pp. 87–105). New York, NY: New Press.

Hill-Jackson, V. (2007). Wrestling Whiteness: Three stages of shifting multicultural perspectives among white pre-service teachers. *Multicultural Perspectives, 9*(2), 29–35.

Hord, S. M., & Sommers, W. A. (2008). *Leading professional learning communities: Voices from research and practice.* Thousand Oakes, CA: Corwin.

Howard, G. R. (2007). As diversity grows, so must we. *Educational Leadership, 64*(6), 16–22.

Irvine, J. J. (2003). *Educating teachers for a diverse society: Seeing with the cultural eye.* New York, NY: Teachers College Press.

Irvine, J. J., & Armento, B. J. (2001). *Culturally responsive teaching: Lesson planning for elementary and middle grades.* New York, NY: McGraw-Hill.

Karpinski, C. F., & Lugg, C. A. (2006). Social justice and educational administration: Mutually exclusive? *Journal of Educational Administration, 44*(3), 278–292.

Kincheloe, J. L. (2004). The bizarre, complex, and misunderstood world of teacher education. In J. L. Kincheloe, A. Bursztyn, & S. R. Steinberg (Eds.), *Teaching teachers: Building a quality school of urban education* (pp. 1–49). New York, NY: Lang.

Knoblauch, D., & Woolfolk Hoy, A. (2008). "Maybe I can teach those kids." The influence of contextual factors on student teachers' efficacy beliefs. *Teaching & Teacher Education, 24*(1), 166–179.

Kozol, J. (1991). *Savage inequalities: Children in America's schools.* New York, NY: HarperPerennial.

Krei, M. S. (1998). Intensifying the barriers: The problem of inequitable teacher allocation in low-income urban schools. *Urban Education, 33*(1), 71–94.

Kunjufu, J. (2002). *Black students middle class teachers.* Chicago, IL: African American Images.

Laczko-Kerr, I., & Berliner, D. C. (2003). In harm's way: How uncertified teachers hurt their students. *Educational Leadership, 60*(8), 34–39.

Ladson-Billings, G. (1994). What we can learn from multicultural education research. *Educational Leadership, 51*(8), 22–26.

Ladson-Billings, G. (1999). Just what is critical race theory and what's it doing in a nice field like education. In L. Parker, D. Deyhele, & S. Villenas (Eds.), *Race is . . . race isn't: Critical race theory and qualitative studies in education* (pp. 7–30). Boulder, CO: Westview.

Ladson-Billings, G. (2000). Fighting for our lives: Preparing teachers to teach African American students. *Journal of Teacher Education, 51*(3), 206–214.

Ladson-Billings, G. (2001). *Crossing over to Canaan: The journey of new teachers in diverse classrooms.* San Francisco, CA: Jossey-Bass.

Leavell, A. G., Cowart, M., & Wilhelm, R. W. (1999). Strategies for preparing culturally responsive teachers. *Equity and Excellence in Education, 32*(1), 64–71.

Levine, A. (2006, September). Educating school teachers. *The Education School Project.* Retrieved June 25, 2012, from http://www.edschools.org/teacher_report.htm

Liston, D., & Zeichner, K. (1991). *Teacher education and the social conditions of schooling.* New York, NY: Routledge.

McCray, C. R., & Beachum, F. D. (2011). Culturally relevant leadership for the enhancement of teaching and learning in urban schools. In I. Bogotch (Ed.), *International handbook on leadership for learning* (pp. 487–501). Van Godewijckstraat, The Netherlands: Springer.

McCray, C. R., & Beachum, F. D. (2014). *School leadership in a diverse society: Helping schools prepare all students for success.* Charlotte, NC: Information Age.

McCray, C. R., & Beachum, F. D. (2014). *School leadership in a diverse society: Helping schools prepare all students for success.* Charlotte, NC: Information Age.

McFadden, C., & Sheerer, M. (2006). A comparative study of the perceptions of teacher preparation faculty and school superintendents. *Action in Teacher Education, 28*(1), 51–71.

Mcintosh, D. K. (1986). Problems and solutions in delivery of special education services in rural areas. *The Rural Educator, 8*(1), 12–15.

Mcintosh, D. K. (1989). Retention of teachers in rural areas. *The Rural Educator, 11*(1), 26–29.

Miller, M. D., Brownell, M. T., & Smith, S. W. (1999). Factors that predict teachers staying in, leaving, or transferring from the special education classroom. *Exceptional Children, 65*(2), 201–218.

Milner, H. R. (2005). Developing a multicultural curriculum in a predominantly White teaching context: Lessons from an African American teacher in a suburban English classroom. *Curriculum Inquiry, 35*(4), 391–427.

Murrell, P. (2001). *The community teacher.* New York, NY: Teachers College Press.

National Center for Education Statistics (NCES). (2005). The condition of education in brief 2005. *Institute of Education Sciences.* Retrieved June 26, 2012, from http://nces.ed.gov/pubsearch/pubsinfo.asp?pubid=2005095

National Collaborative on Diversity in the Teaching Force. (2004). *Assessment of diversity in America's teaching force.* Washington, DC: Author.

National Collaborative on Diversity in the Teaching Force. (2004). *Assessment of diversity in America's teaching force: A call to action.* National Commission on Teaching and America's Future. (2003). *No dream denied: A pledge to America's children.* Washington, DC: Author. Retrieved from http://nctaf.org/wp-content/uploads/no-dream-denied_summary_report.pdf

Obiakor, F. E. (1999). Teacher expectations of minority exceptional learners: Impact on "accuracy" and self-concepts. *Exceptional Children, 66,* 39–53.

Obiakor, F. E. (2001). *It even happens in "good" schools: Responding to cultural diversity in today's classrooms.* Thousand Oaks, CA: Corwin.

Obiakor, F. E. (2006). *Multicultural special education: Culturally responsive teaching.* Upper Saddle River, NJ: Prentice Hall.

Obiakor, F. E. (2007). Multicultural special education: Effective intervention for today's schools. *Intervention in School and Clinic, 42,* 148–155.

Obiakor, F. E. (2008). *The eight-step approach to multicultural learning and teaching* (3rd ed.). Dubuque, IA: Kendall/Hunt.

Obiakor, F. E., & Beachum, F. D. (2005). *Urban education for the 21st century: Research, issues, and perspectives.* Springfield, IL: Thomas.

Obiakor, F. E., Grant, P., & Obi, S. O. (2010). *Voices of foreign-born African American teacher educators in the United States.* New York, NY: Nova Science.

Obiakor, F. E., Harris-Obiakor, P., Garza-Nelson, C., & Randall, P. (2005). Educating urban learners with and without special needs: Life after the *Brown* case. In F. E.

Obiakor & F. D. Beachum (Eds.), *Urban education for the 21st century: Research, issues, and perspectives* (pp. 20–33). Springfield, IL: Thomas.

Olson, K., & Jimenez-Silva, M. (2008). The campfire effect: A preliminary analysis of preservice teachers' beliefs of teaching English learners after state-mandated endorsement courses. *Journal of Research on Childhood Education, 22*(3), 246–260.

Pang, V. O., & Sablan, V. A. (1998). Teacher efficacy: How do teachers feel about their abilities to teach African American students? In M. E. Dilworth (Eds.), *Being responsive to cultural differences—How teachers learn* (pp. 39–58). Thousand Oaks, CA: Corwin.

Payzant, T. (2011). *Urban school leadership*. San Francisco, CA: Jossey-Bass.

Peske, H. G., & Haycock, K. (2006). *Teaching inequality: How poor and minority students are shortchanged on teacher quality: A report and recommendations by the Education Trust*. Washington, DC: Education Trust.

Phuntsog, N. (2001). Culturally responsive teaching: What do selected United States elementary school teachers think? *Intercultural Education, 12*(1), 51–64.

Pohan, C. A. (1996). Preservice teachers' beliefs about diversity: Uncovering factors leading to multicultural responsiveness. *Equity and Excellence in Education, 29*(3), 62–69.

Prater, M. A. (2005). Ethnically diverse rural special educators who are highly qualified: Does NCLB make this impossible? *Rural Special Education Quarterly, 24*(1), 23–26.

Risko, V. J. (2006). Facing teacher education challenges as an insider. *Journal of Reading Education, 32*(1), 5–12.

Rubin, B. C. (2007). Learner identities amid figured worlds: Constructing (in)competence at an urban high school. *The Urban Review, 39*(2), 217–249.

Rushton, S. (2000). Student teacher efficacy in inner-city schools. *Urban Review, 32*(4), 365–383.

Rushton, S. (2001). Applying brain research to create developmentally appropriate learning environments. *Young Children, 56*(5), 76–82.

Shoho, A. R., Merchant, B. M., & Lugg, C. A. (2005). Social justice: Seeking a common language. In F. W. English (Ed.), *The Sage handbook of educational leadership: Advances in theory, research and practice* (pp. 47–67). Thousand Oaks, CA: Sage.

Singleton, G. E., & Linton, C. (2006). *Courageous conversations about race: A field guide for achieving equity in schools.* Thousand Oakes, CA: Corwin.

Siwatu, K. O. (2006). *Preservice teachers' culturally responsive teaching self-efficacy and outcome expectancy beliefs: The role of multicultural and racial attitudes.* Paper presented at the annual Texas Tech University, College of Education Research Conference, Lubbock, TX.

Siwatu, K. O. (2007). Preservice teachers' culturally responsive teaching self-efficacy and outcome expectancy beliefs. *Teaching and Teacher Education, 23*(7), 1086–1101.

Sleeter, C. E. (2001). Preparing teachers for culturally diverse schools. *Journal of Teacher Education, 52*(2), 94–106.

Sleeter, C. E. (2008). An invitation to support diverse students through teacher education. *Journal of Teacher Education, 59*(3), 212–219.

Sorrells, A. M., Schaller, J., & Yang, N. K. (2004). Teacher efficacy ratings by African American and European American preservice teachers at a historically Black college. *Urban Education, 39*(5), 509–536.

Swaminathan, R. (2005). *Building community in urban schools: Promises and challenges. Urban education for the 21st century: Research, issues, and perspectives* (pp. 187–198). Springfield, IL: Thomas.

Theoharis, G. (2009). *The school leaders our children deserve: Seven keys to equity, social justice, and school reform.* New York, NY: Teachers College Press.

Tidwell, M., & Thompson, C. (2009). Infusing multicultural principles in urban teacher preparation. *Childhood Education, 85*(2), 86–90.

Tillman, L. C. (2003, Fall). From rhetoric to reality? Educational administration and the lack of racial and ethnic diversity within the profession. *University Council for Educational Review, 14*(3), 1–4.

Ukpokodu, O. (2004). The impact of shadowing culturally different students on preservice teachers' disposition toward diversity. *Multicultural Education, 12*(2), 19–28.

U.S. Department of Education. (n.d.). *U.S. Department of Education.* Retrieved June 25, 2012, from http://www.ed.gov/

U.S. Department of Education. (1999). *Archived Information: U.S. Department of Education's 1999 Performance Report and 2001 Annual Plan.* Retrieved June 25, 2012, from http://www2.ed.gov/pubs/AnnualPlan2001/index.html

Villegas, A. M. (2007). Dispositions in teacher education: A look at social justice. *Journal of Teacher Education. 58*(5), 370–380.

Villegas, A., & Davis, D. (2007). Approaches to diversifying the teaching force: Attending to issues of recruitment, preparation and retention. *Teacher Education Quarterly, 34*(4), 137–147.

Villegas, A. M., & Lucas, T. (2002). *Educating culturally responsive teachers.* Albany: State University of New York Press.

Villegas, A. M., & Lucas, T. (2007). The culturally responsive teacher. *Educational Leadership. 64*(6), 28–33. Retrieved from http://worldview.unc.edu/files/2014/02/Required-reading1-The-Culturally-Responsive-Teacher.pdf

Weiner, L. (1993). *Preparing teachers for urban schools: Lessons from thirty years of school reform.* New York, NY: Teachers College Press.

Weisman, E. M., & Hansen, L. E. (2008). Student teaching in urban and suburban schools: Perspectives of Latino preservice teachers. *Urban Education, 43*(6), 653–670.

Whitcomb, J., Borko, H., & Liston, D. (2007). Why teach? *Journal of Teacher Education, 59*(1), 3–9.

Wilkins, J. L. M., & Brand, B. R. (2005). *Promoting teacher self-efficacy in elementary mathematics and science methods courses.* Poster presented at the annual meeting of the American Educational Research Association, Montreal, Quebec, Canada.

Yeo, F. L. (1997). *Inner-city schools, multiculturalism, and teacher education.* New York, NY: Garland.

Zeichner, K. M. (2003). The adequacies and inadequacies of three current strategies to recruit, prepare, and retain the best teachers for all students. *Teachers College Record, 105*(3), 490–519.

Zeichner, K., & Hoeft, K. (1996). Teacher socialization for cultural diversity. In J. S. Kula (Ed.), *Handbook of research on teacher education* (2nd ed., pp. 525–547). New York, NY: Macmillan.

Zientek, L. R. (2007). Preparing high quality teachers: Views from the classroom. *American Educational Research Journal: Teaching, Learning, and Human Development, 44*(4), 959–1001.

Zumwalt, K., & Craig, E. (2005). Teachers' characteristics: Research on the demographic profile. In M. Cochran Smith & K. Zeichner (Eds.), *Studying teacher education* (pp. 111–156). Mahwah, NJ: Erlbaum.

Zygmunt-Fillwalk, E. M., & Leitze, A. (2006). Promising practices in preservice teacher preparation. *Childhood Education, 82*(5), 283–288.

CHAPTER 5

INTERDISCIPLINARY COLLABORATION IN TEACHER PREPARATION TO SUPPORT STUDENTS WITH EXCEPTIONALITIES

Shaunita D. Strozier, Margaret M. Flores,
Vanessa Hinton, Margaret Shippen, and Stephanie Taylor

This chapter addresses the importance and critical nature of effective collaboration in preservice teacher preparation. Given the varying needs of students with exceptionalities, multiple service providers are involved in program planning and implementation of individualized education. "Collaboration" means to work with others to achieve a common goal. Within special education, this common goal is the effective implementation of a child's individualized educational program. Professionals work together to provide an environment conducive to learning, effective instruction, and appropriate accommodations (Cook & Friend, 2010). There are various ways in which professionals may approach this task, each cooperating with different levels of participation from group members. Collaborative teams, collaborative consultation, and instructional consultation are typical ways to facilitate communication and problem solving when working toward a common goal.

Critical Issues in Preparing Effective Early Childhood Special Education Teachers for the 21st Century Classroom: Interdisciplinary Perspectives, pages 59–69.
Copyright © 2016 by Information Age Publishing

COLLABORATIVE TEAMS

Groups of professionals work together as teams in order to develop and implement effective educational programs. There are different frameworks through which team members interact: multidisciplinary, interdisciplinary, and transdisciplinary teams. Within a multidisciplinary team, the members maintain separate roles by discipline. The team shares a common goal of program development and accomplishes this goal through the completion of separate tasks by discipline (Koskie & Freeze, 2000). Each team member works separately by conducting separate assessments, designing interventions, and implementing interventions or instruction. Team members communicate with each other regarding their work, but do not share tasks or implement their program plans together. A multidisciplinary team working together in development of an individualized educational program (IEP) would work separately, come together for the meeting to share their work, and implement their portion of the IEP separately.

Interdisciplinary teams differ from multidisciplinary teams in their shared responsibilities. The interdisciplinary team views the educational program as a shared outcome. Team members synthesize their disciplinary expertise to develop program plan. In forming this unified plan, interdisciplinary team members engage in more frequent communication and interaction (Hestenes, Laparo, & Scott-Little, 2009). However, the interdisciplinary team members maintain their own professional identity and implement separate portions of the plan according to discipline.

A transdisciplinary team involves the most collaboration and team interaction. Team members work across disciplines to plan and implement services. Team members share responsibility for program planning and implementation (Zaretsky, 2007). The roles of team members are not separated by discipline, meaning that team members may implement portions of the program developed by team members from other disciplines. In working across disciplines, the transdisciplinary framework seems to involve the most communication, interaction, and sharing of information.

COLLABORATIVE CONSULTATION

In providing effective instruction and services for students with diverse needs, it is likely that multiple professionals from different disciplines will collaborate. This collaboration may involve assisting another professional in service delivery or problem solving, meaning that one professional provides instruction or intervention using strategies or methods recommended by other consulting professionals. The first step in the consulting process is to establish rapport between the consultant and the consultee. It is important that the consultant value the skills and abilities of the consultee and communicate this appreciation and respect. The consulting relationship should be viewed by both parties as two professionals with different expertise working together for a common goal (Thomson, 2013).

In order to provide effective consultation, the student needs within his/her current setting or context should be accurately identified (Musti-Rao, Hawkins, & Tan, 2011). Assessment of student needs may include observation, interviews, review of records, and administration of additional assessments. Interventions and strategies should be developed based on assessment information in addition to their feasibility within the classroom or setting. When providing consultation, the identification of effective strategies is important, but ensuring that they can be used consistently and with fidelity over time is essential (Eisenman, Pleet, Wandry, & McGinley, 2011). For example, a general education teacher with a classroom of 20 students will not be able to provide 20 minutes of one-on-one instruction each day without other support personnel available.

Once appropriate and feasible interventions are identified, the consultant should ensure that the strategy can be implemented, and this may involve demonstration, professional development, and/or coaching. According to professional development literature, one-time demonstrations do not lead to sustained use of educational practices, so follow-up will be necessary (Patti, Holzer, Stern, & Brackett, 2012). Effective consultation entails ongoing support to ensure that the identified intervention or practice can be implemented over time. It may be necessary to modify the original intervention based on changes in the environment over time, and continued contact between the consultant and the consultee will ensure that this can occur.

INSTRUCTIONAL COLLABORATION

With regard to instruction in the classroom, collaboration may take different forms, each serving a different purpose to benefit students with diverse learning needs by improving educational outcomes (Rea, McLaughlin, & Walther-Thomas, 2002; Tremblay, 2013). Friend and Cook (2010) identifed six types of collaborative instructional models: (a) one teaching and one observing, (b) one teaching and one assisting, (c) station teaching, (d) parallel teaching, (e) alternative teaching, and (f) team teaching. Effective collaborative instruction involves the use of multiple models since differentiation of instruction for diverse learners requires flexibility rather than a one-size-fits-all approach. Regardless of the model used, collaborative instruction requires that each professional demonstrate effective communication, interpersonal skills, and expertise in differentiation of instruction based on student needs (Brinkmann & Twiford, 2012; Brown, Howerter, & Morgan, 2013; Friend, Cook, & Hurley-Chamberlain, 2010).

The model in which one professional teaches and the other observes involves active participation from one professional and a less active, but reflective role played by the other professional. This model may be used in situations in which collaboration requires professional development or data collection. When working to meet the needs of learners with disabilities from diverse backgrounds, one professional may have certain expertise or skills that other professionals may need. Through a process of back and forth teaching and observation, instructional skills and methods may be developed or refined. At times, there is a need for observation for the purpose of assessment. One professional may observe during a teaching situation in order to collect data regarding student readiness, engagement, skill acquisition, and/or application of learning.

One teaching, one assisting is another model in which one professional takes a more active role in instruction than another. The purpose of this model is to assist students by making instruction more accessible. The professional who drifts during instruction is free to assist students as needed during an instructional activity. This assistance could include clarification of concepts, assistance with a task or materials, task-related prompts, or redirection. This model allows for group instruction while accommodating the needs of students with diverse learning needs. This model also allows for expedited assistance for students rather than an alternative, which might include interruption of instruction or may involve student frustration as they wait for assistance. This model makes it easier to keep students on-task because of the proximity of the teacher assisting, and it saves time when distributing materials. The supporting teacher can monitor behaviors not seen by the teacher directing the lesson; further, this model requires little or no planning. On the other hand, through the eyes of the students, one teacher (usually the special educator) is viewed as the paraprofessional. One teacher appears to have more control than the other. In addition, the teacher walking around the classroom may be distracting to some students as they begin to expect immediate one-on-one assistance.

Station teaching involves active teaching and cooperative planning by all professionals. Each teaches a small group of students at a station, and students may rotate among stations during instructional time. This allows for differentiation of instruction based on students' needs. For example, station teaching allows for implementation of enrichment and remediation at the same time, meeting the needs of classrooms in which students have diverse learning needs. Instructional groupings and station instructors should be fluid when using this model so as not to unnecessarily call attention to a particular group of students based on skills or abilities. Students who need enrichment should be taught by both a general education teacher as well as a special education teacher. When grouping students, skills and current performance should be considered rather than relying on labels. This model exemplifies a smaller student-teacher ratio, increases response rate, encourages cooperation and independence, allows for strategic grouping, and provides an active learning format. On the other hand, this model requires planning and preparation, increases in noise level, is more difficult to monitor (especially for independent groups), and forces both teachers to know the content.

When using the parallel teaching model, all professionals actively plan and teach the same content. Instruction occurs in two or more heterogeneous groups of students at the same time. Each group of students learns the same content, but this model allows for smaller teacher-to-student ratios and may be more conducive to certain activities in which smaller heterogeneous groups are preferred.

Smaller groupings allow for increased opportunities for student response and practice. This model provides an effective review format, encourages student responses, reduces the student-teacher ratio for group instruction, and gives the special educator an opportunity to add strategies for all students. On the other hand, this model makes it difficult to achieve equal depth of content coverage, is difficult to coordinate, requires monitoring of partner pacing, increases noise level, encourages some teacher-student competition, and forces both teachers to know the content and have planning time.

Alternative teaching allows for greater differentiation of instruction. Students are grouped such that one or more small groups of students will receive instruction that is different than that of the class as a whole. One professional provides instruction that is different based on student needs, such as (a) increased intensity, (b) increased priming of background knowledge, (c) remediation and extra practice, or (d) enrichment of the curriculum. It is important that alternative teaching is not overused or instructional groupings become entrenched in a way that stigmatizes certain students based on particular labels. Using this model sparingly and varying the instructor can reduce this possible risk. This model facilitates enrichment opportunities, offers absent students "catch-up" time, keeps individuals and the class on pace, offers time to develop missing skills, and offers time for preteaching or remediation. On the other hand, this model makes it easy to select the same low-achieving students for help, creates segregated learning environments, makes it difficult to coordinate, and may result in singling out students.

Team teaching is a model in which professionals plan and actively provide instruction together. In a seamless fashion, two or more professionals teach the same lesson to a whole group of students together. Each professional plays an equal and active role in lesson implementation. Examples of team teaching might involve taking turns leading discussion, role-playing, or presentation of different sides of an argument or problem. Team teaching requires cooperative planning, communication, practice, and rapport between professionals. This model provides system observation/data collection; promotes role and content sharing; facilitates individual assistance; models appropriate academic, social, and help-seeking behaviors; teaches questioning and answering; and makes both teachers see themselves as equals during instruction. On the other hand, this model requires considerable planning, requires modeling and role-playing skills, and forces both teachers to be very knowledgeable about the content.

THE TRIADIC RELATIONSHIPS AND COMMUNICATIONS

Triadic relationships encompass partnerships between universities, schools in the community, and the preservice special education teachers (Gardiner & Robinson, 2011). Preservice special education teachers need university supervisors and co-operating teachers to support their emotional development, model evidence-based classroom practices, and promote cognitive processes involved in problem-solving instructional concerns (Goodnough, Osmond, Dibbon, Glassman, & Stevens,

2009). Evidence supports the benefits of the triadic relationship, however, collaboration can be difficult to accomplish because each member of the triad is operating from different perspectives (Valenica, Martin, Place, & Grossman, 2009). Lack of collaboration among the triad impacts preservice teachers' preparation. Lack of continuity between the university supervisor and cooperating teacher negatively impacts preservice teachers' development because the university supervisor is designated to facilitate the relationship between cooperating and preservice teachers as well as provide on-site support and guidance (Beck & Kosnik, 2002; Jabrey & Khamara, 2013; Prater & Sileo, 2004; Ralph & Noonan, 2004). The lack of support and guidance from the cooperating teacher hinders preservice preparation because cooperating teachers provide knowledge, expertise, and professional support during field experiences (Goodnough et al., 2009). To prevent inadequate collaboration, it is important that effective communication occurs.

Communication is defined as the process by which one individual relates to another's ideas (Taylor, Smiley, & Richards, 2009). Effective communication is one of the most important skills needed by each member in the teacher preparation team (Beyene, Anglin, Sanchez, & Ballou, 2002). Conferences, reflective practices, and question and answer sessions enable every member of the triad to communication effectively. To ensure that expectations and goals are being met, the university supervisor, preservice teacher, and cooperating teacher should plan for regularly scheduled conferences for good communication (Sanderson, 2003). Daily conferences are short in length and address matters that are in need of immediate attention. Additionally, daily conferences can coordinate work schedules, adjust plans, as well as identify and solve daily problems with the cooperating teacher. Weekly conferences can be used for long-term planning, evaluation of the student teacher, and analysis of the cooperating teacher (Goodnough et al., 2009). The university supervisor can attend these meetings to help problem-solve concerns that arose during the week.

During the field experiences, there may be concerns and issues that are observed by the preservice teacher. With so many hours of the day being spent educating students with disabilities, at times it may be difficult to conference. However, to ensure that the student teacher is reflecting on his/her experiences, the preservice teacher should journal. Journals are reflective tools that allow prospective teachers to reflect critically upon their field experiences (Lee, 2007). Additionally, the use of journals can increase communication between preservice teachers and their university supervisors to foster self-reflection about their placement and student engagements (Graves, 2013). The university supervisor can also address issues with cooperating teacher that the student teacher is unable or not comfortable enough to state. Thoughtful and meaningful dialogue can be held by passing back and forth a journal of thoughts (Sanderson, 2003). Preservice teachers need to be provided with the opportunity to meet with cooperating teachers and university supervisors to ask questions (Sanderson, 2003). Completing field experiences and university coursework assignments can be challenging. Answering questions could clarify ideas and increase information for the preservice teacher. The expertise of the cooperating teacher and university supervisor should help foster a closer relationship and increase the prospective teacher's self-esteem (Valencia et al., 2009).

FAMILY COMMUNICATION

Communicating with the family is a primary way of establishing effective partnerships that improve outcomes for children (Whitbread, Bruder, Fleming, & Park, 2007). When communicating with the family, it is very important to consider the family-systems theory. With family-systems theory, all family members are interrelated. Therefore, family interactions, characteristics, and functions impact how the family communicates and adapts to critical events (Raver, 2009). Family interactions include the relationships among family members and four subsystems: (a) marital, (b) parental, (c) sibling, and (d) extended family (Turnbull, Turnbull, Erwin, & Soodak, 2006). As a professional, it is important to be aware that each individual in the family has his/her unique set of needs, abilities, and established roles. Family characteristics are attributes that the family unit shares as a whole. Examples of characteristics are socioeconomic status, cultural background, and size. Professionals should understand that family characteristics influence how individuals in the family communicate with other people and adapt to life events. Family functions pertain to the needs that the family is responsible for. This involves daily care, economic needs, recreation, affection, education, and vocational needs. Part of communicating with families involves professionals connecting families to resources and supports.

The Division of Early Childhood of the Council of Exceptional Children recommended that professionals be responsive to the cultural language as well as family characteristics unique to each family unit (Sandall, Hemmeter, Smith, & McLean, 2005). Today, families are culturally, linguistically, and ethnically more diverse (Correa & Heward, 2003). Most professionals, however, are not minorities, and there can be a poor match among the background of professionals and the families professionals are serving (Raver, 2009). Culture and ethnicity influence but do not define the family. Therefore, it is critical that professionals avoid assumptions and stereotypes which expect people within a cultural group to communicate or behave in a predetermined way. Effective communication starts with professionals' commitment to be nonjudgmental about families' values, beliefs, and lifestyles (Zhang & Bennett, 2001). When working with families, Swick and Bailey (2004) made suggestions that could enable a person to be nonjudgmental when communicating with families. They suggest that professionals

1. Model positive nonverbal communication.
2. Learn what the family truly values.
3. Create a relaxed and pleasant atmosphere conducive to conversation.
4. Show respect and support for the family.

1. Share positive feelings about family members.
2. Follow through on commitments to the family.

A commitment to be nonjudgmental is a very good beginning, but it is important to be aware of barriers that prevent families and professionals from communicating efficiently. Barriers to effective communication with family members include professional attitudes, the climate of professional work environment, lack of interdisciplinary collaboration, cultural differences, and policy (Lotze, Bellin, & Oswald, 2010). When communicating with the family, professionals should use specific communication techniques. These include the professional monitoring of his/her own body language, responding to family members' nonverbal communication, and utilizing active listening. For a professional to monitor his/her body language when communicating, he/she must be aware of facial expressions, gestures, posture, and body movements; and make sure to project optimism and confidence in the family (Lotze et al., 2010). Raver (2009) provided tips for effective communication with families. Facial expressions when communicating with family members should involve comfortable eye contact, warmth and concern, and a smile when appropriate. One's posture should express attentiveness and be relaxed, and gestures and body movements should avoid being too expressive or repetitive. Active listening skills are very difficult to build. Active listening acknowledges and emphasizes feelings expressed by family members and uses effective questioning techniques (Cramer, 1998; Gordon, 2003; O'Shea, Algozzine, Hammittee, & O'Shea, 2000; Turnbull & Turnbull, 1990). There are several steps to active listening with family members (McNaughton, Hamlin, McCarthy, Head-Reeves, & Schreiner, 2008). First, the professional makes empathetic statements that acknowledge the feelings of the individual. Then, the professional asks questions which are appropriate to what the family member conveyed. And last, the professional paraphrases what the family member conveyed to ensure verification.

CONCLUSION

In order to meet the diverse needs of children with exceptionalities, preservice teachers must have the skills and abilities to effectively collaborate with families and other professionals. Service development involves the formation of teams, which may take different forms depending on the nature of the needed program. In preparing teachers, instructional and field experiences must allow preservice teachers to observe and participate in different team models, with emphasis on the function and purpose of various team configurations. Preservice teachers also need preparation in their role as consultants for other professionals. Appropriate data collection and interpretation are critical for this role in order to ensure that interventions are developed in ways that are logical and feasible. Consultation also involves clear and effective communication. Preservice teachers should practice effective listening and communication, demonstrating that they understand the needs of other professionals. As a matter of urgency, preservice field experiences should involve modeling and guided practice in the provision of consultative services by seasoned professionals.

It is likely that preservice teachers will work in settings in which collaborative instruction is implemented. It is imperative that preservice teachers have multiple experiences in working with other professionals for the purpose of providing inclusive instruction. In addition, they must understand how to plan collaboratively and implement various models of collaborative instruction based on the content and needs within the classroom. It is critical that they feel comfortable working with other professionals and value the differences between disciplines so that the combined strengths of the instructional team can meet students' diverse learning needs.

Finally, teacher preparation programs must foster the skills and abilities necessary for future educators to effectively work with parents and families to meet the needs of students. Preservice teachers must have experiences working with families from problem solving and tiered intervention to service delivery in order to transition students from special education to postsecondary experiences in the community. They need the preparation in working with other professionals and families. Instructional delivery and support are critical components of the special educator's role, but the development and provision of instruction involves collaboration with others. In the end, teacher preparation programs must provide future teachers the tools necessary to effectively work with others in order to meet the needs of students with exceptionalities.

REFERENCES

Beck, C., & Kosnik, C. (2002). Components of a good practicum placement: Student teacher perceptions. *Teacher Education Quarterly, 29*(2), 81–98.

Beyene, T., Anglin, M., Sanchez, W., & Ballou, M. (2002). Mentoring and relational mutuality: Proteges perspectives. *Journal of Humanistic Counseling, Education and Development, 41*(1), 87–102.

Brinkmann, J., & Twiford, T. (2012). Voices from the field: Skill sets needed for effective collaboration and co-teaching. *International Journal of Educational Leadership Preparation, 7*(3), 1–13.

Brown, N. B., Howerter, C. S., & Morgan, J. J. (2013). Tools and strategies for making co-teaching work. *Intervention in School and Clinic, 49*, 84–91.

Cook, L., & Friend, M. (2010). The state of the art of collaboration on behalf of students with disabilities. *Journal of Educational & Psychological Consultation, 20*(1), 1–8.

Correa, W., & Heward, W. (2003). Special education in a culturally diverse society. In W. Heward (Ed.), *Exceptional children: An introduction to special education* (7th ed., pp. 86–119). Upper Saddle River, NJ: Merrill/Prentice Hall.

Cramer, S. F. (1998). *Collaboration: A success strategy for special educators.* Needham Heights, MA: Allyn & Bacon.

Eisenman, L. T., Pleet, A. M., Wandry, D., & McGinley, V. (2011). Voices of special education teachers in an inclusive high school: Redefining responsibilities. *Remedial and Special Education, 32*(2), 91–104. doi:10.1177/0741932510361248

Friend, M., & Cook, L. (2010). *Interactions: Collaboration skills for school professionals* (6th ed.). Columbus, OH: Merrill.

Friend, M., Cook, L., & Hurley-Chamberlain, D. (2010). Co-teaching: An illustration of the complexity of collaboration in special education. *Journal of Educational and Psychological Consultation, 20*(1), 9–27.

Gardiner, W., & Robinson, K. (2011). Peer placements: Negotiating collaborative relationships. *The Professional Educator, 35*(2),1–11.

Goodnough, K., Osmond, P., Dibbon, D., Glassman, M., & Stevens, K. (2009). Exploring a triad model of student teaching: Pre-service teacher and cooperating teacher perceptions. *Teaching and Teacher Education, 25*(2), 285–296.

Gordon, T. (2003). Teacher effectiveness training. New York, NY: Three Rivers.

Graves, S. (2013). Using dialogue journals in mentoring relationships: Teacher candidates' and mentors' experiences. *Mountainrise, 8*(2), 1–12.

Hestenes, L. L., Laparo, K., & Scott-Little, C. (2009). Team teaching in an early childhood interdisciplinary program: A decade of lessons learned. *Journal of Early Childhood Teacher Education, 30*(2), 172–183.

Jabrey, M. A., & Khamra, H. A. (2013). Special education practicum at the University of Jordan: Preliminary indicator of students' satisfaction and concerns. *International Journal of Special Education, 28*(1), 1–9.

Koskie, J., & Freeze, R. (2000). A critique of multidisciplinary teaming: Problems and possibilities. *Developmental Disabilities Bulletin, 28*(1), 1–17.

Lee, I. (2007). Preparing pre-service English teachers for reflective practice. *ELT Journal, 61*(4), 321–329.

Lotze, G. M., Bellin, M. H., & Oswald, D. P. (2010). Family-centered care for children with special health care needs: Are we moving forward? *Journal of Family Social Work, 13*(2), 100–113.

McNaughton, D., Hamilin, D., McCarthy, J., Head-Reeves, D., & Schreiner, M. (2008). Learning to listen: Teaching an active listening strategy to preservice education professionals. *Topics in Early Childhood Special Education, 27*(4), 223–231.

Musti-Rao, S., Hawkins, R. O., & Tan, C. (2011). A practitioner's guide to consultation and problem solving in inclusive settings. *Teaching Exceptional Children, 44*(1), 18–26.

O'Shea, L., Algozzine, R., Hammittee, D., & O'Shea, D. (2000). *Families and teachers of individuals with disabilities: Collaborative orientations and responsive practices.* Boston, MA: Allyn & Bacon.

Patti, J., Holzer, A. A., Stern, R., & Brackett, M. A. (2012). Personal, professional coaching: Transforming professional development for teacher and administrative leaders. *Journal of Leadership Education, 11*(1), 263–274.

Prater, M. A., & Sileo, T. W. (2004). Fieldwork requirements in special education preparation: A national study. *Teacher Education and Special Education: The Journal of the Teacher Education Division of the Council for Exceptional Children, 27*(3), 251–263.

Ralph, E. G., & Noonan, B. W. (2004). Evaluating teacher-candidates' teaching in the extended practicum. *Brock Education Journal, 14*(1), 1–18.

Raver, S. (2009). *Early childhood special education—0 to 8 years.* Upper Saddle River, NJ: Merrill/Prentice Hall.

Rea, P., McLaughlin, V. L., & Walther-Thomas, C. S. (2002). Outcomes for students with learning disabilities in inclusive and pullout programs. *Exceptional Children, 68*(2), 203–222.

Sandall, S., Hemmeter, M., Smith, B., & McLean, M. (2005). *DEC recommended practices: A comprehensive guide to practical application in early intervention/early childhood special education.* Longmont, CO: Sopris West.

Sanderson, D. R. (2003). Maximizing the student teaching experience: Cooperating teachers share strategies for success. *West Chester University,* 1–14.

Swick, K. J., & Bailey, L. B. (2004). Communicating effectively with parents and families who are homeless. *Early Childhood Education Journal, 32*(3), 211–215.

Taylor, R. L., Smiley, L. R., & Richards, S. (2009). *Exceptional students: Preparing teachers for the 21st century.* New York, NY: McGraw-Hill Higher Education.

Thomson, C. (2013). Collaborative consultation to promote inclusion: Voices from the classroom. *International Journal of Inclusive Education, 17*(8), 882–894.

Tremblay, P. (2013). Comparative outcomes of two instructional models for students with learning disabilities: Inclusion with co-teaching and solo-taught special education. *Journal of Research in Special Educational Needs, 13*(4), 251–258. doi:10.1111/j.1471-3802.2012.01270.x

Turnbull, A., & Turnbull, H. (1990). *Families, professionals, and exceptionality: A special partnership* (2nd ed.). New York, NY: Merrill.

Turnbull, A., Turnbull, R., Erwin, E., & Soodak, L. (2006). *Families and exceptionality* (5th ed.) Upper Saddle River, NJ: Merrill/Prentice Hall.

Valencia, S. W., Martin, S. D., Place, N. A., & Grossman, P. (2009). Complex interactions in student teaching lost opportunities for learning. *Journal of Teacher Education, 60*(3), 304–322.

Whitbread, K. M., Bruder, M. B., Fleming, G., & Park, H. (2007). Collaboration in special education. *Teaching Exceptional Children, 39*(4), 6–14.

Zaretsky, L. (2007). A transdisciplinary approach to achieving moral agency across regular and special education in K–12 schools. *Journal of Educational Administration, 45*(4), 496–513.

Zhang, C., & Bennett, T. (2001). Multicultural views of disability: Implications for early intervention professionals. *Infant-Toddler Intervention, 11*(2), 143–154.

CHAPTER 6

PREPARING TEACHERS TO MAXIMIZE THE POTENTIAL OF YOUNG STUDENTS WITH GIFTS AND TALENTS

Sunday Obi, Festus E. Obiakor, Don Drennon-Gala,
Tachelle Banks, and Satasha Green

In recent years, state and national level attention to students with the highest potential has been diverted to those struggling to achieve at minimum proficiency levels. Meanwhile, school districts wrestle with ensuring that high-ability young students demonstrate annual yearly progress. Decreased school budgets during the current decade have forced many school administrators to consolidate or eliminate specialized services for their most capable students by reallocating funds previously directed toward gifted education. The intent of this chapter is to help general and special educators to maximize the potential of young students with gifts and talents by providing programs and services that match their unique characteristics and needs. These students have a right to an appropriate education, one grounded in the recognition of individual differences and unique learning needs. They also need a curriculum and educators responsive to their individual learning rates, styles, and complexities. This is the goal of this chapter.

Critical Issues in Preparing Effective Early Childhood Special Education Teachers for the 21st Century Classroom: Interdisciplinary Perspectives, pages 71–83.
Copyright © 2016 by Information Age Publishing

WHO ARE YOUNG STUDENTS WITH GIFTS AND TALENTS?

A student with gifts and talents is someone who shows, or has the potential for showing, an exceptional level of performance in one or more areas of expression. Some of these abilities are very general and can affect a broad spectrum of the person's life, such as leadership skills or the ability to think creatively. Students with gifts and talents are identified in grades 1–12 as demonstrating high performance ability or potential in academic and/or artistic areas and therefore require an educational program beyond what is normally provided by the general school program in order to achieve their potential. Programming for these students must include a variety of options, including acceleration, enrichment, in-depth work in selected areas of study, and opportunities for community-based and "beyond the classroom" learning through mentorships and summer and weekend programs. Some of the needs of these students can be met in regular classrooms with adequate teacher training and support services. Teachers who work with these learners must be carefully selected and trained in gifted education; and their curriculum must be designed to be rigorous, deep, and complex.

The historian, Arthur M. Schlesinger (1999) once wrote that "a basic theme of American history has been the movement, uneven but steady, from exclusion to inclusion"—a movement "fueled by ideals" (p. 173). He might well have been talking about the U.S. public education system, where it has become evident some segments of its pupil population have been overlooked or neglected. The good news is that there have been some efforts to ameliorate this problem. However, despite these efforts, there continues to be lingering problems of limited federal leadership, coupled with a singular focus on grade-level proficiency. Apparently, the educational system fails to address the unique learning needs of students with gifts and talents and those who could become high achieving with appropriate support. In fact, the goal should be to maximize the potential of these students by providing programs and services that match their unique characteristics and needs. Success in the 21st century requires a commitment to developing student talents as early as possible. The needs of these students can be met in regular classrooms with adequate teacher training and support services. They are not a homogeneous group with needs that can be satisfied through a single administrative adjustment. It is critical to use a variety of educational services to enable educators to meet the needs of these students.

To address this urgent need, gifted education supporters introduced legislation to amend the Elementary and Secondary Education Act (ESEA) to provide responsible federal leadership in meeting the needs of students with gifts and high abilities. To Aid Gifted and High-Ability Learners by Empowering the Nation's Teachers (TALENT) Act has four key emphases:

- Supporting educator development to ensure academic growth for high-ability students.
- Confronting and addressing the national excellent gap.

- Providing public transparency of student achievement gap.
- Continuing research and dissemination on best practices in gifted education.

The TALENT Act provides commonsense, no-cost strategies to change America's talent trajectory and regain our role as an international leader in education. Far too many students are not achieving to their potential, with every state reporting wide "Excellence Gaps," the achievement gap at the top levels of achievement between low income and their more affluent peers and between minority students and White students. Nationally, on the 2011 NAEP math exam, 9% of White students scored at the advanced level, compared with 1% of African American students and 2% of Hispanic students. The TALENT Act addresses persistent challenges that impede school districts from providing appropriate services to high-ability students. Clearly, the majority of teachers are not trained to recognize high ability and adjust instruction to work with students with high ability and gifts. It is important that principals, teachers, and pupil service personnel have the training to support identification and services for students with gifts and talents, including those who have not been formally identified.

INDICATORS OF GIFTEDNESS

Giftedness lies not so much in the possession of a certain number of traits as it does in the *degree and combinations* in which some of the traits may be present. For example, most children are curious; curiosity in itself does not mean giftedness. However, when a high degree of curiosity is present, in combination with resourcefulness, perseverance, and a drive to organize and perfect, it may take the form of an intense desire to probe until a solution has been found and may well be an indication of giftedness. Below are indicators of giftedness:

- *Heightened Perceptual Skills*: Child is acutely aware of and responsive to his/her environment, uses all senses, is keenly observant and highly alert.
- *Intense Curiosity*: Child probes for answers through verbal questioning, by exploring independently, and/or by manipulating objects.
- *Advanced Problem-Solving Ability and Conceptualization*: Child thinks logically, draws conclusions, makes generalizations, transfers concepts to new settings, and makes good educated guesses.
- *Motivation and Perseverance*: Child has an unusual degree of commitment to tasks (especially self-selected activities), becomes absorbed in work, puts tremendous energy and time into specific topics of interest, and tirelessly pursues interest to point of satisfaction. (These traits may be manifested in hobbies or collections.)
- *Drive to Organize and Perfect*: Child sets what may be impossible high standards for self and for work, and places great importance on the quality of his/her performance.

- *Search for Challenge*: Child welcomes complexity (often selects it over the simple), enjoys games of thought and reason (and resists being provided with the solution), and plays with ideas and words.
- *Originality and Humor*: Child puts elements together in new ways, uses novel approaches to tasks and materials, often displays keen sense of humor, takes risks (often in the form of espousing unconventional or unpopular positions), and is both flexible and fluent in generating ideas.
- *Resourcefulness and Independence*: Child seeks own direction, is self-initiating, and has high tolerance for ambiguity.
- *Fondness for Elaboration*: Child loves to embellish by adding on to ideas, responses, and solutions; generates alternatives and is concerned with detail.
- *Acute Sensitivity*: Child reacts strongly to moral and social issues; feels joy, pain, injustice, sarcasm, and rejection keenly; and has intense empathy. (These abilities may make a child with gifts and talents painfully conscious of his/her separateness from others and highly self-critical. However, at the same time, these very traits may contribute to the child's being well liked by peers and viewed by them as leader. In other words, the social and emotional problems that may result from these traits may lie more in the student's self-image than in others' perceptions.)
- *Abilities and Aptitudes*: These vary in both verbal and nonverbal areas across age, population, sex, disability level, and ethnic group. High aptitude manifests itself in vastly different ways depending on what assessment has been used, students' family and cultural backgrounds, and other areas of talent potential, including the absence or presence of motivation, creativity, and disabilities.
- *Achievement*: This is usually associated with high achievement, but achievement can and does vary across high-potential children and over time (Reis & McCoach, 2000). High-ability children sometimes underachieve because of decreased motivation, social and emotional affect, effort, interest, absence of challenge, engagement, and support. Children with high aptitudes but with learning disabilities, for example, may increasingly demonstrate low motivation in school as they become older, and subsequently, they have lower achievement.
- *Academic Background*: Because of different experiences, academic background results in poor preparation for many young people and adults with high aptitudes. Continuous academic progress depends on strong academic preparation, especially at early ages when brain development progresses at a rapid pace.
- *Culture and Identity*: These are important because children from diverse backgrounds and racial and socioeconomic groups interact with achievement in rich and diverse ways, and we sometimes fail to take their unique identities into account (Ford & Harris, 1999).

- *Effort and Motivation:* No single noncognitive trait is more influential on high levels of performance than effort or motivation. In addition to the aforementioned factors, young people and adults with high potential are most hampered by underchallenging learning or work experiences. High-aptitude students often "coast" through school without having to expend effort, and when they finally do encounter a challenge, some experience a loss of confidence in their abilities resulting in diminished achievement levels (Reis & McCoach, 2000).

- *Interests, Learning Styles, and Creative Opportunities:* These are intimately associated with high performance. All persons recognized in history as gifted contributors in the arts, sciences, humanities, and other areas of human performance have had interests that border on passion for their work, opportunities to pursue this work in a manner compatible with their preferred ways of learning, and environments that provide opportunities for creative expression. Without these factors and environmental conditions, even persons with exceptional cognitive potential may not maximize their potential.

TEACHING STUDENTS WITH GIFTS AND TALENTS

The review of literature shows that during the past, particularly in the last several decades, many experts in the field of gifted education have written descriptions of the characteristics and teaching characteristics they believe to be essential for teachers of the gifted. According to the numerous descriptions in the literature, experts in gifted education believe certain professional and personal characteristics are not only necessary but also essential for teachers of children with gifts and talents. Merlin (1994) believed recognizing and finding "those few good people" can make a world of difference in the life of a child with gifts and talents. Hansford (1985) stated that children with gifts and talents have special educational, social, and emotional needs that differ from those of other children. To meet these needs requires a special type of "good" teacher. As Hansford noted, many of the characteristics of effective teachers of these children (e.g., a thorough understanding of subject matter, self-confidence, a good sense of humor, organizational skills) are characteristics of all effective teachers. However, there are other qualities that are of special significance to teachers of these children and which are as vital as advanced degrees and years of experience. Hansford identified five such qualities. First is openness, which refers to the teacher's ability to be sensitive and accepting. Second is flexibility. Effective teachers of the gifted must be flexible in their approach toward curriculum and learning. Third, a positive sense of self is imperative for teachers of the gifted. Fourth is having strong communication skills, and fifth is intelligence.

Other experts in gifted education highlighted additional characteristics for teachers of the gifted. Freehill (1974) believed desirable teacher attributes are only tentatively inferred from expert opinion, child rating of teachers, and retrospective studies of development. Two qualities stand out: intelligence and empathy. Intelligence is broadly described to include delight in learning, knowledge, curiosity, and a sense of mutuality with children. Empathy appears on most lists of positive qualities. Torrance and Myers (1970) also noted that a teacher must be able to imagine the thinking and feeling of the child in order to respond accurately. Thus, teachers of the gifted must be similar in many respects to those they teach. Newland (1962) found that teachers of the mentally superior must have the so-called essentials. He described the essentials as being emotionally secure in order to withstand the rigors of intellectual bombardment and to enjoy the pursuit of the less well known. Also, teachers should be intellectually curious and agile, concerned with the joy in the act of learning, and prone to seek and experience new structures of experience. In addition, they should have a moderate to high energy level. The teacher with this characteristic is always doing something more, finding and using the extra materials and sources that so many teachers seem to overlook. Professionally, these teachers should have 2 or 3 years of highly effective teaching experience and a broad cultural sensitivity and curiosity.

Many experts agree that standards for teacher training should be established and that the teacher of the gifted should have at least state certification and/or an endorsement in gifted education. Experts also agree that the teacher of the gifted should have high intelligence. Not necessarily gifted themselves, these teachers should have an understanding of giftedness, originality, and self-confidence (Heath, 1997). All in all, just as a struggling student needs a special educator and special accommodations, high-achieving students need to be taught by a qualified teacher and in a specific way to best meet their unique needs. These students must be challenged in a learning environment that provides the opportunity for their knowledge to grow. Teachers must understand and use teaching strategies to support their success.

Most teachers and school administrators have very little or no training in meeting and identifying the unique learning needs of students with gifts and talents. In fact, teachers need training to skillfully modify the curriculum to accommodate the different rates at which students learn as well as their depth of understanding. Teachers of such students need training to create differentiated learning environment in which

- All students have opportunities to work at their challenge levels.
- Differences in learning needs are respected.
- Flexible grouping based on readiness, interests, and learning styles occurs.
- Students can demonstrate and receive credit for previous mastery of standards.
- Opportunities for faster pacing of new material are offered when needed.
- Students' areas of interest are incorporated into their independent studies.
- Research investigations are facilitated.
- Technology is incorporated into differentiated learning opportunities.

When teachers differentiate instructions effectively, there is general improvement in overall achievement for the entire class (Saunders, 2005; Tomlinson, 1999; Winebrenner & Delvin, 2001). This suggests that when teachers learn how to provide what students with gifts and talents need and provide similar opportunities to the entire class, expectations and the levels of learning are raised for all students (Gentry & Kielty, 2001). Many schools, however, do not have specialists for gifted education, and the general education teachers are responsible for differentiating curriculum for students with advanced educational needs. Again, to most effectively understand, teach, and challenge these students, teachers, counselors, and other educators must be formally trained. Unfortunately, most colleges and universities do not offer coursework or degrees in gifted education.

In recent years, the Higher Education Opportunity Act of 2008 (HR 4137) passed both Houses of Congress and was signed by President Bush. Included in the Higher Education Opportunity Act of 2008 are two provisions that included gifted education: In the *Teaching Skills* section, students who are gifted and talented are specifically mentioned, and teacher preparation programs funded by *Title II Teacher Quality Partnership Grants* are required to address the learning needs of students who are gifted and talented. The term "teaching skills" means skills that enable a teacher to

(A) increase student learning, achievement, and the ability to apply knowledge;

(B) effectively convey and explain academic subject matter;

(C) employ strategies grounded in the disciplines of teaching and learning that

    (i) are based on empirically based practice and scientifically valid research, where applicable, on teaching and learning;

    (ii) are specific to academic subject matter;

    (iii) focus on the identification of students' specific learning needs, particularly students with disabilities, students who are limited English proficient, *students who are gifted and talented*, and students with low literacy levels, and the tailoring of academic instruction to such needs.

(D) conduct an ongoing assessment of student learning, which may include the use of formative assessments, performance-based assessments, project-based assessments, or portfolio assessments, that measure higher-order thinking skills, including application, analysis, synthesis, and evaluation;

(E) effectively manage a classroom;

(F) communicate and work with parents and guardians, and involve parents and guardians in their children's education; and

(G) use, in the case of an early childhood educator, age- and developmentally-appropriate strategies and practices for children in early education programs.

Again, teacher preparation programs funded by Title II Teacher Quality Partnership Grants would be required to have their general education teacher candidates possess the skills needed to meet the specific learning needs of students with gifts and talents and differentiate instruction for these students.

EFFECTIVE PROGRAMS FOR LEARNERS WITH GIFTS AND TALENTS

Twenty-first century education must reflect 21st century thinking. All hands must be on deck in looking for new ways of doing things. Different students require different education. In other words, instruction must be differently tiered to meet the needs of students with gifts and talents. *Differentiation* is a broad term referring to the need to tailor teaching environments, curricula, and instructional practices to create appropriately different learning experiences for students with different needs, interests, readiness, and learning profiles Tomlinson (2005, 2011). The reality that gifted learners differ in meaningful ways is the guiding premise of differentiation. The main objective is to engage learners in instruction through different learning modalities, appealing to differing interests, using varied rates of instruction, and providing varied degrees of complexity within and across a challenging and conceptually rich curriculum. Meaningful curriculum differentiation for students with gifts and talents requires that educators and service providers recognize the individual strengths of these learners and acknowledge the inadequacy of the regular curriculum to meet those needs (Kaplan, 2005). Differentiating instruction also "involves a healthy dose of common sense" (Tomlinson, 2011). To go beyond our narrow confines and address future challenges, gifted students must be educated using the following:

1. *Acceleration or Honors Programs.* Many people associate acceleration or honors programs with gifted and talented programs. These programs may include skipping grades, early entrance, and early graduation, credit by examination, nongraded classes, and advanced placement classes. Some students with gifts and talents who seem bored in school may benefit from an accelerated program that provides an academic challenge and keeps them involved in school. However, it may be difficult to identify these students who initially may not be seen as gifted. Honors courses are classes designed to present students with higher levels of content, process, product, and pacing. Honors courses are not exclusively for these students, but they may be clustered within an honors section, providing a higher-level curriculum that can be further differentiated.

2. *Mentor Programs.* Another program model for gifted and talented education is the mentor program. Mentors provide role models for students and give them an opportunity to interact with adult professionals. Through the Higher Achievement Program in Washington, DC, elementary and junior high school students from low-income neighborhoods are tutored by volunteers two nights a week. To be eligible for the program, students must show a high level of motivation and pass a qualifying examination. One night each week is devoted to verbal skills such as reading comprehension, vocabulary, and writing; the second night is devoted primarily to mathematics and related skills. The mentor program has many psychological and social benefits for students and is a low-cost program if the school district recruits area professionals as volunteers. School districts located near universities can encourage them to establish a course in which official credit is given to university students who participate as mentors. If mentors are sensitive to the needs of particular groups, they can provide positive role models for students. The mentor program concept can be a solution to difficult budget constraints and has been used by numerous school districts around the country.

3. *Enrichment Programs.* The most common program model for students with gifts and talents is probably an enrichment program, in which students receive instruction in addition to their regular classroom instruction. Enrichment programs provide learning experiences designed to extend, supplement, or deepen understandings within specific content areas (Dannenberg, 1984). Some enrichment programs provide academic services and cultural opportunities for students. For example, students with gifts and talents at Louis S. Brandeis High School in New York City (Cochran & Cotayo, 1983) attend operas and museums and, in this way, become a part of American culture. Another example of activities in an enrichment program would be to have students studying the prehistoric era, watch films on dinosaurs, draw pictures of them, and go to a natural history museum to see a dinosaur exhibit.

4. *Resource Rooms.* Resource room is usually staffed by a resource teacher. Students may visit the resource room to do special assignments or to check out various educational games or puzzles. In a kindergarten/first grade gifted and talented program in Albuquerque, New Mexico (Beam, 1980), parents were able to check out items for their children. The resource room provides an excellent opportunity for parents and students to bridge the gap between home and school. However, in many inner-city schools, special programs may be needed to obtain the desired levels of parental support. Also, the establishment of a resource room usually requires physical space for the room, sufficient operating funds, and a resource teacher who has expertise in the area of giftedness.

5. *Parent Involvement Programs.* Many programs include a strong parent involvement component in which parents can help support their children's development at home while the school can be used as an additional resource. Although it is important for all parents to be involved in their children's education, it is particularly critical to develop a strong link between the home and the school for school children. Many programs provide parents with checklists to help assess their children. In addition, programs often provide booklets of home activities through which parents can encourage critical thinking and creativity.

6. *Curriculum Compacting.* Many students with gifts and talents have already mastered much of the content of the general education curriculum before the school year begins. *Curriculum compacting* involves compressing the instructional content and materials so that academically able students have more time to work on more challenging materials (Reis & Renzulli, 2005).

7. *Tiered Lessons.* A tiered lesson provides different extensions of the same basic lesson for groups of students of differing abilities. For example, after the whole class is exposed to a basic lesson on a poem, three groups of students might work on follow-up activities or assignments of basic, middle, and high difficulty.

8. *Using Bloom's Taxonomy in Phrasing Questions and Assigning Student Products.* Bloom and his colleagues (Bloom, Englehart, Furst, Hill, & Krathwohl, 1956) formulated a taxonomy of educational objectives that has proven very useful for differentiating curriculum. The original, *Bloom's Taxonomy* contains six levels or types of cognitive understanding: knowledge, comprehension, application, analysis, synthesis, and evaluation. In 2001, the taxonomy was revised (Anderson et al., 2001). Nouns have become active verbs in the revised taxonomy. Knowledge is called *remember,* comprehension is called *understand,* application is *apply,* analysis is *analyze,* evaluation is *evaluate,* and synthesis is called *create.*

9. *Cluster Grouping.* Cluster grouping is the grouping of a limited number of identified students with gifts and talents in a heterogeneous setting with a teacher trained in the appropriate special needs of gifted students for the purpose of receiving differentiated educational experiences matched to the student's needs, interests, and abilities.

10. Independent Study. Independent study is the self-directed exploration of a topic or a course under the supervision of a teacher or college/university personnel.

Other instructional strategies that should be used for students with gifts and talents are

1. Individualized programming.

2. Ability grouping.
3. Flexible scheduling (i.e., students attend class less than peers, perhaps only four days each week).
4. Faster-paced, higher-level materials.
5. Field trips.
6. Community resource persons at school.

Various kinds of special classes are available for students with gifts and talents. They include

1. Honors classes and seminars.
2. Extra coursework.
3. Special course offerings (i.e., Junior Great Books).
4. Use of resource room or itinerant teacher on a weekly basis.
5. Segregated "pullout" program for part of the day or week.
6. Full-time placement in a special class.
7. Special study centers.
8. Magnet schools (i.e., one may specialize in science, another in language arts; students choose to enroll in a school that will serve them best).
9. School within a school (i.e., a portion of the school is reserved for gifted students in specialized classes).
10. Specialized schools for gifted (e.g., Bronx High School of Science).

Offerings before and after school and during lunch periods, weekends, and summers can provide other alternatives for students with gifts and talents. These offerings include

1. Extracurricular clubs.
2. Early-bird classes (i.e., special classes held before school).
3. Extended day.
4. Extended school year.
5. Saturday or after-school workshops, classes, excursions.
6. Summer courses.
7. Evening courses.

Off-campus options can be made available to students with gifts and talents. They include

1. Mentorships.
2. Individual study with a community member.
3. Internships (e.g., working in the field with a specialist).
4. Outreach activities (e.g., programs developed for the gifted at local museums, colleges, and businesses).
5. Residential summer institutes and Governor's Schools.
6. Community-based career education.

7. Student exchange programs.
8. Credit for educational experiences outside school (e.g., travel).

CONCLUSION

In this chapter, we addressed how to prepare teachers to maximize the potential of students with gifts and talents. As facilitators of learning seek to improve educational practices in schools, they must not only raise the base level of expectations for all but also expand at the top to allow students with gifts and talents to go beyond and reach their potential. Efforts to provide students with gifts with equitable educational opportunities have been inundated with problems despite the range of educational programming and service delivery options (e.g., enrichment, accelerated, mentoring, and combination programs; cluster programs, pull-out programs, special classes, and ability grouping). For some reason, most teachers and school administrators have very little or no training in meeting the unique learning needs of their students. Many of the existing programs do not infuse critical elements that provide for the individual needs of students with gifts and talents. It is known, however, that these students perform at high levels when they receive instruction under a qualified or certified teacher. In fact, teachers and service providers who lack a repertoire of practical ideas, strategies, and techniques within a diverse classroom are inept in their interpretation of the affective social, emotional, psychological, and motivational needs of students with gifts and talents. This ineptness must not be allowed to exist in a society or schooling that is competing in a global education and economy. Schools have a crucial role to play in helping to prepare teachers to maximize the potential of all students. All educational programs and services should be about gift and talent development and about providing appropriate gifted programs for all students. In the end, students with gifts and talents deserve the most challenging instruction possible.

REFERENCES

Anderson, L. W., Krathwohl, D. R., Airasian, P., Cruikshank, K. A., Mayer, R. E., Pintrich, P. R., ... Wittrock, M. C. (2001). *A taxonomy for learning, teaching, and assessing: A revision of Bloom's Taxonomy of Educational Objectives.* New York, NY: Longman.

Beam, G. C. (1980). *A kindergarten/primary program for culturally different potentially gifted students in an inner city school in Albuquerque, New Mexico* (Final Report). Albuquerque, NM: Albuquerque Special Preschool.

Bloom, B. S., Englehart, M., Furst, E., Hill, W., & Krathwohl, D. (1956). *Taxomony of educational objectives: The classification of educational goals. Handbook 1: Cognitive domain.* New York, NY: Longmans Green.

Cochran, E. P., & Cotayo, A. (1983). *Louis D. Brandeis high school. Demonstration bilingual enrichment college preparatory program.* New York: New York City Public Schools.

Dannenberg, A. C. (1984). *Issues in education for the gifted.* In A. H. Passow (Ed.), *The gifted and the talented: Their education and development.* Chicago, IL: University of Chicago Press.

Ford, D. Y., & Harris, J. J. (1999). *Multicultural gifted education.* New York, NY: Teachers College Press.

Freehill, M. F. (1974, Winter). Intelligence, empathy and methodological bias about teaching the gifted. *The Gifted Child Quarterly, 18*(4), 247–248.

Gentry, M., & Kielty, W. (2001). Rural and suburban cluster grouping: Reflections of staff development as a component of program success. *Roeper Review, 26*(3), 147–155.

Hansford, S. J. (1985, October). What it takes to be a G/T teacher. *Gifted Child Monthly,* 15–17.

Heath, W. J. (1997). *What are the most effective characteristics of teaching of the gifted.* Reston, VA: ERIC.

Kaplan, S. (2005). Layering differentiated curricula for the gifted and talented. In F. A. Karnes & S. M. Bean (Eds.), *Methods and materials for teaching the gifted* (2nd ed., pp. 107–132. Waco, TX: Prufrock.

Merlin, M. S. (1994, March/April). A few good people. *Gifted Child Today, 17*(2), 14–19.

Newland, E. T. (1962). Some observations on essential qualifications of teachers of the mentally superior. *Exceptional Children, 29,* 111–114.

Reis, S. M., & McCoach, D. B. (2000). The underachievement of gifted students: What do we know and where do we go? *Gifted Child Quarterly, 44*(3), 152–170.

Reis, S. M. & Rensulli. (2005). Curriculum compacting: An east start to. Storrs, CT: The National Research Center on the Gifted and Talented.

Saunders, R. (2005). *A comparison study of the academic effect of ability grouping versus heterogeneous grouping in mathematics instruction.* Unpublished doctoral dissertation. Arizona State University, Tempe, Arizona.

Schlesinger, A., Jr. (1999). What is an American? In S. Heckney (Ed.), *One America indivisible: A national conversation on American pluralism and identity.* Washington, DC: National Endowment for the Humanities.

Tomlison, C. A. (1999). The differentiated classroom: Responding to the needs of all learners. Alexandria, VA: Association for Supervision and Curriculum Development.

Tomlinson, C. A. (2005). *How to differentiate instruction in mixed ability classrooms* (2nd ed.). Upper Saddle River, NJ: Pearson.

Torrance, E. P., & Myers, R. W. (1970). *Creative learning and teaching.* New York, NY: Mead.

Winebrenner, S., & Delvin, B. (2001). Cluster grouping of gifted students: How to provide full-time services on a part-time budget. *ERIC Digest E538.*

CHAPTER 7

PREPARING TEACHERS AND PRACTITIONERS TO WORK WITH CHILDREN WITH AUTISM SPECTRUM DISORDERS

Lynn Adams

Autism Spectrum Disorders (ASD) impact 1 in 68 families in the United States, according to the Center for Disease Control (CDC, 2014) data. Additionally, autism impacts boys (1 in 42) more often than girls (1 in 210). This is a 30% increase over the last 2 years. In about 1985, autism was considered a relatively rare disorder with a reported rate of 4–5 in 10,000 (Adams, 2013). Several theories point to the noted increase in reported cases of ASD. Some have attributed the increase to better identification, and some have given the credit to revision of criteria. Regardless of why there is a noted increase in children identified with ASD, public school teachers must be prepared to address the needs of all children, including those with ASD. This chapter focuses on how teachers and practioners can be prepared to work with children with ASD.

CONCEPTUAL FRAMEWORKS

The ASD population of students will spend a fair amount of time in regular educational placements as their academic skills are often at or near expected levels of

Critical Issues in Preparing Effective Early Childhood Special Education Teachers for the 21st Century Classroom: Interdisciplinary Perspectives, pages 85–97.
Copyright © 2016 by Information Age Publishing

performance. Limited information is available about the preparation of teachers of children with ASD. Recent studies have shown that teacher training improves outcomes for children with ASD (Browder, Trela, & Jirnenez, 2007; Koegel, Koegel, Frea, & Green-Hopkins, 2003). Additionally, with such practice, students with ASD are properly identified, assessed, placed, and taught.

In 1943 and 1944, respectively, Leo Kanner and Hans Asperger described children with communication and social deficits (Adams, 2013). Each man noted behaviors of concern including communication and social deficits as well as behavioral concerns. In the United States, Asperger Syndrome did not become widely known until the early 1980s, when Dr. Asperger's work was translated into English. At that time, the striking similarities between the two disorders came to the forefront. Children in both groups demonstrated deficits in communication and social interaction skills. Differences between the two groups began to emerge when it was noted that those with Asperger Syndrome demonstrate at least average cognitive functioning, while persons with autism may have a range of cognitive abilities. As a result of these differences, it is essential for educators and service providers to be prepared to address the needs of children on the autism spectrum.

The Individuals with Disabilities Education Act (IDEA) was enacted in 1990, and its reauthorization in 2004 specifically to address the needs of persons with disabilities (U.S. Department of Education, Office of Special Education and Rehabilitative Services, Office of Special Education Programs, 2005). IDEA requires as one of its mandates that all persons without regard to disability have the right to a free and appropriate public education. IDEA defines autism as a developmental disability that significantly affects verbal and nonverbal communication and social interaction. These deficits are generally present prior to age 3 years. Additional characteristics may include engagement in repetitive activities, resistance to change in routine, and unusual sensory responses. IDEA also mandates the use of evidenced-based treatment strategies. While evidence is emerging and some treatment approaches show potential, no one approach addresses the needs of all persons with ASD. In fact, data exists to show that most successful programs for persons with ASD are those designed to meet the precise and individual needs of the person. The increase in diagnosis of ASD has had a dramatic impact on the educational system (Sansosti, 2008). According to the Department of Education (2007), the rate of ASD in schools *quintupled*, from accounting for .8% of all noted to have a disability in 1997 to approximately 3.8% in 2006. Between 1994 and 2004, a 500% increase in the number of children served under the classification of autism was noted (OSEP, 2007a, 2007b; US Government Accountability Office, 2005).

While identification and surveillance programs seem to be working well for students with ASD, it appears that training and support for school personnel who must address the educational needs of this population have not been sufficiently addressed. Data indicate that many teachers and service providers have little to no training in the educational needs of children with ASD (Teffs & Whitbread, 2009). An attempt to address the problem of burgeoning populations and a dearth of trained personnel began in 2002 with the TEACH Acts of 2002 and 2007. These Acts provided grants to allow state educational agencies to improve outcomes for students with ASD. To date, while $5 million has been allocated, no data is available to examine the impact of these Acts. There is an obvious need to provide effective educational opportunities for students with ASD. One of the ways that will happen is by the training and preparation of education professionals. The lack of adequately trained professionals is noted among several studies (Dymond, Gibson & Myran, 2007; Sack-Min, 2008; Scheuermann, Webber, Boutot & Goodwin, 2003; Simpson, 2004).

DIAGNOSIS OF ASD AND CHALLENGES

In May of 2014, the Diagnostic and Statistical Manual (DSM) was revised to remove the diagnosis category of Asperger Syndrome along with an expansion of the criteria for autism diagnosis. Additionally, a new category called "social-communication disorder" was created to capture those who might not fit the criteria for ASD but for whom social communication exchanges are challenging. The result is the newly minted label of "autism spectrum disorder" (ASD). The revisions were intended to simplify the diagnostic process. These changes should have minimal impact on the provision of special education services in schools, but understanding the changes is prudent for all teachers. Proper diagnosis will be impossible unless the specific areas of need are known. Communication, social skill deficits, and unusual sensory needs are often the most predominant characteristics of ASD in children. Without effective management of these three areas, the child with ASD may demonstrate problem behaviors in the classroom that are ultimately unrelated to the academic task at hand, but disruptive to the child's learning of said task.

Communication

With regard to communication, if a child cannot effectively communicate their wants, needs, thoughts, feelings, and knowledge, he or she might present behaviors that interfere with learning. Communication is the combination of speech (actual sounds we use to form words) and language (the conventional system of rules that govern word combinations). Communication results when the child can effectively utilize speech and language skills. For example, if the child does not understand the vocabulary included in the lesson, he or she may not be successful in completing the lesson. Children with high-functioning autism are often fully included in the regular education setting while still demonstrating language challenges.

It is vital that educators have high expectations for children with ASD. It is also important that these expectations be realistic. The acquisition of even the most rudimentary communication skills (gesture, sign, vocalization, picture-based) allow for learning opportunities. Opportunities for choice making and getting needs met have as a side benefit of increasing the likelihood that the child will attempt to communicate again. "Educators who learn to respond to the initial communicative attempts and shape these into more elaborate systems of communication are not only facilitating the learner's ability to acquire new skills, but also have worked to enhance the overall quality of life" (Hall, 2013, p. 26). There are seven important ways that educators can enhance communication skills in a student with ASD (Hall, 2013). They are

1. *Communication Partners.* The effective partner is aware of his or her role in supporting the communicative exchange.
2. *Providing Frequent Opportunities.* The effective partner provides frequent and varied chances for communication to assist in skill development.
3. *Working with Learner Motivation.* The effective partner finds what motivates the student and uses that to facilitate skill acquisition.
4. *Acknowledge Communication Attempts.* The effective partner recognizes and responds to communication attempts even if these attempts are atypical or ungrammatical.
5. *Embed Communication in Ongoing Routines.* The effective partner uses daily routines to embed communication opportunities and support learning.
6. *Incorporate Affect and Enjoyment.* The effective partner is emotionally attached and enjoys the communicative interaction.
7. *Elaborating Communication Duration and Complexity..* The effective partner assists the student in using more elaborate language as skills allow.

Social Skills

Children with ASD often present social skill deficits that can impact their performance in the classroom. They do not always follow the rules of conversation and may interrupt the speaker. They often do not understand the importance of greetings (Hi, bye) and polite terms (please, thank you). Some will need explicit instruction in the use of these social niceties. Many children with ASD are excellent rule followers and many social issues can be avoided if the rules of the classroom are clearly communicated. The effective educator will have the rules of the classroom clearly posted in the early grades. It is best to avoid value statements such as "Be respectful of others" in favor of the specific behaviors the respectful child should demonstrate. The use of figurative language is particularly challenging for the student with ASD who may not understand the implied meaning of "respectful." By way of example, the following rules are offered:

- Raise your hand and wait to be called on by the teacher.
- Sit in your chair.
- Do not touch other people's things.
- Use an inside voice in the classroom.

The aforementioned rules are clear, concrete, and direct. As children mature, the rules may change. At about third or fourth grade, it seems that the rules are no longer posted but rather assumed by the teacher and students. This may pose a particular challenge to the child with ASD, who may not realize rules are still in effect. The educator or service provider should consider either maintaining printed, visible rules or providing the child with ASD a personal copy of the rules.

Sensory Needs

Many students with ASD have unusual sensory needs and reactions. The child may have a "sensory diet" in place that affords him or her a variety of sensory stimulation activities that help to maintain attention and a calm demeanor. Others with ASD will find it quite challenging to sit quietly without having an object to manipulate. Often referred to as "fidgets," the successful educator will recognize the value of allowing the student to stretch putty or squeeze a stress ball. Some children with ASD also have difficulty sitting in the same manner as their peers. Some may benefit from a therapeutic cushion. Others will benefit from being allowed to sit in their preferred position, even if it deviates from the norm. Still others will respond well to being allowed to stand at times. A flexible educator will appreciate individual needs. Other neurotypical students may note that this seems unfair. The successful educator helps students understand that it not about fairness or about everyone receiving the same thing but rather everyone receiving what they need to succeed.

INSIDE THE CLASSROOM OF A STUDENT WITH ASD

The successful teacher combines many factors and skills in order to be successful. According to Carlson, Hyunshik, and Schroll (2004), the most important factor is experience, followed by credentialing, self-efficacy, professional activities, and finally, selected classroom practices. Just as every successful teacher has a combination of skills and strategies, so does a student with ASD.

No one set of skills and behaviors can be used to describe children with ASD; however, data is available to provide broad categories of educational concern. Generally, by age 6 years, any cognitive and linguistic deficits have been noted (Adams, 2013). As a result, the behavior of a child with ASD is likely to be different relative to his or her neurotypical peers. A lack of peer relationships, the challenge of pretend play, the presence of repetitive actions, and marked social deficits can all contribute to this difference. Between the ages of 6 and 12, the student with ASD will experience numerous transitions, new places, new people, and new topics.

There is no one-size-fits-all treatment approach for persons with ASD. However, there are many treatment strategies that can be easily implemented in the regular classroom that may help the student with ASD, along with his or her neurotypical peers. Integrating these strategies in the entire classroom allows the student to access the support without being singled out for specialized attention when it might not be needed. To date, only 12 states appear to offer a specific endorsement or certificate in ASD. Furthermore, it should be noted that this information is not centrally located, meaning that no single agency is tracking the endorsements/certificates currently offered. A search of the U.S. Department of Education website did not yield a list of states offering endorsements/certificates for ASD. Rather, a search via a popular search engine helped to determine the approximate numbers of states granting the same.

The child with ASD is frequently impacted by what is referred to as the "hidden curriculum" (Myles & Simpson, 2001). The hidden curriculum refers to the slang of the students and the rules that "everyone knows" but that are not explicitly stated. One teacher might allow quiet discussion in the room whereas another might not, but neither teacher has those rules posted. The child with ASD is not likely to understand what behaviors are pleasing to the teacher, as he or she is egocentric in his or her thinking and does not know the teacher needs to be pleased. The hidden curriculum of the community includes things like not talking to strangers, but, for instance, a policeman is a stranger and if he is asking the child with ASD a question, he is expecting an answer. Children with ASD usually have all or nothing rules, very black and white distinctions that do not allow for exceptions (Myles & Simpson, 2001). In spite of all these challenges, there are particular strategies that work in the classroom with students with ASD. These strategies are discussed in the sections below.

Visual Schedules

Nearly all of us use visual schedules in some form or another, but we do not always consider their use with young children. For the young child who is not yet reading, a picture-based schedule can be used to detail the day's events. Furthermore, minipicture schedules can be developed to assist the child in the independent completion of tasks. For example, a minischedule could be placed on the student's desk detailing the steps to successful task completion (Do your daily grammar practice. Put the completed work in your notebook. Place the notebook on Mrs. Smith's desk when finished). For some children, a mini- or embedded schedule can be created to illustrate the steps of many tasks. Visual schedules are always oriented in a top-down fashion so that they can be differentiated from communication systems that are oriented from left to right. Generally, the sooner schedules can be implemented in the daily life of the child, the better. The schedule can serve to diminish problems with transitions from one activity to the next and can reduce anxiety and fears with regard to what is coming next. Ultimately, visual schedules can foster independence as the child learns to move throughout the day with little or no need for adult intervention. The schedule can and should grow with the child. For the young child, an object- or picture-based schedule can be used, always with accompanying print. As the child develops skills, the schedule may transition to a print-only format. This can take the form of a laminated schedule placed on a desk/work space, or a daily planner. Some older children can demonstrate skills to utilize electronic devices such as a personal digital assistant (PDA) (Ferguson, Myles, & Hagiwara, 2005). As technology develops by leaps and bounds, cell phones now include calendar functions as well as phone and address books to allow for successful personal organization and self-management.

Teachers frequently post the class schedule on the board for all students to reference. These schedules often include times for each item/subject. It should be noted that many children with ASD are attuned to time and will alert others when the schedule is not being followed. While the teacher and other practitioners may not be concerned by being "off schedule," the child with ASD may be quite concerned. This child may point the issue out to the teacher, thereby disrupting the learning process. The successful teacher may find that omitting the specific time constraints from the daily schedule may result in fewer concerns and potential problems.

Checklists

Certainly, we have all made a list of things that we have to do. Perhaps our lists name chores or tasks that we hope to accomplish over a week's time. For the child with ASD, the list might be for things that the child needs to accomplish in the next hour. If the child is in study hall, the checklist may include the list of assignments facing the child. He or she may complete the items and check them off the list. Later, the list may be referenced again at home to ensure that all assignments are completed prior to the next schoolday.

For maximum flexibility, dry erase boards are available in all shapes and sizes. Many boards come with magnets allowing them to be placed on home appliances or inside a school locker. Items can be checked or marked off the list and the boards can be easily erased and a new list created as needed. The markers for such boards also come in a variety of colors allowing color coding of tasks to facilitate organization. School-related tasks might be written in red, while play or sports related tasks could be written in blue. This makes the list easily scanned by adults and helps children learn to categorize similar tasks or events (Adams, 2013).

Color Coding

To address executive function issues (e.g., planning, organizing, task completion), color-coded materials may prove helpful. Families and teachers are encouraged to utilize systems using color to help the child with autism develop and maintain self-management skills. Using colored file folders and closable colored plastic sleeves, the child's schoolwork can be organized by subject. Placing the file folder for assignment pages, worksheets, homework, a notebook, and pencils/pens in the plastic sleeve, along with texts and workbooks, creates a manageable packet he or she can retrieve for each class or subject. This is particularly helpful when children with autism enter the later elementary grades and middle and high school where they have to change classes and have more materials to keep up with. By placing a legend on the child's desk or inside the locker, the child can match the appropriate packet for the next class. At the end of the day, the child can place the packets needed for homework or other class work in the book bag to take home.

For the home, color coding on a monthly calendar can help the child with autism know which days are schooldays and which are not. Using colored adhesive disks, the parents and child can place one color on schooldays and another color on weekends and holidays. This can be particularly helpful as teacher workdays can disrupt a child's rhythm. Most schools announce workdays and holidays well in advance allowing for this type of planning. Additional colors can be added for sports, therapies, and other daily/weekly events. Color coding allows children with autism and Asperger Syndrome to develop self-management skills and learn to prepare themselves for the day's events by recognizing the colors. For example, colored file folders can be used for organizing a child's work (Adams, 2013).

Cue Cards

When the child with ASD is faced with delivering a verbal message, the stress of the situation may impact the child's ability to transmit that message. A cue card allows the child to relay a message by referencing the card. The child can use the card as a cue to assist in transmitting the verbal message, or if that proves too challenging, the child can simply pass the card to the communication partner (Janzen, 2003). Cue cards can be printed for a variety of situations, color coded for topics, laminated, hole punched, and then placed on a C ring. The ring allows for the easy addition or removal of cards. It also allows the cards to be clipped to the child's belt loop or book bag. Cue cards can be expanded to include a short list of options for addressing a social situation, like how to enter a conversation. The key to using the cue card is not to overwhelm the user with excessive information or language. It should be kept clear and concise. A situation that might lend itself to cue cards is greeting a new person. The cue card contains the language needed for the greeting and helps the child know that he or she has been successful in the exchange. It also lets him or her know when the exchange is completed. Again, the advent of technology may allow the student to merely post cues in a memo file on a phone or other device.

Choice Making

Studies have demonstrated that offering choices to children with ASD can decrease problem behaviors (Dunlap et al., 1994; Foster-Johnson, Ferro, & Dunlap, 1994). The ability to control some aspects of one's life can decrease problem behavior while increasing independence. Dunlap et al. (1994) studied the relationship between choosing between two tasks versus having no choice in task selection. They found that the choice-making condition was superior to the other condition with regard to task engagement. Additionally, disruptive behavior decreased in the choice-making condition. In a similar vein, Foster-Johnson et al. (1994) found that participation in preferred curricular activities reduced problem behavior and increased desirable behavior.

Social Stories

Social stories serve as scripts that provide the learner with information for appropriate behaviors and social skills. According to Barry and Burlew (2004), social stories utilize empirically supported components, including repetition, priming, practice, and feedback. Social stories have been found to aid in decreasing inappropriate behaviors (Adams, Gouvousis, VanLue, & Waldron, 2004; Kuoch & Mirenda, 2003; Kuttler, Miles, & Carson, 1999), while increasing positive social skills (Adams et al., 2004; Barry & Burlew, 2004; Ivey, Heflin, & Alberto, 2004). Social stories are descriptions of social situations, including relevant social cues and appropriate responses. A social story is effective because it presents information visually, identifies relevant social cues, describes accurate information and expected behavior, and lessens social interference. The need of the student provides the topic of the story. The perspective of the student provides the focus of the story. Social stories are useful because what we see as misbehavior may result from confusion. Often, we assume that the child with autism knows what behavior we expect, and we are frequently wrong when we make these assumptions. By reading the story immediately prior to the situation, one can provide the child with the script for the situation and facilitate success. According to Simpson (2004), social stories have shown a promising degree of evidentiary support. They can be written by anyone who can observe a problem situation. This includes parents, extended family, teachers, and other professionals. Sometimes children with autism can participate in writing their own stories. In order to write a social story, one must target a behavior or situation that is difficult for the student, spend time looking at the situation, and practice describing the situation from the student's perspective. The story writer must consider the child's motivations, fears, current response to the situation, and the observations of others. Often, it is advantageous for more than one person to observe and consider the situation as subtle nuances may be overlooked.

Social stories consist of descriptive sentences—*The teacher says when it is time for lunch. The children line up at the classroom door;* directive sentences—*I am sitting at my desk. The teacher says, "Line up for lunch." I get my lunch bag from my desk and get in line*; perspective sentences—*The teacher is happy when all the children line up for lunch. The teacher likes it when I line up with my lunch bag*; and control sentences—*I get my lunch bag and line up when my teacher tells me. When the teacher says to line up it is time for lunch.* When crafting a social story, it is important to keep several rules in mind. While one can put one to three sentences on a page, only one concept should be addressed per page. The use of pictures or photographs may be helpful, but some children respond very concretely and fail to generalize the story beyond that represented in the illustrations. For example, a mother wrote an excellent story addressing the tying of shoes, complete with photographs of the shoe from the child's perspective. The story failed to generalize in that the child only tied the shoes depicted in the story. The writer is also encouraged to avoid negative statements such as *I will not run in line to lunch*, but rather use *I will try to walk in line to lunch*. Positive statements explaining what the child *should* do are preferred over stories that simply tell the child what *not* to do. Topics for social stories are determined by noting challenging social situations or specific social skills which need attention. As stories are generated, copies should be made and placed in notebooks. Stories that are useful at home can also be read any time at school, and those for school issues can and should be read in the home in addition to the school. It is essential, however, that a story for a specific event be read immediately before the event. In other words, the story for the playground must be read right before the class goes to the playground. There are several volumes of generic social stories available to allow for personalization and editing as needed (Gray, 2010). The successful teacher might have a variety of social stories crafted and available for reading by all students. Common story topics applicable to all might include *being the line leader, waiting my turn, going to other rooms (art/music)*, and *asking for help*. Having these stories available to all may ensure that all students understand and experience the classroom consistently.

CONCLUSION

Successful classroom teachers find that children with ASD both inspire and puzzle them. These children may allow the teacher to see a task in a completely different way than ever before. They are among the most challenging students to educate, especially for classroom teachers who are not prepared, for example, for a student with ASD who can recite science facts but cannot tolerate minor changes in the daily class schedule. Many teachers are confused when a kindergarten child can read but does not follow simple directions. Children with milder ASD may be enrolled in regular education classes, often with little need for special education support beyond resource class assistance. This happens because the latest public law, IDEA (2004) and the 2001 policy of No Child Left Behind (NCLB), noted that a diagnosis of autism does not automatically result in the development of an

Individualized Education Plan (IEP). Unless a child's autism results in academic difficulties, the child may not qualify for an IEP.

Clearly, current laws have increased the accessibility of services for children with ASD by emphasizing not only academic performance but also how the challenges affect other aspects of their life. In other words, school teams must consider not only academic issues but also academic setting. The academic setting is defined as encompassing regular education classrooms, other education-related settings, and extracurricular and nonacademic activities. This means that not only must the classroom impact be considered but also the impact on communication at recess, on the bus, at lunchtime, and in interactions with peers during school-sponsored clubs and activities (Adams, 2013). Classroom teachers and service providers who see students with ASD experience social-communication failure, despite academic ability, are encouraged to advocate on behalf of those children. In addition, they are encouraged to seek out continuing education opportunities that can help them build a "tool kit" that will facilitate student learning and success. Finally, they are encouraged to recognize that all children with ASD are individuals with individual needs, skills, and talents. As the old saying goes, "Once you meet one child with ASD, you have met *one* child with ASD!"

REFERENCES

Adams, L. (2013). *Parenting on the autism spectrum: A survival guide* (2nd ed.). San Diego, CA: Plural.

Adams, L., Gouvousis, A., VanLue, M., & Waldron, C. (2004). Social story intervention: Improving communication skills in a child with autism spectrum disorder. *Focus on Autism and Other Developmental Disabilities, 19*(2), 87–94.

Agency for Healthcare Research and Quality (AHRQ). (2013). *Evidence-based practice center systematic review protocol. Project title: Autism Spectrum Disorder—An update.* Retrieved from http://www.effectivehealthcare.ahrq.gov/ehc/products/544/1724/autism-update-protocol-130920.pdf

Barry, L., & Burlew, S. (2004). Using social stories to teach choice and play skills to children with autism. *Focus on Autism and Other Developmental Disabilities, 19*(1), 45–51.

Browder, D., Trela, K., & Jimenez, B. (2007) Training teachers to follow a task analysis to engage middle school students with moderate and severe developmental disabilities in grade appropriate literature. *Focus on Autism and Other Developmental Disabilities, 22*(4), 206–219.

Carlson, E., Hyunshik, L., & Schroll, K. (2004). Identifying attributes of high quality special education teachers. *Teacher Education and Special Education, 27*(4), 350–359.

Centers for Disease Control and Prevention (CDC). (2014). *Autism spectrum disorders (ASD).* Retrieved from http://www.cdc.gov/ncbddd/autism/data.html

Dunlap, G., dePerczel, M., Clarke, S., Wilson, D., Wright, S. White, R., & Gomez, A. (1994, Fall). Choice making to promote adaptive behavior for students with emotional and behavioral challenges. *Journal of Applied Behavior Analysis, 27*(3), 505–518.

Dymond, S. K., Gibson, C., & Myran, S. P. (2007). Service for children with autism spectrum disorders. *Journal of Disability Policy Studies, 18*(3), 133–147.

Ferguson, H., Myles, B., & Hagiwara, T. (2005). Using a personal digital assistant to enhance the independence of an adolescent with Asperger Syndrome. *Education and Training in Developmental Disabilities, 40*(1), 60–67.

Foster-Johnson, L., Ferro, J., & Dunlap, G. (1994, Fall). Preferred curricular activities and reduced problem behavior in students with intellectual disabilities. *Journal of Applied Behavior Analysis, 27*(3), 493–504.

Gray, C. (2010). *The new social story book.* Arlington, TX: Future Horizons.

Hall, L. J. (2013). *Autism spectrum disorders: From theory to practice* (2nd ed.). Upper Saddle River, NJ: Pearson.

Ivey, M., Heflin, J., & Alberto, P. (2004). The use of social stories to promote independent behaviors in novel events for children with PDD-NOS. *Focus on Autism and Other Developmental Disabilities, 19*(3), 164–176.

Janzen, J. (2003). *Understanding the nature of autism: A guide to the autism spectrum disorders* (2nd ed.). San Antonio, TX: PsychCorp.

Koegel, L., Koegel, R., Frea, W., & Green-Hopkins, I. (2003) Priming as a method of coordinating educational services for students with autism. *Language, Speech, and Hearing Services in Schools, 34*(3), 228–235.

Kuoch, H., & Mirenda, P. (2003). Social story interventions for young children with autism spectrum disorders. *Focus on Autism and Other Developmental Disabilities, 18*(4), 219–227.

Kuttler, S., Miles, B., & Carson, J. (1999). The use of social stories to reduce precursors to tantrum behavior in a student with autism. *Focus on Autism and Other Developmental Disabilities, 13*, 176–182.

Loveland, K. A., & Tunali-Kotoski, B. (1997). The school age child with autism. In D. J. Cohen & F. R. Volkmar (Eds.), *Handbook of autism and pervasive developmental disorders* (pp 247–287). Hoboken, NJ: Wiley.

Myles, B., & Simpson, R. (2001). Understanding the hidden curriculum: An essential social skill for children and youth with Asperger Syndrome. *Intervention in School and Clinic, 36*(5), 279–286.

Office of Special Education Programs (OSEP). (2007a). *Students ages 6 through 17 served under IDEA, Part B, by disability category and state: Fall 007.* Retrieved January 21, 2009, from https://www.ideadata.org/TABLES31ST/AR_1-16.htm

Office of Special Education Programs (OSEP). (2007b). *Students ages 6 through 21 served under IDEA, Part B, by disability category and state: Fall 007.* Retrieved April 8, 2014, from https://www.ideadata.org/TABLES31ST/AR_1-3.htm

Sack-Min, J. (2008). The cost of autism: Educating children with this complex condition puts a strain on budgets and staff, but some schools are making great strides. *American School Board Journal, 195*(3), 18.

Sansosti, F. (2008). Teaching social behavior to children with autism spectrum disorders using social stories: Implications for school-based practice. *Journal of Speech-Language Pathology and Applied Behavior Analysis, 2.4–3.1*(Special Compiled Issue), 36–45.

Scheuermann, B., Webber, J., Boutot, E. A., & Goodwin, M. (2003). Problems with personnel preparation in autism spectrum disorders. *Focus on Autism and Other Developmental Disabilities, 18*(3), 197–206.

Simpson, R. L. (2004). Finding effective intervention and personnel preparation practices for students with autism spectrum disorders. *Exceptional Children, 70*(2), 135–144.

Teffs, E. E., & Whitbread, K. M. (2009). Level of preparation of general education teachers to include students with autism spectrum disorders. *Current Issues in Education, 12*(10). Retrieved March 18, 2014, from http://cie.asu.edu/ojs/index.php/cieatasu/rt/captureCite/172/4/

U.S. Department of Education, Office of Special Education and Rehabilitative Services, Office of Special Education Programs (2005). *26th Annual (2004) Report to Congress on the Implementation of the Individuals with Disabilities Education Act, 1.* Washington, DC: Author.

U.S. Government Accounting Office (2005, February 15). *Reports and Testimonies. Special education: Children with autism.* Retrieved February, 2014, from http://www.gao.gov/products/GAO-05-220

CHAPTER 8

PREPARNG TEACHERS FOR ADAPTIVE PHYSICAL EDUCATION FOR YOUNG CHILDREN WITH SPECIAL NEEDS

Eugene F. Asola

The United Nations Education, Science and Cultural Organization (UNESCO) International Charter of Physical Education and Sport (1978), in its Article 1 states, "Every human being has a fundamental right of access to physical education and sport, which are essential for the full development of his personality." Article 2 states, "Physical education and sport form an essential element of lifelong education in the overall education system," and Article 3 states, "Physical education and sport programmes must meet individual and social needs." Over the years, the United States has led the way in the area of research and development in an effort to enrich the lives of its citizens holistically as stated by the UNESCO Charter. Many private and public sector stakeholders have supported these efforts through national and state legislative activities in providing donor funding opportunities for education and research. Although these efforts have been beneficial to some

Critical Issues in Preparing Effective Early Childhood Special Education Teachers for the 21st Century Classroom: Interdisciplinary Perspectives, pages 99–110.
Copyright © 2016 by Information Age Publishing
99

extent, they have fallen short of recognizing the need for preparing quality teachers for adapted physical education for young children with special needs.

Teacher preparation for adaptive physical education in the United States, like any other teacher preparation program, has grown and developed over the years. The passage of several legislative instruments in support of individuals with disabilities, further provided impetus for implementing federal laws for individuals with disabilities in especially physical education. In 1961, PL 87-276 (Special Education Act) was enacted by the U.S. Congress with a focus on training professionals to teach children with hearing impairments. By 1965, the PL 89-10 (the Elementary and Secondary Education Act) was also passed to enable states and local school districts to develop programs for economically disadvantaged children with the use of federal funds. A year later, Public Law 89-750 (Amendments to the Elementary and Secondary Education Act) led to the creation of the Bureau of Education for the Handicapped. These trends in legislative events brought change for individuals with disabilities and continued until 1990, when the PL 101-476 (the Individuals with Disabilities Education Act; IDEA) was passed. This law was designed to replace and extend the provisions of PL 94-142 (the Education of the Handicapped Act) and to further guarantee the educational rights of students with disabilities. Changes were made to this Act with the enactment of IDEA 2004, requiring that all students with disabilities be provided with physical education, "unless the public agency enrolls children without disabilities and does not provide physical education to children without disabilities in the same grades" (Cornell Law School, n.d.). Currently, about 14 states have responded to the need for Adapted Physical Education personnel by creating a separate teaching license or credential (California, Louisiana, Missouri, Minnesota, Wisconson, Indiana, and Ohio) in response to IDEA 2004. While one course model has been adapted by many states for initial certification, high quality programs also exist in some states without separate licenses (Virginia, New York, Utah, and Texas or more). Therefore, there is a significant need for the preparation of highly qualified and effective adaptive physical education teachers and service providers. Even though recent research results show that obesity and sedentary lifestyles may negatively affect children with disabilities, there is a cautious optimism that effective evidence-based practices can lead to enhanced motor and physical skills of children with special needs. As Macphail (2011) explained, personnel development in adapted physical education can lead to meaningful student success and positive education outcomes. This is the thrust of this chapter. Adapted Physical Education (APE) involves adapting or modifying developmentally appropriate physical activities that are as appropriate for persons with disabilities as they are for persons without a disability. These may include but are not limited to the following (See U.S. Department of Education, 2011):

- Autism
- Cerebral Palsy

- Down Syndrome
- Hearing impairment
- Intellectual impairment
- Multiple disabilities
- Orthopedic impairment
- Serious emotional disturbance
- Specific learning disability
- Speech or language impairment
- Traumatic brain injury
- Visual impairment
- Other health impairment

The APE teacher is expected to provide direct services to children with special needs and not consider it a related service, since physical education for children with disabilities is a federally mandated component of special education services (U.S.C.A. 1402 [25]). Those special services in education involve the physical educator differentiating instruction to meet the needs, interests, and abilities of each individual student. Differentiation of instruction might involve the teacher selecting appropriate physical activities and adapting/modifying the content, process, environment, and/or student assessment to meet the needs of children with special needs.

APE or physical education (PE) teachers qualified to teach adaptive curricular activities need to learn how to design an achievement-based program, implement high quality instruction, and demonstrate leadership and advocacy. APE teachers also should provide standard placement for students with disabilities, whether in a general physical education class (Inclusion), in a separate adapted physical education class (Least Restrictive Environment; LRE), or a combined setting. It is pertinent to note that LRE mandates that any child with disability must be included whenever and wherever possible (Columna, Davis, Lieberman, & Lytle, 2010), unless this cannot otherwise be achieved satisfactorily as planned even if supported with supplemental aids. A clear example is when the child with disability may be of danger to others in the same classroom, therefore making it impossible to accommodate for LRE.

Teacher education programs and APE or PE teacher candidates should be taught how to design developmentally appropriate physical education programs, evaluate general PE curriculum for applicable or appropriate activity, and utilize adapted PE information to design individualized PE programs. They should learn how to monitor student progress toward Individual Education Plan (IEP) goals/ objectives so as to provide instruction tailored to maintaining students' healthy lifestyles within the community. Shriner and DeStefano (2003) found that providing training can influence teachers' participation and accommodation decisions, improve the way in which decisions are documented on IEPs, and increase consistency between intended and actual accommodation. In addition, APE candidates should be learning more about special needs children. Learning all they can about the type of disability and consequently the level of function will help them understand that no two kids are the same no matter the disability. APE teacher candidates' knowledge about sensory integration (Columna et al., 2010), as it relates to physical education, can also help them breakdown motor skills so that each special needs student will participate no matter the activity. It is critical that APE teacher candidates hear life stories from the parents of these kids to understand how far and well they function in different conditions or environments for planning, monitoring, and assessment purposes.

PREPARING HIGH QUALITY APE TEACHER CANDIDATES

Auxter, Pyfer, Huettig, Zittel, and Roth (2009) argued that the ultimate goal of physical education for children with disabilities is to equip them with motor skills that contribute to independent living. For this to occur systematically, it is important to clearly distinguish the levels of functionality of each student with specific disability that contribute to the acquisition of many sports' skills. Auxter et al., (2009) describe three levels that contribute to independent functioning uniquely; (1) *basic input function*, which deals with processing information in the central nervous system, but is most likely to be overlooked by physical educators regarding purposeful movement; (2) *general abilities*, such as basic input functions/sensory input functions like balance and spatial awareness (prerequisite skills acquisition); and (3) *specific skills*, considered the uppermost level of functioning involving motor behavior that are either specific to a sport or specific to functional living.

Certified PE/APE teacher education programs should be designed to provide quality instruction based on individual state/local APE requirements in addition to the federal mandate. The foundation for quality instruction for children with special needs can be tied to the implementation of effective classroom behavioral management strategies, whereby teacher candidates are provided with opportunities to experience firsthand what happens in the real world. It is very important that teacher candidates acquire both content knowledge and pedagogical content knowledge to ensure that activities they implement are age-appropriate and based on best practices. Teacher candidates should be educated on how to evaluate or assess individual performance and to determine the strengths and needs of each student (Macphail, 2011). This is particularly important for teacher candidates to know in order to modify an activity when students are either successful or unsuccessful. To ensure student learning, it is critical for teacher candidates to know when to modify the environment, equipment, and specialized or assistive devices to meet students with special needs outcomes. A quality instructional program incorporates technology such as communication boards/smart boards (e.g., Wii, Xbox, Kinect, etc.) to keep students motivated and focused. This is equally very necessary for meeting differentiated learning needs, because some special needs students may understand planned-content activity better when a preferred learning or teaching style is used with a particular technology/equipment. For instance, cooperative learning is an instructional model that shifts the focus of learning to the student. The goal must be to make each student become a meaningful participant in learning. By doing this, students work together in small, structured, heterogeneous groups to master the content (Dyson, Griffin, & Hastie, 2004).

Various organizations such as the Adapted Physical Activity Council (APAC), under the umbrella of the American Association of Physical Activity and Recreation (AAPAR), promote both practical and theoretical endeavors in the area of physical activity, recreation, and sport for individuals with disabilities to buttress active lifestyles and healthful qualities of life. The Council advocates and encourages programs, policies, standards, and research that will positively affect opportunities for physical activity and recreation available to individuals with disabilities (AAPAR, 2010). APE teacher candidates should be encouraged to join such organization to enjoy benefits such as excellence in professional practices and preparation. Clearly, the AAPAR sponsors presentations and activities designed to foster growth of practitioners working with individuals with disabilities in schools and communities. To a large measure, APE teacher candidates must be prepared by respective programs to be knowledgeable on how to

- Promote positive attitudes in all students irrespective of their disabilities in the gymnasium.
- Stay up-to-date with IDEA and other federal, state, or local laws and policies (e.g., the Law on Fitness and Athletics Equity Act).
- Seek collaboration with other professionals in delivering related services, such as physical therapists, learning specialists, speech-language pathologists, and other special educators.
- Be active as critical participants in the IEP team process when they get a job.
- Be up-to-date on current issues, through reading research journals and actively participating in professional state and national organization activities.
- Plan, implement, and evaluate instructional programs for students based on selected goals.
- Work with special needs students with different or multiple disabilities through hands-on experiences with local school and communities through outreach programs.

Finally, APE teacher preparation must provide knowledge and skills in

- PE content, assessment, and evaluation in pre-K–12 curriculum/program objectives (e.g., object control, body management, health-related fitness, aquatics, outdoor activities, and adventure pursuits).
- What constitutes psychomotor, cognitive, and affective domains and how to state an achievable objective.

- Knowing physical education content standards (NASPE, 2004). Many states have their own physical education standards which teacher candidates should know.
- What is appropriate or inappropriate for special needs students (e.g., safety, integrity of objectives, challenge, success, and feasibility).
- Implications of physical activities on individuals with disabilities; teacher candidates should be taught to understand a wide range of disabilities and their associated characteristics (i.e., physical, cognitive, and affective). In addition, these candidates must know how specific individual characteristics can influence movement skill functioning and acquisition of relevant skills.
- The use of documentation to improve physical activity and health outcomes through physical education knowledge and skills in IEP development and implementation.
- Presenting levels of performance and annual goals as well as individualized and meaningful progress reporting of student outcomes.
- How to conduct a focused educational intervention in different physical activity settings.
- How to develop, implement, and evaluate IEPs.
- Creativity in long- and short-term planning for students with special needs.
- Collaborative planning with special education personnel, related service personnel, parents, and community providers.
- Other documentation alternatives beyond standardized testing for students with special needs.

ASSESSMENT AND ACCOMMODATION PRACTICES IN APE

Assessment, in many ways, consists of activities carried out by teachers, students, and other organizations such as schools, districts, or states to provide information used as feedback to modify teaching and learning activities for specific or general education. Such information generated could also be used to make judgment about achievements. IDEA 2004 mandates that all students with disabilities participate in statewide and districtwide testing "with appropriate accommodations and alternate assessments where necessary and as indicated in their respective individualized education programs" (IDEA, 2004). The law also requires that alternative assessments be available to students who need it, as decided by IEP teams. Alternative assessments are designed to evaluate progress of students who may not be able to participate in a regular assessment. APE teacher candidates should be taught how to use a variety of assessment tools to ascertain current levels of student performance. Assessment areas include motor development skills (psychomotor), physical fitness knowledge (cognitive), and social/emotional/behavior (affective). Below are some examples of assessment tools:

- Physical Fitness Tests

- Fitnessgram Physical Fitness Test
- Brockport Physical Fitness Test
- Motor Development
- Test of Gross Motor Development-2 (TGMD-2)
- Peabody Developmental Motor Skills 2
- Motor Performance
- Adapted Physical Education Assessment Scale
- Bruininks-Oseretsky Test of Motor Proficiency
- Aquatics
- Red Cross Skill Progression
- Aquatics Skills Checklist

While it may be beneficial to use many forms of assessments, depending on the level and needs of individuals with disability, it is imperative that authentic assessments are used. Authentic assessments link closely to instruction and take place in real-life situations, thereby making it relevant for student learning (Wiggins, 1989). They directly measure skills students need for successful participation in physical activities. Accommodations, particularly for students whose disabilities interfere with performing simple and complex learning tasks (Luke & Schwartz, 2007), especially in physical activity, play an important role in educational settings and levels. A critical part of teaching and assessing students with disabilities is to provide them with accommodations that support learning while supporting their ability to show what they can do in the physical education classroom (Pitoniak & Royer, 2001). The question then becomes, What accommodations are appropriate for which students? How do accommodations affect students' learning and their performance on different physical activity tasks? A critical challenge for APE teacher candidates is deciding which accommodations help students learn new skills and knowledge—and which will help them demonstrate what they have learned (Shriner & Destefano, 2003). Whatever accommodations are needed by individual students and consequently "permissible," to a great extent, may vary from state to state and/or district to district. Whatever accommodation will work for one student may not address another's needs at all, therefore, decisions about accommodations must be made on a student-by-student basis. Research results indicate that raised expectations can lead to increased participation supported appropriately with individualized accommodations, improved instruction, and thus performance (Ysseldyke et al., 2004). The majority of states distinguish between standard accommodations—those that do not alter the nature of what a test is designed to measure—and nonstandard accommodations—those with the potential to significantly change what is being tested (Thurlow & Wiener, 2000). This is usually very difficult to apply in many cases for physical activity. Therefore, APE teacher candidates who know that a particular disability can pose a serious challenge to learning should be asked to demonstrate such knowledge and abilities fully (Luke & Schwartz, 2007). This will help them understand what type of accommodations help students. Appropriate accommodations will help students overcome or minimize the barriers presented by their disabilities, which is why federal law requires their use when necessary (Elliott, Kratochwill, & Schulte, 1999; McDonnell, McLaughlin, & Morison, 1997; Pitoniak & Royer, 2001). Luke and Schwartz (2007) argued that students with disabilities bring an extremely broad range of strengths and weaknesses with them to testing environments (especially in the physical education class). They however agreed that it is possible for two students with very similar disabilities to require very different accommodations. For example, individuals who use wheelchairs may have different functional levels according to their categories, therefore requiring different accommodations. This premise makes it emphatically relevant for APE teacher education to provide practical guidance in selecting appropriate accommodations for individual students for improving and informing decision-making. However, the availability of these valuable commodities can vary even in the same district or school (Helwig & Tindal, 2003; Hollenbeck, Tindal, & Almond, 1998; McDonnell et al., 1997; McKevitt & Elliott, 2001; Tindal & Fuchs, 2000).

FUTURE PERSPECTIVES

Physical education being predominantly performance based is a very unique subject compared to other disciplines, making it more challenging for APE teacher candidates to handle students with special needs. It is therefore recommended that practical guidance opportunities be provided as part of program learning to help teacher candidates understand such challenges hands-on, such as the characteristics of regular class teachers, the nature of activities children with special needs will perform, and available support services (Auxter, Pyfer, & Huettig, 1993). Once APE teacher candidates are predisposed to these learning phenomena in real-life settings, they will learn how to make the right instructional decisions in physical education with time and practice.

In many cases of students with multiple disabilities, there is always the likelihood that such students will have a combination of various disabilities that include speech impairment, limited physical mobility, learning disability, mental impairment, visual or hearing impairments, brain injury, and other forms. With multiple disabilities, they may exhibit sensory losses and behavioral or social problems. In order to establish and categorize levels of functional abilities of students with special needs and develop and present age-appropriate tasks, it is important for teacher candidates to know that students with multiple disabilities will vary in severity and characteristics. While some students may exhibit weakness in auditory processing and have speech limitations, others may show limited physical mobility as an area of need. Some of these students may have difficulty attaining and remembering skills and transferring these skills from one condition or activity to another. Therefore, a variety of teaching styles will be needed to address individual and group learning. Obviously, some type of support will be needed beyond the confines of the classroom in extreme cases. There are also medical implications with some of the more severe multiple disabilities, which could include students with cerebral palsy and severe autism and brain injuries, thereby facing many educational challenges and implications for APE teachers.

High quality physical education for special needs students will develop many aspects that include physical and motor fitness; fundamental motor skills and patterns; as well as skills in aquatics, dance, and individual and group games and sports. The application of laws in various states and district levels has many implications for the success and impact of any APE program within the state or district. IDEA is intended to integrate all children within instructional and extra class programs with emphasis on individualized instructional strategies. APE teacher candidates must understand that some activities may have more restrictions than others and some will be less vigorous than others, depending on the needs of each individual child. Usually, the APE teacher, in conjunction with other paraprofessionals, will decide if the physical education program requires mild, moderate, or limited participation, based on IEP evaluations. More often, this leads APE teachers to adapt, modify, and change the activity and/or equipment to meet the needs of the special needs student. It may also involve the use of different size balls, bats, partner/peer assistance, using different body parts, and providing more rest time in between activities. Requiring APE teacher candidates to follow best practices will ensure that children with special needs are progressing and having some form of success in the physical education class.

APE may be offered to students with gross motor delays or other disability and related difficulties that may make them unable to participate, thereby seen as unproductive in a regular physical education class. This is especially challenging in the case of those with profound/severe disabilities. To help develop or refine fine motor skills and increase socialization among students who use wheelchairs, for example, the APE teacher candidate can begin with organizing students in groups close together to pass a volleyball around. Students can also be asked to pull on some isotonic bands as a warm-up activity while the instructor sets up stations for the main activity. She/he can then explain what he/she will do at each station and let students decide where they want to start and how long they will participate at each station. Ramps can be used to launch a ball at targets like bowling pins or markings on the floor. Students can do shuffleboard, box hockey, goal ball, bowling, or any target game of their choice. Regardless, APE teacher candidates must be taught to make sure the rules and adaptations allow for maximum participation and learning. Wheelchair aerobics and wheelchair dance tapes can be used to add variety to the curriculum. Other options may include wheelchair racing and wheelchair basketball. APE teacher candidates can possibly simplify the rules as needed to address students' intellectual level, and with good planning, they can have high expectations for their students.

Some strategies for meeting potential challenges dealing with students with special needs include (a) the physical arrangement of the gym needed to best accommodate them, (b) the use of special equipment and assistive devices/technology if necessary, and (c) integrating students into peers activities to assist with social development. In addition, instructors must ensure that all students demonstrate respect for those with multiple disabilities and vice versa. APE teacher candidates should have knowledge of the extent to which students with physical disabilities face challenges when it comes to fitness or fitness activities. These students may have limited mobility and feel exhausted more easily than other students. Such students may need special equipment or other forms of assistance to participate in physical activity. Potentially, a combination of these limitations with other obstacles such as the effect of medications or sensory issues can compound physical inactivity issues resulting in a high risk for obesity.

CONCLUSION

Preparing teachers for adaptive physical education to handle young children with special needs in the world today can be challenging, especially in meeting every child's basic needs and in recognizing the fundamental right of access to physical education and quality APE programs. Therefore, designing and planning developmentally appropriate instruction has the potential to address a variety of issues related to children with special needs education. Teaching and learning related needs may include but are not limited to physical, mental/intellectual, psychological, emotional, and social. It is obvious that APE teacher preparation programs need the support of many stakeholders such as policymakers, parents, administrators, educators, healthcare professionals, and other service providers to deliver quality services to the needy children. Legislative instruments like the IDEA of 2004 will ensure quality program implementation and delivery.

Quality professional training for APE teachers includes planning instruction, behavior management, and assessment processes to enhance student learning. It is therefore important to emphasize that states and districts be consistent and efficient in service delivery to children with special needs. Service providers at all levels must endeavor to collaborate in their efforts to provide quality services and encourage leadership and advocacy in APE program institutions. For example, assessments and accommodation practices must be consistent with best practices required by the APE profession across states and districts while allowing for the use of modern innovative technologies. It is recommended that teacher educators use authentic measures for assessing students (Goodman, Arbona, & De Rameriz, 2008). The overreliance on traditional assessment forms tends to ignore the unique nature of children (with special needs) in physical education classes (Kritt, 1993). Authentic assessment will provide educators with the most meaningful ways of assessing games and activities in physical education (Dyson et al., 2004). APE Programs must embrace standards such as instructional strategies and adaptations which aim to (a) provide knowledge for APE candidates; (b) emphasize comprehensive curriculum planning, content standards, lesson and unit plans, behavior management, collaboration and consultation; and (c) teach transition planning to comply with various legislatives mandates (APENS, 2011). While it is important for APE teacher preparation to focus on program goals that address the needs and challenges facing children with special needs, institutions that offer APE certification programs must equip teacher candidates with current knowledge, skills, and strategies to confront the challenges of the 21st century.

REFERENCES

Adapted Physical Education National Standards (APENS). (2011). *Welcome.* Retrieved 2014, from http://apens.org

American Association for Physical Activity and Recreation (AAPAR). (2010). *Eligibility criteria for adapted physical education services.* Retrieved 2014, from http://www.shapeamerica.org/advocacy/positionstatements/pe/loader.cfm?csModule=security/getfile&pageid=4599

Auxter, D., Pyfer, J., & Huettig, C. (1993). *Principles and methods of adapted physical education and recreation* (7th ed.). New York, NY: McGraw-Hill.

Auxter, D., Pyfer, J., Zittel, L., Roth, K., & Huettig, C. (2009). *Principles and methods of adapted physical education and recreation.* (11th ed.). Dubuque, IA: McGraw-Hill.

Columna, L., Davis, T., Lieberman, L., & Lytle, R. (2010). Determining the most appropriate physical education placement for students with disabilities. *Journal of Physical Education, Recreation & Dance. 81,* 30–37.

Cornell Law School. (n.d.). *34. CFR 300.108—Physical education.* Retrieved 2014, from http://www.law.cornell.edu/cfr/text/34/300.108

Dyson, B., Griffin, L. L., & Hastie, P. (2004). Sport education, tactical games, and cooperative learning: Theoretical and pedagogical considerations. *Quest. 56*(2), 226–240.

Elliott, S. N., Kratochwill, T. R., & Schulte, A. G. (1999). *Assessment accommodations guide.* Monterey, CA: CTB/McGraw-Hill.

Goodman, G., Arbona, C., & De Rameriz, R. D. (2008). Authentic assessment and academic achievement. *Journal of Teacher Education, 59*(1), 24–39.

Helwig, R., & Tindal, G. (2003). An experimental analysis of accommodation decisions on large-scale mathematics tests. *Exceptional Children. 69*(2), 211–225.

Hollenbeck, K., Tindal, G., & Almond, P. (1998). Teachers' knowledge of accommodations as a validity issue in high-stakes testing. *Journal of Special Education, 32,* 175–183.

Individuals with Disabilities Education Improvement Act of 2004. H.R. 1350, 108th Cong. (IDEA). (2004). Retrieved from http://idea.ed.gov/download/statute.html

Kritt, D. (1993). Authentic, reflection, and self-evaluation in alternative assessment. *Middle School Journal, 25*(2), 43–45.

Luke, S. D., & Schwartz, A. (2007). Assessment and accommodations. *Evidence for Education. Volume 2*(1), 1–11

Macphail, A. D. (2011). Professional learning as a physical education teacher. *Physical Education and Sports Pedagogy. 16*(4), 435–451.

McDonnell, L. M., McLaughlin, M. J., & Morison, P. (Eds.). (1997). *Educating one and all: Students with disabilities and standards-based reform.* Washington, DC: National Academies Press.

McKevitt, B. C., & Elliott, S. N. (2001). *The effects and consequences of using testing accommodations on a standardized reading test.* Madison: University of Wisconsin.

National Association for Sport and Physical Education (NASPE). (2004). *National physical education standards: General description of standards.* Retrieved 2014, from http://wheresmype.org/downloads/NASPE%20Standards%202004.pdf

Pitoniak, M. J., & Royer, J. M. (2001). Testing accommodations for examinees with disabilities: A review of psychometric, legal, and social policy issues. *Review of Educational Research, 71*(3), 53–104.

Shriner, J. G., & Destefano, L. (2003). Participation and accommodation in state assessment: The role of individualized education programs. *Exceptional Children, 69*(2), 147–161.

Thurlow, M., & Wiener, D. (2000, May). Non-approved accommodations: Recommendations for use and reporting. (Policy Directions No. 11). *NCEO.* Minneapolis: University of Minnesota, National Center on Educational Outcomes. Retrieved 2014, from http://cehd.umn.edu/NCEO/OnlinePubs/Policy11.htm

Tindal, G., & Fuchs, L. (2000). *A summary of research on test changes: An empirical basis for defining accommodations.* Lexington, KY: Mid-South Regional Resource Center.

UNESCO. (1978, November 21). *International charter of physical education and sport.* Retrieved 2014 from http://portal.unesco.org/en/ev.php-URL_ID=13150&URL_DO=DO_TOPIC&URL_SECTION=201.html

U.S. Department of Education. (2011). *Creating equal opportunities for children and youth with disabilities to participate in physical education and extracurricular athletics.* Report.

Wiggins, G. (1989). A true test: Toward more authentic and equitable assessment. *The Phi Delta Kappan, 70*(9), 703–713.

Ysseldyke, J., Nelson, J. R., Christenson, S., Johnson, D. R., Dennison, A., Triezenberg, H., . . . Hawes, M. (2004). What we know and need to know about the consequences of high-stakes testing for students with disabilities. *Exceptional Children, 71*(1), 75–95.

CHAPTER 9

PREPARING EDUCATORS THROUGH RELATIONSHIPS BETWEEN SCHOOLS, FAMILIES, AND COMMUNITIES

Sullivan Literacy Center

Gina M. Doepker

It's wonderful to be a part of the most powerful group of people that spend time helping kids. Please tell Dr. Doepker I said thanks. Sullivan Literacy Center #1 Fan
            —*Parent D. Horton, personal communication, August 12, 2013*

Building positive relationships between schools, families, and communities has become a popular notion in teacher education literature as national and state policymakers and teacher education programs fully understand that families, cultures, and communities have major influences on educational processes and student learning outcomes (Christenson & Sheridan, 2001; Teacher Leadership Exploratory Consortium, 2011). It is essential for teacher educators to build these partnerships, as the resounding benefits for children, families, as well as preservice teachers are numerous. This chapter discusses the Valdosta State University Sul-

Critical Issues in Preparing Effective Early Childhood Special Education Teachers for the 21st Century Classroom: Interdisciplinary Perspectives, pages 111–124.
Copyright © 2016 by Information Age Publishing

livan Literacy Center, which exemplifies such a successful partnership between schools, families, and communities.

SULLIVAN LITERACY CENTER AND SERVICE LEARNING

The Sullivan Literacy Center is an educational center in the Department of Early Childhood and Special Education in the Dewar College of Education and Human Services at Valdosta State University, which has been in existence since August 2011. The mission of the Sullivan Literacy Center is to be an integrated system of care for children and families of Valdosta and the surrounding areas with the goal of increasing the reading and writing motivation, confidence, and skills. The Sullivan Literacy Center currently services children in grades kindergarten through fifth grade. Several literacy programs and services were created which are in direct alignment with the mission and goal statement.

"I take it that the fundamental unity of the newer philosophy is found in the idea that there is an intimate and necessary relation between the processes of actual experience and education" (Dewey, 1938, p. 20). Learning by doing is a simple yet powerful concept. Could you imagine yourself getting your car brakes fixed by a car mechanic who had only read car repair instructional guides, or undergoing surgery by a doctor who only learned the art of medicine through lectures and large textbooks, or even taking a flight on a plane that was flown by a pilot who only read numerous flight manuals? The answer is probably a resounding "No." Throughout the centuries, people have been learning their various crafts and trades through lectures, through textbooks and manuals, and by seeing examples, but the most powerful means of learning has been by the act of doing. As teacher educators, we can present information to our students through lectures and discussions, we can have our students read numerous textbooks and research articles about best practice, we can even show numerous examples exhibiting what works, but until our students go out and do it, they will not have a complete understanding of how to do it. Herman and Marlowe (2005) suggested that teacher educators as leaders in their respective disciplines should move from a "classroom" mentality. Similar to the car mechanic, the doctor, and the pilot, learning how to teach reading is best accomplished by actually teaching reading.

Service learning is one experiential method of instruction to prepare preservice teachers to be effective literacy teachers in the 21st century classrooms. In a study completed by Wilkinson, Doepker, and Morbitt (2012), they concluded that "service-learning experiences in the undergraduate course in reading had beneficial effects on prospective teacher education students' ability to make connections between theory and practice and on their overall experience of the course" (p. 118). Service learning takes place as participants purposefully interact in the social environment of the particular target community; and the learning is socially constructed by virtue of personal experiences in serving the community. Dewey (1966) surmised,

The social environment . . . is truly educative in its effect in the degree in which an individual shares or participates in some conjoint activity. By doing his share in the associated activity, the individual appropriates the purpose which actuates it, becomes familiar with its methods and subject matters, acquires needed skill, and is saturated with its emotional spirit. (p. 22)

In service learning, participants not only provide a needed service within the social context, but they also acquire subject-matter knowledge and skills simultaneously. When done correctly, service learning can be a win-win situation for all those involved.

The Educational Context

The Valdosta State University undergraduate and graduate students take a variety of courses in different disciplines that require experiential learning opportunities which can be completed by working with children and families in the Sullivan Literacy Center. These disciplines include early childhood education, special education, middle-grades education, mathematics education, gifted and talented education, communication science and disorders, nursing, psychology, as well as marriage and family therapy. The degree of experiential learning depends on individual course requirements as well as the particular service needed.

LITR 3110—Emergent Literacy.

For the first professional semester course *LITR 3110—Emergent Literacy,* preservice teachers are required to work as partners to prepare and implement an interactive read-aloud lesson with a small group of children. They complete this requirement in the Sullivan Literacy Center *Reading is R.A.D.* (Radiant, Aromatic, Delicious) literacy program. These preservice teachers plan the interactive read-aloud by first choosing a developmentally appropriate high quality children's literature book based on children's particular grade range (i.e., K–1st, 2nd–3rd, 4th–5th). They then plan comprehension extension activities that are engaging and likewise pique the children's interest through sensory stimulation such as smell, taste, touch, sight, and sound. The goal is to have children experience the overall pleasures of reading through seeing the **R**adiance, smelling the **A**roma, and tasting the **D**elicious stories of high quality children's literature. Through this experiential field work, these preservice teachers are learning and applying course content related to emergent literacy such as developmentally appropriate children's literature, phonemic awareness, fluency, and comprehension. They are also serving the literacy needs of these community children.

LITR 3120—Early Literacy.

For the second professional semester course *LITR 3120—Early Literacy,* preservice teachers are required to work as partners to plan, implement, and reflect on weekly guided reading and guided writing lessons. They complete this requirement in the Sullivan Literacy Center *Blazing LitES* (Literacy Education Success) literacy program. These preservice teachers plan and implement developmentally appropriate guided reading, decoding, fluency, and comprehension instruction every Monday with a small group of children. They also plan and implement word work, phonics, sight words, vocabulary, and guided writing instruction every Wednesday. These preservice teachers must complete their experiential fieldwork with the same small group of children each week. These children range in grades from kindergarten through fifth grade, but small groups are formed based on their instructional reading levels and not necessarily their grade level. This experiential fieldwork lasts for 10 weeks and is purposeful in helping preservice teachers to learn and apply course content related to early literacy such as phonemic awareness, alphabetic principle, phonics, sight words, vocabulary, fluency, comprehension, and process writing. They are also serving the literacy needs of these children.

LITR 4120—Literacy Assessment and Application.

For the third professional course, *LITR 4120—Literacy Assessment and Application,* preservice teachers work one-on-one with a struggling/reluctant reader and writer in the Sullivan Literacy Center **L.E.A.P.** (Literacy Education Assessment Program) literacy program. These children range in grades from kindergarten through fifth grade and were identified as needing individualized literacy support either by their classroom teachers and/or parents or guardians. The literacy assessment and instruction take place every Monday and Wednesday from 4:00 to 4:50 for a ten-week period of time. Preservice teachers first pretest the child's current literacy skills. They analyze their assessment data to determine prominent reading and writing goals based on their child's individual literacy needs. They then plan and implement purposeful literacy instruction that is developmentally appropriate and based on the child's identified reading and writing goals. Throughout the semester, preservice teachers are required to monitor the child's progress through continual assessments such as performing running records and reflecting on the success of their instruction as it directly relates to the child's progress. This reflection informs their next instructional step. Preservice teachers then posttest their child to determine if there was any growth in the child's literacy skills after implementation of their purposeful literacy instruction. Finally, they prepare a final summary report of findings which they present to the parents at the end of the program. The report includes information regarding the child's literacy goals, literacy strengths, literacy weaknesses, as well as recommendations for future literacy support. This experiential fieldwork is purposeful in helping the preservice teachers to learn and apply the course content related to literacy assessment, literacy instruction, and correction of reading difficulties. They are also serving the specific literacy needs of these children.

Multidisciplinary Child Advocacy Team—M-CAT

In response to the Sullivan Literacy Center mission statement to be an integrated system of care, it was necessary to recruit many departments throughout

Valdosta State University as well as community organizations to provide services as needed. As a result, partnerships were formed with over 20 different university departments and 7 community organizations. This team of service providers became known as the *Multidisciplinary Child Advocacy Team* or **M-CAT** for short. University departments that are partners in *M-CAT* have their undergraduate and graduate students participate in these service learning experiences for the purpose of serving the community while learning their course content at the same time.

M-CAT Content Area Tutors.

When the Sullivan Literacy Center first started, parents had an overwhelming request for their children to also receive content-area tutoring that is in addition to the literacy support they were already receiving. Parents were specifically requesting one-on-one math tutoring for their children. In response to this request, undergraduate and graduate students are actively recruited each semester to serve as *M-CAT* content-area tutors. The Department of Mathematics and Computer Science as well as the Department of Middle Grades Education are two *M-CAT* partners that have their students provide this needed math support for children of the Sullivan Literacy Center. The Department of Middle Grades Education preservice teachers choose two content areas of study in preparation to become a future middle-grades teacher. One of the content areas that they can choose is math. This experiential field experience specifically helps these undergraduate and graduate students in both departments to learn and apply the math content related to their courses. They are also serving the math needs of these children.

The Center for Gifted Studies.

The Center for Gifted Studies is an *M-CAT* partner that provides services for exceptional children enrolled in the *R.E.C. Center*. The **R.E.C. Center** (**R**eading **E**nrichment **C**lub) is a literacy program in the Sullivan Literacy Center that is reserved for those children in grades kindergarten through fifth grade who exceed their grade-level literacy proficiencies. The facilitator of the *R.E.C. Center* is a graduate student in the Center for Gifted Studies who is seeking an endorsement in gifted and talented education. This graduate student plans and implements instruction that is meaningful, relevant, purposeful, and challenging for children in the *R.E.C. Center*. These children in the center likewise receive literacy instruction based on choice, inquiry, and interest. They participate in project work, self-directed learning, literature-based reading, problem-based learning, reflective practice, and writing. They are encouraged to become academic leaders in their schools and families with an emphasis on leadership in reading and writing. This experiential fieldwork is purposeful in helping the graduate student to learn and apply course content related to their studies in gifted and talented education. They are also serving the advanced literacy needs of these children.

Blazing Through Books.

The *Blazing Through Books* literacy program is a feeder program for *L.E.A.P.* This program is available for all children in grades kindergarten through fifth grade who need supplementary literacy support and who are waiting to be accepted into the *L.E.A.P.* program. Preservice teachers in their first professional semester volunteer their time to work with these children by implementing and monitoring rotating literacy centers. The Sullivan Literacy Center graduate assistants who are completing reading endorsements plan and organize all of the literacy centers for volunteers and children. These children are divided into three groups based on their current grade levels (i.e., K–1st, 2nd–3rd, 4th–5th), and likewise the literacy centers are developmentally appropriate based on children's academic levels. The *Blazing Through Books* literacy program helps the preservice teacher to experience supplementary literacy materials that they may consider using in their future classrooms to help their future students' literacy development. This experiential fieldwork is also helpful for graduate assistants in planning and organizing research-based literacy centers which support their reading endorsement coursework. The *Blazing Through Books* literacy program focuses on serving the literacy needs of community children while helping preservice teachers and graduate students to gain valuable knowledge regarding effective literacy instruction.

Health Screenings.

The College of Nursing as well as the Department of Communication Sciences and Disorders are both *M-CAT* partners. Graduate and undergraduate students in both departments actively participate in providing healthcare screenings on children of the Sullivan Literacy Center. The College of Nursing students perform vision and hearing screenings, while the Department of Communication Sciences and Disorders students perform speech and hearing screenings as well. At the end of the screenings, these students write final reports that they present to parents. These final reports include their diagnostic assessment results as well as recommendations for treatment when deficiencies in vision, speech, and/or hearing are detected. This experiential field experience helps all of these students to learn and apply these different health screenings, as well as writing diagnostic reports necessary for their particular field of work. They are also serving children and families by providing early detection of health-related issues.

The Department of Psychology and Counseling is an *M-CAT* partner that has its graduate students perform requested and/or needed screenings on children of the Sullivan Literacy Center in the ***ABC***: *Responding to the Needs of Children: Academic, Behavioral, and Consultative Psychological Support* program. These graduate students perform a variety of academic and behavioral screenings on children which are based on individual academic and/or behavioral needs. These screenings include personal interviews with the child as well as with the parent or guardian. At the end of the screening, graduate students write and present a final comprehensive report that outlines all of the screenings administered along with results of screenings. Graduate students then plan and participate in a consultative follow-up meeting with the parent or guardian to explain and discuss results of screenings as well as recommend further action that may or may not be necessary. This experiential fieldwork helps these graduate students to learn and apply different comprehensive assessments as well as diagnostic reporting and consultative practices which are essential for their particular field of work. They are also serving these children and families by providing early detection of academic and behavioral issues.

The Department of Marriage and Family Therapy is another *M-CAT* partner. Their graduate students provide counseling services as requested or needed by families of the Sullivan Literacy Center. Two graduate students provide on-the-spot counseling by actually coming to the Sullivan Literacy Center during the tutoring hour to meet and talk with parents and guardians while children participate in the various literacy programs. These impromptu counseling sessions are very informal, nonthreatening, and noninvasive. Follow-up sessions with the whole family are frequently made in order to provide the needed support for each member of the family. This experiential fieldwork helps graduate students to learn and apply counseling services and consultative procedures that are essential for their field of work. They are also serving families by providing a free, safe, and supportive counseling service.

SCHOOL PARTNERSHIP

School partnerships are very important to the preparation of preservice teachers. According to the National Council for Accreditation of Teacher Education (2010), "All teacher education programs should be accountable for—and their accreditation contingent upon—how well they address the needs of schools and help improve P–12 learning" (p. iii). The Sullivan Literacy Center partners with two local schools specifically; S.L. Mason and Westside Elementary have historically partnered with the Department of Early Childhood and Special Education in the Dewar College of Education and Human Service. Preservice teachers specifically work with struggling/reluctant readers and writers in the first grade at S.L. Mason, and work with struggling/reluctant readers and writers in the third grade at Westside Elementary. These children have been identified for supplementary literacy services by classroom teachers or school reading specialists. In the past, preservice teachers participated in literacy assessment and one-on-one instruction with the children of the two schools. This tutoring has been improved through *L.E.A.P.* (Literacy Education Success Program). As a part of the *L.E.A.P.* program, field requirements are now more rigorous. Preservice teachers are required to plan and implement literacy lessons every Monday and Wednesday that follow the research-based *Reading Recovery* model. "Every day in Reading Recovery, children develop phonological and orthographic awareness and learn to make the connections they need to construct words in writing and to read words within continuous text" (Fountas & Pinnell, 1999, p. 13). Through these research-based lessons, preservice teachers implement a prescribed cycle of instruction (i.e., familiar read, running record, word work, guided writing, and guided reading) that helps children to build their reading and writing skills. Preservice teachers actually travel to individual schools to implement literacy assessments and instruction.

For the past 2 years, all of the third-grade students at Westside Elementary, including students who received the supplementary literacy support from preservice teachers, passed the reading portion of the Criterion-Referenced Competency Test (CRCT). According to the Georgia Department of Education,

> The CRCT is designed to measure how well students acquire the skills and knowledge described in the state mandated content standards in reading, English/language arts, mathematics, science and social studies. The assessments yield information on academic achievement, at the student, class, school, system, and state levels. This information is used to diagnose individual student strengths and weaknesses as related to the instruction of the state standards, and to gauge the quality of education throughout Georgia. (2014, para. 1)

The 2-year pass rate on the CRCT reading assessment may not be solely credited to the preservice teachers, but their supplementary literacy support helped these struggling/reluctant readers and writers to learn and experience research-based reading and writing strategies that may have contributed to their success on the test. The quality of literacy education increases through this intensive one-on-one literacy support.

Valdosta Enrichment Program (V.E.P.)

The *Valdosta Enrichment Program (V.E.P.)* is a literacy program that was developed for struggling/reluctant readers and writers in the third grade at Westside Elementary. The Sullivan Literacy Center Director, along with graduate assistants who were completing a reading endorsement, planned and implemented meaningful, relevant, and purposeful literacy enrichment activities with these children. The purpose of this literacy enrichment program is to build these children's reading and writing confidence, motivation, skills, and excitement. Past activities included writing letters to U.S. Olympic athletes participating in a nationwide "Ask the Olympic Athlete" project (these Westside third graders represented the whole state of Georgia), reading Olympic athletic event trade books, writing book recommendation scripts, filming book recommendations, and posting the film to YouTube in the first episode of the *Lights, Camera, Read! Blazer Books Series*. All of these literacy enrichment activities are highly motivating and help these children to get excited about reading and writing. These experiences help graduate assistants to see the power in planning and implementing literacy enrichment activities that are highly engaging. These enrichment activities do not come from a traditional textbook or teacher's manual, yet they support the Core Curriculum Georgia Performance Standards (CCGPS) for reading and writing.

FAMILY AND COMMUNITY PARTNERSHIP

Sewell (2012) noted that "it is vital for both early childhood teacher prepara-tion programs and in-service trainers to ensure pre-service students and practicing teachers are adequately prepared to partner with families in order to best serve the needs of the child and family" (p. 262). As stated earlier, the Sullivan Literacy Center mission is to be an integrated system of care for children and families of the Valdosta community and surrounding areas. As a result of this mission, several service programs were developed and/or created to strengthen this family and community partnership.

Community Service Programs

As indicated, the Sullivan Literacy Center provides needed services for chil-dren and families of Valdosta and surrounding areas. These services are not lim-ited to literacy development exclusively, but also include health-related service as well. According to the National Human Services Assembly Policy Brief No. 19 (2007) on Family Literacy, "Family literacy is an evidence-based, family centered educational approach that can improve the basic reading and mathematics skills, English language proficiency, and life skills of both parents and children" (p. 1). Valdosta State University preservice teachers, as well as other undergraduate and graduate students throughout the university, either participate in or take the lead in most of the services provided by the Sullivan Literacy Center.

Community Service Initiative.

The Sullivan Literacy Center, in partnership with the local geotechnical engi-neering corporation *TTL, Inc.*, has collaborated on an ongoing community service initiative. The *Spring Into Reading—Family Literacy Event* was the first com-munity service event planned for children and families of the Sullivan Literacy Center as well as all of Valdosta and surrounding areas. This event involved indi-vidual break-out sessions for the parents as well as individual literacy sessions for the children. Free high quality children's books and literacy materials were given to parents and children throughout the event. Individual parent sessions were fa-cilitated by professors in the Department of Early Childhood and Special Educa-tion as well as the preservice teachers in the department. Preservice teachers also facilitated the children's literacy sessions as well. There were four different parent break-out sessions, namely,

1. *The Electric Slide: No Longer Just a Dance*: In this session the parents explored ways to promote literacy using current and developmentally appropriate technology resources.
2. *Toon Into Reading: Kids LOVE comics!*: The details in the pictures make children want to read the words. Comics beg for repeated readings and let both emerging and reluctant readers enjoy stories with a rich vocab-

ulary. In this session, parents explored how to use TOON books and graphic novels in an interactive, engaging, and educational way.

3. *Using Sign Language with Old Macdonald Had a Farm*: The goal of this session was for parents to learn sigh language that can be useful with children or relatives who are deaf. Parents learned signs of the American Sign Language that goes along with Old Macdonald Had a Farm. Preservice teachers read the book while teaching them the signs of animals. After reading the book and learning the signs, the parents followed along with the CD signing animals in the book.

4. You Read to Me, I'll Read to You: Very Short Fairy Tales to Read Together: In this session, the parents experienced easy and fun ways to share reading with their children. They explored how to use simple books, personal stories, and even daily routines as the basis to write and read their own short stories to read aloud.

The children's literacy sessions were broken into two sessions where the preservice teachers led the children in engaging and interactive comprehension activities centered around the books Pete the Cat—I Love My White Shoes by Eric Litwin and James Dean and A Bad Case of Stripes by David Shannon. The different break-out sessions for both the parents and children helped the preservice teachers to experience working with families on building their literacy engagement and motivation.

Parent Education Series.

Each semester, parents of the children in the Sullivan Literacy Center are asked to complete a questionnaire regarding different topics that they would be interested in learning more about. Different topics are chosen by parents and may or may not be related to literacy. Education series sessions occur at the same time that children are participating in different literacy programs. Parents are also actively participating in their own learning activities instead of just sitting and waiting for the children to finish. Past educational topics presented to parents included phonics strategy instruction, fluency strategy instruction, comprehension strategy instruction, discipline, stress management, childhood learning disabilities, and childhood obesity. Undergraduate and graduate students in the Department of Early Childhood and Special Education as well as from across the university help the faculty to facilitate different sessions. The *Parent Education Series* is a very meaningful and educational experience for these undergraduate and graduate students in presenting topics that they are learning in their own coursework.

Scholastic Book Fair.

Each semester, the Sullivan Literacy Center hosts a *Scholastic Book Fair* for children and families of Valdosta and surrounding areas, which include the Valdosta State University faculty, staff, students, and families as well. The book fair is a university and community-wide event. The *Scholastic Book Fair* offers high quality, low cost books for children ages birth through high school to purchase, which promote reading enjoyment and reading engagement. The Sullivan Literacy Center graduate assistants facilitate and monitor the fair while preservice teachers throughout the Dewar College of Education and Human Services volunteer their time to work different fair shifts. The *Scholastic Book Fair* helps these preservice teachers to be exposed to different high quality children's books that they can potentially use in their future classrooms.

Southern Regional Helen Ruffin Reading Bowl.

The Sullivan Literacy Center hosts the *Southern Regional Helen Ruffin Reading Bowl* every February for coaches, children, and families all throughout South Georgia. The Helen Ruffin Reading Bowl was started by Helen Ruffin, who was a media specialist from DeKalb County Georgia. Her purpose for starting the Reading Bowl was to get children in grades 4 through 12 to read and increase their comprehension skills through friendly team competition. Children read books recommended by the Georgia Children's Book Award nominees and Georgia Peach Teen Book Award nominees throughout the year and then compete through county, regional, divisional, and finally state Bowl competitions. The Helen Ruffin Reading Bowl is an annual event that first started in 2003 (DeKalb County School System, n.d.). The Sullivan Literacy Center hosts the annual southern regional Bowl. Just recently, there were over 600 people, including coaches, children, families, and supporters, in attendance for this year's Bowl. Faculty and preservice teachers in the Department of Early Childhood and Special Education volunteer their time to work at the Bowl by being a team personal assistant, time keeper, console judge, runner, scorekeeper, or moderator. The *Southern Regional Helen Ruffin Reading Bowl* helps preservice teachers to consider how they can get their future students involved in highly engaging and motivational reading experiences such as the Reading Bowl.

Moody Air Force Base community outreach.

The Moody Air Force Base is an *M-CAT* partner with the Sullivan Literacy Center. The Sullivan Literacy Center Director and graduate assistants have participated in the Moody Air Force Base Child Expo in disseminating information to the Moody Air Force Base families regarding different services and programs offered by the Sullivan Literacy Center. As a result, there are several children and families from Moody Air Force Base that have registered for and participate in different programs at the Sullivan Literacy Center. The Moody Air Force Base Child Expo is a great event that helps graduate assistants to see the importance and need for community outreach programs. Active Moody Air Force men and women also serve as pen pals for children of the Sullivan Literacy Center in the *Dear Blazer Buddy Pen Pal Program.* Preservice teachers help children to write their pen pal letters during the guided writing portion of their literacy lessons in

the *Blazing LitES* and *L.E.A.P.* literacy programs. Many children who participate in different literacy programs in the Sullivan Literacy Center have had many
negative and unsuccessful reading and writing experiences which have depleted
their confidence in reading and writing. The *Dear Blazer Buddy Pen Pal Program*
gives these children positive, successful writing experiences which boost their
confidence and desire to write. The *Dear Blazer Buddy Pen Pal Program* helps
preservice teachers to plan and implement meaningful, relevant, and purposeful
writing instruction that is highly motivating for these struggling and often reluctant writers.

Children's Illustration Art Gallery Event.

The children of the Sullivan Literacy Center participated in a *Children's Illustration Art Gallery Event.* The Sullivan Literacy Center in partnership with
the Valdosta State University Art Education Department worked together on this
project to merge our passions for literacy and the visual arts. The Sullivan Literacy Center Director and graduate assistants planned and implemented a visual
arts comprehension enrichment activity which involved having the children first
choose a Caldecott Award–winning children's book. The children then created
original illustrations based on the book content using different art media (e.g.,
watercolors, colored pencils, cut paper, chalk, marbleized foam, and paint). This
was a highly motivating and engaging way for these struggling readers to use
visual literacy to showcase their comprehension of the books. Children's original
illustrations were displayed in the Annette Howell Turner Center for the Arts in
downtown Valdosta. Children and families were invited to attend the exclusive
opening day gala event. The *Children's Illustration Art Gallery Event* helped
graduate assistants to plan and implement alternative comprehension enrichment
activities using the visual arts that are highly engaging and motivating for these
struggling and reluctant readers.

FUTURE PERSPECTIVES

The Sullivan Literacy Center Director has future plans to begin a preschool literacy program, middle-grades literacy program, and high school literacy program.
There have been discussions regarding starting a middle-grades reader's theater
program in conjunction with mentorships with the Valdosta State University College of the Arts undergraduates. These undergraduates majoring in theater would
work with and mentor these middle-grades students to rehearse and perform different reader's theaters on the stage. There has also been talks proposing that
international students and students in the English Language Institute at Valdosta
State University would partner with local high school students to work on reading, writing, foreign language, and cultural studies. All of these programs would
involve Valdosta State University graduate and undergraduate students participating in these meaningful service learning opportunities, which would enhance their
course content knowledge as well.

The ultimate long-term goal includes building a literacy center that houses individual tutoring stations, classrooms, conference rooms, central office, parent lounge, healthcare clinic, materials library, mailroom, state-of-the-art computer lab, music studio, art studio, television studio, soundstage, photography lab, printing and copy center, book bindery, movie theater, theatrical stage, and auditorium. Children would be (a) writing and publishing books, poems, jokes, articles, letters, and scripts; (b) creating and performing monologues, speeches, plays, musicals, comedy routines, commercials, videos, and movies; (c) composing and performing original song lyrics and music videos; (d) learning phonemic awareness, phonics, fluency, vocabulary, comprehension, as well as the writing process including spelling, conventions, and content development; and (e) designing their own course of study based on their interests and under the guidance and supervision of preservice teachers. Valdosta State University undergraduate and graduate students would be in charge of planning, managing, organizing, and facilitating the learning experiences for the children and families of Valdosta and the surrounding areas. This would be a meaningful, relevant, purposeful, and highly motivational learning experience for these VSU students and children. The focus would be on building children's reading and writing motivation, confidence, and skills, as well as helping preservice teachers apply content knowledge or theory to practice. They would be learning by doing; and the possibilities and potential lessons learned will be endless.

CONCLUSION

Preparing future educators can be accomplished through building partnerships with schools, families, and communities. As state-mandated standards become increasingly rigorous, the emphasis on application-based field experiences is crucial. These educational field experiences can be accomplished through service learning that focuses on service to children, service to families, and service to communities. The Sullivan Literacy Center is one example of the positive outcomes experienced from building these essential relationships through service learning. As Wilkinson et al. (2012) reported, "Incorporation of service-learning made the course content more meaningful for students and helped further their understanding of concepts and principles as well as their professional growth in areas relevant to practice in the field" (p. 115). Preservice teachers learn how to help build literacy confidence, motivation, and skills in struggling and reluctant readers and writers, while at the same time see the value in providing literacy instruction that is meaningful, relevant, and highly engaging. The Sullivan Literacy Center is a center for service and a center for learning. Clearly, service learning is a win-win situation for all involved.

REFERENCES

Christenson, S. L., & Sheridan, S. M. (2001). *Schools and families: Creating essential connections for learning.* New York, NY: Guilford.

DeKalb County School System. (n.d.). *Helen Ruffin Reading Bowl.* Retrieved from http://www.dekalb.k12.ga.us/hrrb/

Dewey, J. (1938). *Experience and education.* New York, NY: Collier.

Dewey, J. (1966). *Democracy and education: An introduction to the philosophy of education.* New York, NY: Free Press.

Fountas, I. C., & Pinnell, G. S. (1999). How and why children learn about sounds, letters, and words in Reading Recovery lessons. *The Running Record, 12*(1), 1–14.

Georgia Department of Education. (2014). *Criterion-referenced competency tests (CRCT): What is the purpose of the CRCT?* Retrieved from http://www.gadoe.org/curriculum-instruction-and-assessment/assessment/pages/crct.aspx

Herman, D. V., & Marlowe, M. (2005). Modeling meaning in life: The teacher as servant leader. *Reclaiming Children and Youth, 14*(3), 175–178.

National Council for Accreditation of Teacher Education. (2010). Transforming teacher education through clinical practice: A national strategy to prepare effective teachers: Report of the Blue Ribbon Panel on clinical preparation and partnerships for improved student learning. *ERIC.* Retrieved from http://eric.ed.gov/?id=ED512807

National Human Services Assembly. (2007). *Family literacy. Policy brief no. 19.* Retrieved from http://eric.ed.gov/?id=ED500005

Sewell, T. (2012). Are we adequately preparing teachers to partner with families? *Early Childhood Education Journal, 40*(5), 259–263. doi:10.1007/s10643-011-0503-8

Teacher Leadership Exploratory Consortium. (2011). The standards. *Teacher Leader Model Standards.* Retrieved September 30, 2012, from http://www.teacherleaderstandards.org

Wilkinson, I. A. G., Doepker, G. M., & Morbitt, D. (2012). Bringing service-learning to scale in an undergraduate reading foundations course: A quasi-experimental study. *Journal of Excellence in College Teaching, 23*(2), 93–122.

CHAPTER 10

PREPARING TEACHERS TO TEACH WITH COMICS LITERATURE IN K–12 CLASSROOMS

Alicja Rieger, Ewa McGrail, and J. Patrick McGrail

Comics literature is emerging as a powerful and innovative tool that can be used to meet the needs of today's increasingly visually and media-oriented generation of students (Afrilyasanti & Basthomi, 2011; Syma & Weiner, 2013). These learners are also "savvy multi-taskers, text-messagers, and Internet sophisticates" (Mortimore, 2009, p. 257). At the same time, the findings of the report of the Commission on the Future of Higher Education (U.S. Department of Education, 2006) indicated that teacher preparation programs should require from their teacher candidates a noticeably different set of competencies from that of just a few generations ago. These competencies should put an emphasis on creative and innovative approaches to both teaching and learning practices. The inculcation of comics literature into the curriculum is an excellent and relevant example of such an emphasis. Alvermann (2005) viewed such an innovative approach as "transitioning to teaching in 'newer' times" (p. 10), and she called upon educators to expand their perception of text to include multiliteracies such as comics

Critical Issues in Preparing Effective Early Childhood Special Education Teachers for the 21st Century Classroom: Interdisciplinary Perspectives, pages 125–139.

and graphic novels in order to close the literacy achievement gap. As she explained, "Because many struggling or reluctant readers find their own reasons for becoming literate—reasons that go beyond reading to acquire school knowledge of academically sanctioned texts—it is important to offer them a variety of reading materials" (p. 12). In addition, the newly implemented Common Core State Standards (CCSSI, 2010) now explicitly called for the use of alternative media, including comic and graphic novels in the curriculum. This chapter uncovers the potential of comics literature in the classroom and encourages teachers across disciplines to innovate in their instruction and to include this alternative medium in their teaching arsenal.

WHY COMICS LITERATURE?

Comics literature, which might be termed sequential art, is considered a legitimate and effective form of reading and has its roots in the oldest forms of communication (Bitz, 2009). Of course, comics are not always funny; the term "comics literature," as used here, refers rather to images and words arranged next to each other in space and time to tell a story (Eisner, 2008). In this way, comics literature encompasses many kinds of graphic and sequential narratives, each bound by its own conventions (Wolk, 2007). Popular comics literature includes a multitude of forms and techniques, which include comic strips, comic books, the neologism "comix," and graphic novels.

Comics literature is experiencing a "best of times" in education today. In the words of Wolk (2007), "If there is such a thing as a golden age of comics, it's happening right now" (p. 10). Indeed, over the past several years, comics literature has gained a recognition and place in the classroom curriculum and instruction (Bakis, 2012; Hammond, 2012; Syma & Weiner, 2013; Upson & Hall, 2013). As a result, comics and graphic novels have been incorporated into classroom curricula alongside the traditional literary canon (Mortimore, 2009; Rubin, 2013). This is because "comic art can carry as much truth, beauty, mystery, emotion, and smart entertainment as any other, more traditional, media of expression" (Arnold, 2007, p. 12). Graphic novels in the classroom "can be used to motivate reluctant readers and aid comprehension for less skilled readers who may have had difficulty transitioning from picture books to print only text" (Hammond, 2012, p. 25). With its visual modes of communication, comics literature has been also deemed an effective scaffold for second-language learners (Liu, 2004). Similarly, due to the interplay of words with visual images, comics literature has been considered an effective and motivational medium in educational settings for students with disabilities (Gavigan, 2011; Smetana & Grisham, 2012) and those with behavior problems (Elder, Caterino, Chao, Shacknai & De Simone, 2006; S. Ozdemir, 2008). These are but a few reasons for using comics literature across curricula; and there are many untapped possibilities of comics for classroom use.

Comics Literature and Literacy Skills Development

With the implementation of the new Common Core State Standards (CCSSI, 2010), increased expectations in English Language Arts (ELA) are placed on all students, including students with disabilities (Straub & Alias, 2013). Research has, however, found comics literature to be an effective instructional tool for improving literacy skills, especially when students are engaged concurrently in reading and creating comic books in their language arts instruction (Stoermer, 2009). "Graphic novels, after all, are the perfect blend of word and picture, story as text and story as art. As such, they offer important, unique, and timely multiliteracy experiences" (Carter, 2007, p. 7).

That said, Morrison, Bryan, and Chilcoat (2002) demonstrated that students in their study were able to improve their literacy skills because comic books allowed them to be engaged in the artistic process of words flowing intuitively with pictures. Specific gains were reported in areas such as sequencing, decoding, nonverbal communication, and making inferences (Lyga, 2006), as well as comprehension and thinking skills (Frey & Fisher, 2008). As Bitz (2004) pointed out, 733 children, in grades 5 through 8 who were identified as low-performing students, reluctant readers and writers, and had a limited English proficiency but who had participated in an after-school literacy program in New York City, the Bitz's Comic Book Project, demonstrated significant gains in their literacy and motivation skills. More specifically, Bitz's (2004) research indicated that 86% of children demonstrated an improvement in their writing skills. They also met all components of standards in reading and writing. This included reading, writing, listening and speaking for information and understanding, paying attention for literacy response and expression, for critical analysis and evaluation, and for social interaction. They brainstormed, outlined, sketched, wrote, and designed individual comic books. Similarly, Sonnenschein, Baker, Katenkamp and Beall (2006), who studied the Comic Book Initiative sponsored by the Maryland State Department of Education, found the lessons that utilized award-winning graphic novels and related materials to be effective in improving literacy skills among elementary-grade students. When asked to estimate the percentages of students in their classes who mastered the specified objectives of each lesson, teachers across varied classrooms indicated that 77% to 88% did so. The program targeted 3rd-grade students specifically; it consisted of lesson plans and lesson guidelines supporting the development of reading, vocabulary, and writing.

Comics literature helps English-language learners (ELLs) to advance their literacy skills. For instance, Cary (2004) found that when ELLs were attuned to illustrations in the comics literature, they made better sense of the text. This facilitated their reading comprehension and second-language acquisition. Liu (2004) reported that these learners who were low-performing students but who were coached into using high-level text with comics improved their information recall up to 38.7% in comparison to their low-level ESL peers who used only the traditional readings and maintained only 19.4% information recall. Smetana and Grisham (2012) used an experimental design and the Dynamic Indicators of Basic Literacy Skills (DIBELS) to assess student learning in their research on graphic novels. They found them to be a powerful and impactful genre for improving reading comprehension, vocabulary, and word recognition, as well as oral reading fluency among a Tier 2 Response to Intervention students with learning disabilities. Graphic novels have also been found to be an effective tool for improving achievement among students with hearing impairment, learning disabilities, and autism spectrum disorders (Gavigan, 2011; Smetana, Odelson, Burns, & Grisham, 2009). There is evidence that graphic novels can challenge more advanced and gifted students, since they allow for the integration of higher-level thinking with writing and reading skills (McTaggert, 2008).

Comics Literature and Motivation

Comics literature has been found to be a powerful tool for increasing student attention and motivation. Comic books apparently help to create a positive emotional affect in the minds of students for unusual and idiosyncratic pictorial representation, motivating them to maximize their learning (Bitz, 2004; Sonnenschein et al., 2006; Syma & Weiner, 2013). For example, Syma and Weiner (2013) noticed that when students read comics, "Their minds are lively" (p. 5). Students cannot learn if they are not attending to the material at hand (Morrison, 2008). Earlier, in Bitz's study (2004) of the Comic Book Project among low-performing readers, 92% of students indicated that they liked to write their own stories in a comic book format and 94% indicated that they loved to draw pictures that went along with their stories, thus improving student motivation and engagement for reading and writing. Likewise, the findings by Sonnenschein et al. (2006) from the pilot study of the Comic Book Initiative indicated a very high degree of student interest in the program, with mean ratings above 4.0, ranging from 3.4 to 4.6 on a scale of 1–5. The project was sponsored by the Maryland State Department of Education. This statewide program had been launched to encourage the use of award-winning graphic novels and other comic book materials in the classroom (see http://www.marylandpublicschools.org/msde/programs/recognition-partnerships/md-comic-book.html).

Dallacqua's recent study (2012) found a positive change in 5th-grade students' attitudes toward reading after exposure to graphic novels. These students made a direct connection between a graphic novel and the format of film during their discussion of their experience with reading a graphic novel. Dallacqua concluded that the students' acknowledgement of this visual connection between graphic novel and film increased their engagement and motivation in reading and literacy instruction. Dallacqua explained that

> Both media fit the description of sequential art, showing a progression of action through the images. The reader is able to watch action unfold, see what a character

looks like, and experience the setting illustrated in the background while reading a graphic novel. And in a graphic novel, these images are not additions to the story; they are part of the story. Each image in a graphic novel gives important information to the reader and pushes the plot forward. (p. 65)

Earlier, Gavigan (2011) showed the effectiveness of graphic novels with struggling 8th-grade male adolescent readers. These readers made significant improvement in their value of reading and moderate improvement in their self-concept as readers as measured by the Adolescent Motivation to Read Profile (AMRP). Additionally, increased engagement and motivation have been observed during graphic novel book club reading sessions.

Comics Literature and Social Interaction

Given the fact that many students of the current generation are already aficionados of comics and graphic novels and are eager to share them with other comic book fans and age- appropriate peers (Mortimore, 2009), utilizing comics literature can be a powerful social factor in promoting social-skills development and authentic social interactions. For example, Bitz (2004) reported that students demonstrated increased levels of social development and interaction as a result of participation in the Comic Book Project. Working collaboratively on comic books provided these students with the opportunity to negotiate different ideas and to problem-solve disagreements among group members, leading eventually to improved peer-to-peer relations and communication. Bitz explained that "the effect seemed to be children's better understanding of themselves and those around them—a positive social interaction" (p. 584). Similarly, based on 4 years of qualitative study of the original site for the Comic Book Project, Bitz (2009) discovered that *manga* (a Japanese style of writing and drawing comics) that featured characters who lived in troubled neighborhoods emerged as a uniting factor for both male and female students. One of the reasons why this form of comics was so appealing to students in this project was that it allowed them to discuss their own lives and to analyze their inner fears and vulnerabilities within their immediate social contexts. More specifically, these young authors' comic books told stories about gang violence, drug abuse, family violence, and other difficult moments in their lives as new immigrants to the United States. Sharing these experiences with their peers opened opportunities for getting to know each other and creating a community as well.

Other research studies (e.g., Mortimore, 2009; Norton, 2003) have supported the notion that student-authored comic books tell stories with charisma and depth, and that they also help young readers connect in meaningful and relevant ways to the lives of the characters in these books. Having the ability to relate to others and their experiences or viewpoints is an important interpersonal and social development skill. It is also an indicator of a child's healthy emotional life (American Academy of Pediatrics, n.d.). Mortimore (2009) explained that "through the critical investigation of the picture, the word, and the world, students can begin to connect both personally and culturally to the ideas and themes inherent in these texts" (p. 18). In addition, graphic novels and comic books have been found to be an ideal format to engage students in conversation about topics such as friendship or racial and ethnic identity (Karp, 2010). Indeed, Lu (2010) reported that reading and discussing graphic novels helped inner-city children understand larger social issues such as discrimination, oppression, and institutional inequities. The comic book format also provided a forum for expressing their own concerns, emotions, and feelings, as is evident in these titles of graphic novels: *Mom is in Jail Because of NSF Checks and Hard Drugs*, *A Broken Family*, or *We Met Bullies at Trick or Treat* (p. 13).

After having experienced "vicariously the children's emotions of sorrows, anxiety, fears, worries, conflicts, concerns, frustration, etc." (p. 14), Lu (2010) urged teachers to give the struggling learners the opportunity to "use multimodal transformations to express social injustices." She also encouraged teachers to use student "authentic artifacts" (p. 14) as a call for social justice as well.

Seidler (2011) reported on the effective classroom use of comics to fight disability stereotypes. More specifically, in her classroom, she asked 6th-grade students with and without disabilities to examine stereotypes about people living with disabilities and then to challenge these stereotypical perceptions through the creation of comic strips that included affirmative representations of disability. The latter representations portrayed a disability as a positive and an integral part of a person's identity. According to Seidler, engagement in such comic book creation helped her students improve their disability awareness and to dispel common stereotypes about disability and disability issues. It also empowered them to take a stand against discriminatory practices and disability stereotypes. Additionally, reading social stories was found to be effective in reducing disruptive behaviors in the mainstream classroom and in meeting the social and behavioral needs of children with autism (Özdemir, 2008) and Asperger's Syndrome (Elder et al., 2006). Conducting comic strip-based conversations has helped to improve social skills among students with autism (Attwood, 2000). Later, Epp (2008) found that teaching conflict-resolution skills by reading and creating therapeutic comic strips to be more effective with children with autism spectrum disorders than using traditional guided discussion or role playing.

Comics Literature and Content Area Instruction

The benefits of comic books in all content area instruction, and for students with a wide range of abilities, from struggling to gifted students, have been documented for some time (Carter, 2007). For example, outside the area of ELA, comic books have been identified as an effective medium with which to teach science concepts and ideas to 6th-grade students who participated in science instruction aided with science comics. They more readily improved in comparison to their peers whose science instruction was provided only with standardized science texts (Özdemir, 2010). Hosler and Boomer (2011) found that the incorporation of the science comic book *Optical Allusions* (Hosler, 2008) was received positively by biology nonmajors who demonstrated initial deficits in understanding certain science concepts as measured on their performance tests. In addition to enhancing the cognitive comprehension of the science content, the results indicated an increased interest in and motivation to learn biology among students who engaged in reading the science comic book.

Analogous positive results have been observed in social studies content area instruction that included a comics-based learning component in the presentation of history to students. Mallia (2007) conducted an experiment on 90 students (average ages: 14–15 years; 45 girls and 45 boys) that incorporated a **text-only version** about Maltese history, an **illustrated text version,** and the **comics version** of the same text. He found that the comics version of the text had been as effective as the two other versions of the text in improving student performance on "knowledge and procedural recall" (para. 25).

MAKING COMICS LITERATURE WORK IN K–12 CLASSROOMS

As evidenced above, comics literature can be a powerful tool for improving teaching and learning for all students, and in different subject areas. However, that potential can only be realized when educators and service providers know how to use such literature to its full potential. In the following sections, we provide essential steps and resources to support educators in this effort.

Teaching Key Aspects of a Comics Genre

Comics literature, like any other genre, operates within its own conventions. The panel is the "box" in which the main art and word balloons are placed for each entry in the sequence of images in the story. The panel is equivalent to a single visual shot in a motion picture, though some have most of the elements of a full scene. Each panel plays a critical role in ensuring the flow of the story, allowing for changes within the progression of the storyline and helping the reader to pace their reading (Mortimore, 2009; Tilley, 2008). Word balloons are used to communicate the dialogue effectively between the characters. Narrative boxes, like contextual clues, are meant to be read as messages outside of the dialogue, as they hold the pertinent information for understanding the story (Mortimore, 2009). Singular panels, side-by-side (stacked together) panels, or narrow panels are sometimes interspersed with wide panels. Frames and borders around the panels are also often used to communicate actions and evoke emotions in the reader. That is, they are meant to create action through conflicts that must be resolved (Tilley, 2008). An equally important convention of comics is the use of gutters, or the space between panels (Tilley, 2008). Gutters are there to help the reader to "fill in the 'gaps' (the space between each panel) with their imagination" (Mortimore,

2009, p. 72). As such, they help the reader to understand the detail and the depth of the story.

Critical thinking, along with understanding of key characteristics and conventions of comics, is needed to read comics literature with full comprehension. The reason is that much emotional knowledge is required of the reader, consisting of what must be understood by him or her as the contextual framework of the comic, what is suggested by it, and what is developed fully and differently for each individual reader. This is in contrast with television and film, in which every iota of narrative is motionally depicted and elaborated upon. Both teachers and students need to familiarize themselves with comic art conventions. Fortunately, there are texts available that can be powerful tools to aid educators and students in this task. For instance, McCloud's (2006) *Making Comics: Storytelling Secrets of Comics, Manga, and Graphic Novels* can assist educators and students in understanding what goes on inside varied types of comic books, how they are composed, and how to read and understand them. Other books that instruct on comic book conventions include *Using Graphic Novels in the Classroom: Grades 4-8* (Hart, 2010), *Teaching Graphic Novels: Practical Strategies for the Secondary ELA Classroom* (Monnin, 2010), and *The Graphic Novel Classroom: POWerful Teaching and Learning with Images* (Bakis, 2012).While Hart's book is designed for elementary and middle school students and Bakis' for high school audiences, both texts demonstrate literary analysis of the comic books genre and provide strategies and lessons for developing a comic book or graphic novel story. In addition, the teacher should share examples of different kinds of comics literature and illustrate the difference between a comic strip, a comic book, and a graphic novel. These websites provide such examples: Sample Comics: http://www.wikihow.com/Make-a-Comic-Strip and Comic Books Collection: http://www.pixton.com/collection/Pixton.

Modeling Reading and Critical Analysis of Comics Literature

Since comic books are complex texts with rich content and multifaceted relationships that can be communicated through pictorial and textual means, inexperienced readers may experience cognitive overload (Hammond, 2012). Therefore, it is critical that students are provided with systematic instruction and modeling on how to engage in reading and critical analysis of comics literature. Kelley (2010) advised using picture walk strategies and modeling, that is, how to read first just a single panel and then to move to reading multiple panels. This type of scaffold provides the reader with an effective strategy for reading text structure and making meaning of the texts. Kelley also recommended engaging students in conversations about text content and structure and asking the following questions to make their analysis of and conversation about the comic book and graphic novel text deeper and richer:

1. What is the story in this panel? How do we know? Is there more to this story than we're aware of? How do we know?
2. What happens if we add a second panel, telling the story of this panel from a different perspective? Do we see the story the same way?
3. Have we learned anything new about the character, the setting, or the situation from the addition of a second panel? (p. 12)

This strategy focuses on interpreting visual, textual, and verbal clues in context and from various perspectives, leading to a critical text analysis, which is required from all students in language arts and other curricula.

Teaching critical text analysis of comic/graphic books involves coaching students on how to make "Text-to-Self, Text-to-Text, and Text to-World Connections" and on how to establish connections with the characters and events they read about in the text—"a task necessary for successful reading of sequential art—the task of integration" (Kelley, 2010, p. 17). To assist students in such an analysis, Langer (1995) offered a framework that consists of four stances the readers must employ to arrive at an understanding or "envisionment" (p. 10). The stances are

1. *Being Out and Stepping In*: Readers make their initial contact with a book based on prior knowledge, including knowledge of history, culture(s), or other texts (the reader brings in all kinds of prior knowledge associations).
2. *Being In and Moving Through*: Readers build a personal envisionment or understanding (using personal experience, values, or ideas, the text, and the context).
3. *Being In and Stepping Out*: Readers reflect on the way(s) in which a book relates to their own life and the lives of others, other cultures, and people.
4. *Stepping Out and Objectifying the Experience*: Readers reflect on the story as a crafted object/literary work (they reflect on the sum of the text—the overall message—and can think about the ways other characters or readers can see the text). (p. 18)

It is critical that students read and respond to both the text and the image in the comic/graphic book first independently, using the four reading stances. Then they can discuss these stances in small groups, explaining which ones they assumed and when they assumed them while reading the story. This two-step process allows for an analytical look at the text from the personal viewpoint as well as from the perspectives of others. The multilevel method also gives students the opportunity to reread the complex graphic/comic book text and thereby enables them to hone their comprehension and close-text analysis skills.

Providing Opportunities to Create Comics in the Classroom

The extensive literature cited above shows the power of comics literature reading to enhance comprehension, improve motivation and affect, and increase reading in general. However, new tools exist for students to create their own comic literature. Carter and Evensen (2011) recommended the following steps to guide this production process: "planning, plotting, editing, scripting, revisions, collaborative writing, publishing and more" (p. 151).

Planning and plotting involves coming up with ideas, events, and the people that students would like to write about in response to the literature they read and discuss in class. *Scripting* is like making a movie, which involves deciding on the setting, the cast, and actions. Like movie-making, creating comics should be a collaborative endeavor, and students should be invited to take on different roles, such as the scriptwriter who will write the dialogue, the artist who will sketch illustrations or select images, and the designer who will plan the layout, change angles, and organize the story on the comic strip. The *editor* will ink in the artist's pencil drawings, erase pencil marks, and proofread the entire text.

To help students with scriptwriting, teachers may use a comic script template and examples of scripts from this website: http://www.comicbookscriptarchive.com/archive/the-scripts/. A recommended resource is the *Comic Book Show and Tell* lesson on the ReadWriteThink professional development website, available at http://www.readwritethink.org/classroom-resources/lesson-plans/comic-book-show-tell-921.html. The ReadWriteThink website includes a handout with the roles for developing a comic book and a handout with instructions for scriptwriting as well. Students can hand draw illustration and write dialogue for their comic book or they can use software. For comic strip/book applications, instructors may go to these websites: MakeBeliefsComix, available at http://www.makebeliefscomix.com/Comix/; ToonDoo: Free Online Comic Maker, available at http://www.boxoftricks.net/2007/12/free-comic-strip-creating-website/; and Chogger: http://chogger.com/. While the MakeBeliefs and ToonDoo websites offer free comic book and strip makers and examples of comic book creations, Chogger also allows for importing and working with webcam pictures. A good recommendation is the Pixton comic book software, if you have access to funds, available at http://www.pixton.com/. The Pixton software offers a wide range of comic book templates and a greater degree of customization than the free comic book maker websites.

Instructors can end the comic book production process with viewing and discussing of the comics in a *Show and Tell* session to which guests can be invited. Also, they should consider publishing student creations on the Web as well. Some possible outlets include the Comic Book Project: http://www.comicbookproject.org/, Super Action Comic Gallery: http://www.artisancam.org.uk/flashapps/superactioncomicmaker/gallery.php, and Chogger: http://chogger.com/. There is evidence that following a session of comic book making, all students will become profoundly more interested in text, story, and narrative flow—in essence, all of the ingredients for reading, comprehending, and enjoying fictional and nonfictional material. More advanced students will enjoy the challenge in creating something that looks like the best of what they have read and perused; and struggling students will find that comics literature provides them with its own multiliteracies, as it buttresses picture with dialogue and dialogue with narrative box elaboration. The arresting, dramatic images aid in memory retention, and the timely, gripping narratives spark the imagination of students from different races, genders, circumstances, and geographical locations.

IMPLICATIONS FOR TEACHER PREPARATION

If we wish teachers to use comics in the K–12 classroom as an innovative instructional strategy, then teachers require education that includes immersion in and analysis of graphic novels and comics literature as genres. Such an education should involve exploring both the unique language (terminology) of comics as well as the conventions of the comics genre, including the study of comic book components such as the earlier described script, panels, borders and gutters, speech and thought balloons, story layout, drawings, lettering and sound effects. There are specialized terms for each of these components, such as an *inset panel* (a panel contained with a larger panel) and *tailless balloons* (word balloons that function as voiceover or off-panel dialogue). Adopting various styles for panels, borders, gutters, or lettering can be used to communicate different moods, images, types of dialogue, plot structures, or even characters and their ways of being, believing and talking (Bennett, n.d.). Studying both the language and conventions of comics books will thus expand teachers' own understandings and beliefs about comics literature as a genre and about its potential for education. It will also prepare them to teach it to their students as a powerful means for the communication and expression of complex ideas and thoughts while connecting with their interests and motivation.

We believe the best way to acquire sophisticated understandings of comics literature as a genre is through review and critique of many exemplars, including various formats (print-based traditional comic books, manga, or TV cartoon/comic book series), styles (rich in color or text), content and topics, and genres (e.g., fiction, nonfiction, memoir, novel, or play). Such hands-on explorations will also help teachers develop the quality criteria for comics literature as appropriate for various styles, media, and genres, and for teaching different content that they can employ to select quality and age-appropriate comics literature for their own classroom use in the future.

Another great way to learn about the language and conventions of a comics genre is for teachers to create a comic or graphic novel of their own. Teacher candidates should be provided with such opportunities in teacher education programs. Wurdinger and Carlson (2010) agreed that experiential learning (learning by doing and critical reflection on action) will assist teachers in mastering not only the unique characteristics of the genre itself but also the processes involved in creating powerful stories, fiction, or media products through this medium of expression. Such knowledge will prepare teachers to help their students to recognize quality comics literature and the process that is involved in creating good comics stories. The experiential learning in which the teachers will engage in the college classroom will also serve as example of how to teach with comics literature different content using a hands-on minds-on instructional approach in their own teaching contexts and situations.

Although a language arts or a literature methods course may seem like the most natural contexts for engaging teachers in analyzing and creating comic book literature, we report from the studies in various content areas in our literature review. For example, Attwood (2000), Dallacqua (2012), Gavigan (2011), Mallia (2007), and Özdemir (2010) noted that content area, general education, or special education programs might serve well as alternative spaces for teacher explorations of comic literature as well. We make this recommendation based on our conviction that teaching reading and writing, indeed, teaching literacy in general is not, and should not be, the sole responsibility of the language arts, reading, or writing teachers (Alvermann, Phelps, & Ridgeway, 2010). Any content area methods course where teachers are involved in studying to understand, critique, and communicate through text, whether it is a literary text, information text, or discipline-specific text, can yield rich explorations and creations in comics literature and lead to helpful suggestions as to how to teach it to students. This will eventually produce teachers who have developed the ability to communicate such experiences to students in several different content areas as well as enhance their ability to implement such pedagogy in their own classrooms.

CONCLUSION

As evident in our literature review, comics literature, far from a passing fad or momentary diversion, is a durable and rich means of written and graphic expression. Certain notable features make comics literature particularly appropriate for today's literacy and reading classrooms and content area education. First, as is apparent and prevalent through the genre, main textual points are made clear through both dialogic and external narrative means. Moreover, many of these points are illustrated graphically, allowing avid readers and less sophisticated readers, English-language learners, as well as those students who have a disability to have an alternate means of absorbing the meaning, context, and connotation of the narrative arc of the comics piece, fiction or nonfiction.

Teachers who may be less familiar with popular comics and graphic novel literature than some of their students should familiarize themselves with the best that has been produced in these genres. This is because comics literature is an involving, intricate, challenging, and fun way to engage all learners by studying and crafting these visuotextual pieces in their classrooms.

REFERENCES

Afrilyasanti, R., & Basthomi, Y. (2011). *Adapting comics and cartoons to develop 21st century learners. Language in India, 11*(11), 552–568.

Alvermann, D. E. (2005). Literacy on the edge: How close are we to closing the literacy achievement gap? *Voices from the Middle, 13*(1), 8–14.

Alvermann, D. E., Phelps, S. F., & Ridgeway, V. G. (2010). *Content area reading and literacy: Succeeding in today's diverse classrooms* (6th ed.). Boston, MA: Pearson.

American Academy of Pediatrics. (n.d.). The social emotional development of young children: Resource guide for healthy start stuff. *National Healthy Start Association.* Retrieved from http://www.nationalhealthystart.org/site/assets/docs/NHSA_SocialEmotional_1.pdf

Arnold, A. (2007). Comix poetics. *World Literature Today, 81*(2), 12–15.

Attwood, T. (2000). Strategies for improving the social integration of children with Asperger Syndrome. *Autism, 4*(1), 85–100.

Bakis, M. M. (2012). *The graphic novel classroom: POWerful teaching and learning with images.* Thousand Oaks, CA: Corwin.

Bennett, A. (n.d.). Visual language: Writing for comics. *Big Red Hair.* Retrieved from http://www.bigredhair.com/work/comics.html

Bitz, M. (2004). The comic book project: The lives of urban youth. *Art Education, 57*(2), 33–39.

Bitz, M. (2009). *Manga high: Literacy, identity, and coming of age in an urban high school.* Cambridge, MA: Harvard Education Press.

Carter, J. B. (2007). *Building literacy connections with graphic novels: Page by page, panel by panel.* Urbana, IL: National Council of Teachers of English

Carter, J. B., & Evensen, E. (2011). *Super-powered word study.* Gainesville, FL: Maupin House.

Cary, S. (2004). *Going graphic: Comics at work in the multilingual classroom.* Portsmouth, NH: Heinemann.

Common Core State Standards Initiative (CCSSI). (2010). *English language arts standards: Reading: Informational text.* Retrieved June 21, 2013, from http://www.corestandards.org/ELA-Literacy

Dallacqua, A. K. (2012). Exploring the connection between the graphic novel and film. *English Journal, 102*(2), 64–70.

Eisner, W. (2008). *Comics and sequential art: Principles and practices from the legendary cartoonist.* New York, NY: Norton.

Elder, L. M., Caterino, L. C., Chao, J., Shacknai, D., & De Simone, G. (2006). The efficacy of social skills treatment for children with Asperger Syndrome. *Education and Treatment of Children, 29*(4), 635–663.

Epp, K. M. (2008). Outcome-based evaluation of a social skills program using art therapy and group therapy for children on the autism spectrum. *Children & Schools, 30*(1), 27–36.

Frey, N., & Fisher, D. (Eds.). (2008). *Teaching visual literacy: Using comic books, graphic novels, anime, cartoons, and more to develop comprehension and thinking skills.* Thousand Oaks, CA: Corwin.

Gavigan, K. (2011, June 14). More powerful than a locomotive: Using graphic novels to motivate struggling male adolescent readers. *Journal of Research on Libraries and Young Adults. Retrieved from* http://www.yalsa.ala.org/jrlya/2011/06/more-powerful-than-a-locomotive-using-graphic-novels-to-motivate-struggling-male-adolescent-readers/

Hammond, H. (2012). Graphic novels and multimodal literacy: A high school study with American Born Chinese. *Bookbird, 50*(4), 22–32.

Hart, M. (2010). *Using graphic novels in the classroom: Grades 4-8.* Westminster, CA: Teacher Created Resources.

Hosler, J. (2008). *Optical allusions.* Columbus, OH: Active Synapse.

Hosler, J., & Boomer, K. B. (2011). Are comic books an effective way to engage nonmajors in learning and appreciating science? *CBE Life Sciences Education, 10*(3), 309–317.

Karp, J. (2010). Truth and justice!: Graphic novels for the social studies curriculum. *Book Links, 20*(1), 26–26.

Kelley, B. (2010). Sequential art, graphic novels, and comics. *SANE Journal, 1*(1), 3–26. Retrieved from http://digitalcommons.unl.edu/cgi/viewcontent. cgi?article=1009&context=sane

Langer, J. A. (1995). *Envisioning literature: Literary understanding and literature instruction.* New York, NY: Teachers College Press.

Liu, J. (2004). Effects of comic strips on L2 learners' reading comprehension. *TESOL Quarterly, 38*(2), 225–243.

Lu, L. Y. (2010). Inner-city children's graphics call for social justice. *English Language Teaching, 3*(3), 11–19.

Lyga, A. W. (2006, March 1). Graphic novels for (really) young readers. *School Library Journal.* Retrieved December 19, 2007, from http://www.schoollibraryjournal.com/article/CA6312463.html

Mallia, G. (2007). Learning from the sequence: The use comics in instruction. *ImageText: Interdisciplinary Comics Studies.* Retrieved from http://www.english.ufl.edu/imagetext/archives/v3_3/mallia/

McCloud, S. (2006). *Making comics: Storytelling secrets of comics, manga, and graphic novels.* New York, NY: Harper.

McTaggert, J. (2008). Graphic novels: The good, the bad, and the ugly. In N. Frey & D. Fisher, (Eds.), *Teaching visual literacy: Using comic books, graphic novels, anime, cartoons, and more to develop comprehension and thinking skills* (pp. 27–46). Thousand Oaks, CA: Corwin.

Monnin, K. (2010). *Teaching graphic novels: Practical strategies for the secondary ELA classroom.* Gainesville, FL: Maupin House.

Morrison, M. K. (2008). *Using humor to maximize learning: The links between positive emotions and education.* Lanham, MD: Rowman & Littlefield Education.

Morrison, T. G., Bryan, G., & Chilcoat, G. W. (2002). Using student-generated comic books in the classroom. *Journal of Adolescent & Adult Literacy, 45*(8), 758–767.

Mortimore, S. R. (2009). *From picture to word to the world: A multimodal, cultural studies approach to teaching graphic novels in the English classroom.* Western Michigan University. *ProQuest Dissertations and Theses,* , 335-n/a. Retrieved from http://search.proquest.com/docview/305032758?accountid=14800. (305032758)

Norton, B. (2003). The motivating power of comic books: Insights from *Archie* comic readers. *The Reading Teacher, 57*(2), 140–47.

Özdemir. E. (2010). *The effect of instructional comics on sixth grade students' achievement in heat transfer.* Unpublished doctoral dissertation. Middle East Technical University. Ankara. Turkey.

Ozdemir, S. (2008). The effectiveness of social stories on decreasing disruptive behaviors of children with autism: Three case studies. *Journal of Autism and Developmental Disorders, 38*(9). 1689–1696.

Rubin. D. I. (2013). "Remember, remember the fifth of November:" Using graphic novels to teach dystopian literature. In C. K. Syma & R. G. Weiner (Eds.), *Graphic novels in the classroom: Essays on the educational power of sequential art* (pp. 84–90). Jefferson. NC: McFarland.

Seidler, C. O. (2011, November). Fighting disability stereotypes with comics: "I cannot see you. but I know you are staring at me." *Art Education, 64*(6). 20–23.

Smetana. L.. & Grisham, D. I. (2012). Revitalizing Tier 2 intervention with graphic novels. *Reading Horizons, 51*(3), 181–208.

Smetana. L. D.. Odelson, D.. Burns. H., & Grisham. D. L. (2009). Using graphic novels in the high school classroom: Engaging Deaf students with a new genre. *Journal of Adolescent and Adult Literacy, 52*(8). 228–240.

Sonnenschein. S.. Baker. L.. Katenkamp. A.. & Beall. L. (2006. October 1). *Evaluation of the "Maryland Comics in the Classroom" pilot program.* Retrieved from http://www.marylandpublicschools.org/NR/rdonlyres/24F49CEE-0E05-4E7B-B9CE-A7C692E4DCC3/17094/Comics_in_the_Classroom_Evaluation_Exec_Summary_06.pdf

Stoermer. M. (2009). *Teaching between the frames: Making comics with seven and eight year old children, a search for craft and pedagogy.*(Indiana University). *ProQuest Dissertations and Theses, 333*-n/a. Retrieved from http://search.proquest.com/docview/304902585?accountid=14800. (304902585)

Straub. C.. & Alias. A. (2013). Next generation writing at the secondary level for students with learning disabilities. *Teaching Exceptional Children, 46*(1), 16–24.

Syma. C. K.. & Weiner, R. G. (2013). *Graphic novels in the classroom: Essays on the educational power of sequential art.* Jefferson. NC: McFarland.

Tilley. C. L. (2008). Reading comics. *School Library Media Activites Monthly. 24*(9). 23–26.

Upson. M.. & Hall. C. M. (2013). Comic Book Guy in the classroom: The educational power and potential of graphic storytelling in library instruction. *Kansas Library Association College and University Libraries Section Proceedings. 3*(1). 28–38. Retrieved from http://newprairiepress.org/cgi/viewcontent.cgi?article=1032&context=culsproceedings

U.S. Department of Education. (2006). *A test of leadership: Charting the future of U.S. higher education: A report of the commission appointed by Secretary of Education Margaret Spellings.* Retrieved from http://www2.ed.gov/about/bdscomm/list/hief-future/reports/final-report.pdf

Wolk. D. (2007). *Reading comics: How graphic novels work and what they mean.* Philadelphia. PA: De Capo.

Wurdinger. S. D.. & Carlson. J. A. (2010). *Teaching for experiential learning: Five approaches that work.* Lanham. MD: Rowman & Littlefield Education.

CHAPTER 11

USING TECHNOLOGY TO PREPARE TEACHERS AND LEADERS IN EARLY CHILDHOOD SPECIAL EDUCATION

**Sunday Obi, Floyd Beachum, Festus E. Obiakor,
Carlos McCray, Elizabeth Omiteru, and Marty Sapp**

A fundamental shift in the most beneficial way to provide services to young children with special needs is taking place. Infusing technology into the curriculum is now widely accepted as one of the best ways to educate all children. Technology makes it possible for young children with special needs to be included in public and private schools, childcare centers, preschool programs, Head Start programs, and family childcare. And aspiring special educators and leaders must be familiar with all the tools and strategies available in early childhood special education. Also, teachers and leaders in early childhood special education must continue to work together to develop a plan and then establish a system of ongoing communication that enables them to address changes in technology as they arise. However, many of them are overwhelmed by the impact that technology has had on their

Critical Issues in Preparing Effective Early Childhood Special Education Teachers for the 21st Century Classroom: Interdisciplinary Perspectives, pages 141–154.
Copyright © 2016 by Information Age Publishing

ability to be effective teachers and leaders. They often have little training in infusing technology in the curriculum or in the use of assistive devices. Although special educators may be experts when it comes to working with children with special needs, they frequently lack experience in the integration of technology in the curriculum planning and implementation that is necessary for a successful educational program.

The commitment to effective education for early childhood programs is well established in Individuals with Disabilities Education Improvement Act (IDEIA)—this law continues to support many solutions to providing effective education to children with disabilities. They include

> supporting high-quality, intensive pre-service preparation and professional development for all personnel who work with children with disabilities in order to ensure that such personnel have the skills and knowledge necessary to improve the academic achievement and functional performance of children with disabilities, including the use of scientifically based instructional practices, to the maximum extent possible; and supporting the development and use of technology, including assistive technology devices and assistive technology services, to maximize accessibility for children with disabilities.

In perspective, recent technological advancements and demographic and cultural forces have dramatically changed the education landscape around the world. In other words, teaching and learning have changed dramatically over the years. Technology has become an integral part of the lesson plan and an indispensable part of the classroom. However, seamlessly integrating technology into the curriculum can be a challenge. All infants and young children, no matter how significantly challenged or disabled, will benefit from those best practices that create supportive and motivating learning environments for all young children. In this chapter, we discuss the importance of technology in early childhood special education. Embedded in our discussion are the impacts of technology on students, teachers, and leaders.

IMPORTANCE OF TECHNOLOGY IN EARLY CHILDHOOD SPECIAL EDUCATION

Technology in education is most simply and comfortably defined as an array of tools that might prove helpful in advancing student learning. It refers to material objects of use to humanity, such as machines or hardware, but it can also encompass broader themes, including systems, methods of organization, and techniques. Some modern tools include but are not limited to overhead projectors, laptop computers, and calculators. Newer tools include smartphones, software, as well as Internet applications such as wikis and blogs. Digitized communication and networking in education started in the mid-1980s and became popular by the mid-1990s, in particular through the World Wide Web (WWW), email, and forums. Students are now growing up in a digital age where they have constant exposure to a variety of media. No aspect of their lives is untouched by the digital era, which is transforming how they live, relate, and learn (Craft, 2012).

The use of computers and other digital technologies continues to rise in early childhood programs, and technology is being used as a tool for improving program quality in many interesting ways. We routinely use high-tech tools like cellphones, PDAs, personal computers, the Internet, email, and digital cameras in our homes, at work, and in our classrooms. Now cellphones have built-in digital cameras that send photos and receive text messages and email via wireless Internet. Acronyms like PC, CD, DVD, PDA, DSL, eBay, and .com are part of our professional vocabulary right alongside ECE, DAP, ADA, and NAEYC (Donohue, 2003). For better or worse, technology has changed the way we keep records, write programs, give presentations, teach children, and train teachers. The question is not if we should use technology, but how and why we use technology to improve program quality, increase responsiveness to parents, and expand opportunities for professional development. When used effectively, technology tools can support and enhance learning, teaching, documentation, program management, customer service, staff and parent communication, staff development, networking, and advocacy. Today, childcare programs are using technology in many creative ways. For example, developing a website for marketing and access to information, posting lunch menus on the Web, distributing the newsletter electronically, sending digital photos of children to parents via email, participating in listservs, online discussion groups and webcasts for networking and advocacy, and taking online courses (Donohue, 2003). Teachers are also using the Internet as a resource for curriculum ideas and research, taking children on virtual field trips, and as a powerful tool to help children explore ideas and access information. The uses of digital technologies and the Internet in the classroom are as open-ended as the imagination and creativity of the teacher.

The focus on assistive technologies and the provision of inclusive childcare are important trends today. *Tech for Tots* is one example. The University of Southern California University Affiliated Program (UAP) at Children's Hospital, Los Angeles has developed a comprehensive awareness-level training for use in teacher education and professional training. The program focuses on the value of assistive technology for children with disabilities and addresses concerns about children ages birth to 3 being underserved with assistive technology (Donohue, 2003). As educators, we are always on the lookout for innovation, and uses for educational technology in the classroom are endless. When used appropriately, today's technology options can motivate and enhance student learning while promoting early literacy. Clearly, educators should use technology in the classroom because its wide range of uses and forms has the potential to reach students of all learning styles, as well as be more efficient. The interest and motivation that technology induces in students makes its usage in schools important. In addition, educators better prepare students for the future when using technology aimed at addressing each learning style. There are age-appropriate uses of technology that include

1. *Computer Software*: Computers are powerful tools that provide students with a place to practice what they are learning. Most children learn how to manipulate a mouse by the time they reach preschool age. You can use computer software programs in the preschool classroom to strengthen students' abilities and provide them with the opportunity to use their imagination through the use of software programs. It is critical to choose software that contains music and sound and that builds on what they already know.

2. *Welcome to the Internet*: The Internet has an endless amount of games for early childhood education. There are thousands of websites that provide educational games for students to practice what they are learning. When choosing which games to play, it is critical to search for sites that tailor to pre-K and younger children such as pbskids.org. When one visits this website, he/she will see it has links for both parents and teachers.

3. *SMART Boards*: An Internet white board is another way to provide a hands-on approach to the early childhood classroom. Teachers can have students experience integration with their lessons by showing them how to use their finger or a special pen to write on the board. The SMART Board is scratch-resistant and durable enough for little hands to use. Using this interactive approach to learning will only entice students to learn.

4. *Meet the iPad*: Apple's iPad is the newest trend in educational technology today. Teachers are incorporating the iPad into their classroom as a way of motivating their students. For age-appropriate use of the iPad in early childhood classrooms, teachers can download applications specific for their student group. The iPad is easy for little hands to use; by just the use of their fingertips, they will play educational games in no time.

5. *Digital Camera and Camcorders*: Digital recording is another great tool to use in the early childhood classroom. The use of this technology is simple. Teachers can record or take photos of students' performances and have them watch. Another use for this technology is to share photos with parents that students have taken.

6. *Tape Recorder:* This may be viewed as an "old" use of educational technology, but it still serves the same purpose. Having students record stories, poems, or songs and then hear them back is great fun and captures their enthusiasm. Going beyond that to translate their story into print is a great way for children to understand how sound translates to print. Children can also learn this concept through books on tape.

USING TECHNOLOGY TO PROMOTE POSITIVE EDUCATIONAL CHANGE: ROLES OF EDUCATORS AND LEADERS

Knowledgeable and effective teachers and leaders are extremely important in determining types of technology needed to improve learning for all children. However, some teachers and leaders tend to be uncomfortable providing leadership in technology areas. They may be uncertain about implementing effective technology leadership strategies in ways that will improve learning, or they may believe their own knowledge of technology is inadequate to make meaningful recommendations. Because technology is credited as being a significant factor in increasing productivity in many industries, some people believe more effective use of technology in schools could do more to improve educational opportunities and quality. Research indicates that while there are poor uses of technology in education, appropriate technology use can be very beneficial in increasing educational productivity (Byrom & Bingham, 2001; Clements & Sarama, 2003; Mann, Shakeshaft, Becker, & Kottkamp, 1999; Valdez et al., 2000; Wenglinsky, 1998). Teachers and leaders must operate in both the present and the future. The present operations, however, must be viable foundations for the future. As James pointed out:

> You need to understand how the currents of technological change will affect your life and your work, how economic changes will affect your business and its place in the global market, how demographic and cultural change will alter your self-perception, your perception of others and of human society as a whole. (p. 24)

Managing a childcare program involves many complex tasks and daily challenges. To succeed in our digital information age, teachers and leaders in early childhood special education need access to technology; technology training; opportunities for online learning and professional development; access to the wealth of information; resources and services available on the Internet; and the ability to link electronically with parents, staff, and other childcare professionals. Technology tools can make these tasks more manageable (Donohue, 2003). There are several reasons why educators and leaders are expected to know and utilize instructional technology, especially those technologies related to computer use for accessing and finding information and for creating and communicating new knowledge. These reasons include the need to (a) prepare students to function in an information-based, Internet-using society, (b) make students competent in using tools found in almost all work areas, and (c) make education more effective and efficient. School leaders need to help students become technology literate, as outlined in *enGauge 21st Century Skills: Literacy in the Digital Age* School leaders also need to consider increasing educator technology effectiveness and modeling it after nationally accepted guidelines, such as the *National Educational Technology Standards for Teachers.* The integration of technology in early childhood special education is no longer a "new" idea. And teachers, leaders, and change agents can interface to maximize the potential for effective use of technology.

IMPACT OF TECHNOLOGY ON CHILDREN

Today's students, surrounded by digital technology since infancy, are fundamentally different from previous generation (McHale, 2005) and are no longer the people our educational system was designed to teach (Prensky, 2001). As a result, a widening gap has formed between the knowledge and skills children are acquiring in schools and the knowledge and skills needed to succeed in the increasingly global, technology-infused 21st century workplace (Partnership for 21st Century Skills, 2005). As a first step toward bridging this gap, the No Child Left Behind (NCLB) Act, requires states to demonstrate that "every student is technologically literate by the time the student finishes the eighth grade, regardless of the student's race, ethnicity, gender, family income, geographic location, or disability" (U.S. Department of Education, 2001). Universal Design for Learning (UDL) takes advantage of the opportunity brought by rapidly evolving communication technologies to create flexible teaching methods and curriculum materials that can reach diverse learners and improve student access to the general education curriculum (Rose & Meyer, 2002). UDL assumes that students bring different needs and skills to the task of learning and that the learning environment should be designed to both accommodate and make use of these differences (Bowe, 2000; Rose & Meyer, 2002). To promote improved access to the general curriculum for all learners, including learners with disabilities, Rose and Meyer (2002) identified key principles or guidelines for UDL, namely, (a) presenting information in multiple formats and multiple media, (b) offering students multiple ways to express and demonstrate what they have learned, and (c) providing multiple entry points to engage student interest and motivate learning.

As an instructional tool, technology helps all children, including students with disabilities, master, basic, and advanced skills. Because of technology, parents communicate more with their children and their children's teachers, are more aware of their children's assignments, and increase their own computer skills. Technology helps students to

- *Analyze and Interpret Data*: Students must have the ability to crunch, compare, and choose among the glut of data now available on Web-based and other electronic formats.
- *Understand Computational Modeling*: Students must possess an understanding of the power, limitations, and underlying assumptions of various data-representation systems, such as computational models and simulations, which are increasingly driving a wide range of disciplines.
- *Manage and Prioritize Tasks*: Students must be able to manage the multitasking, selection, and prioritizing across technology applications that allow them to move fluidly among teams, assignments, and communities of practice.
- *Engage in Problem Solving*: Students must have an understanding of how to apply what they know and can do to new situations.
- *Ensure Security and Safety:* Students must know and use strategies to acknowledge, identify, and negotiate 21st century risks.

Technology offers several advantages over traditional methods of student assessment. For example, multimedia technology expands the possibilities for more comprehensive student assessments that require students' active participation and application of knowledge. The immense storage capacity enabled by technology such as CD-ROMs allows schools to develop electronic portfolios of students' work. A single CD can hold exact copies of students' drawings and written work, recordings of the child reading aloud, and video images of plays, recitals, or class presentations. By saving work samples on different subjects at different times during the year, teachers can display them in rapid succession to demonstrate and assess growth.

IMPACT OF TECHNOLOGY ON TEACHERS AND LEADERS

As technology advances, it becomes difficult to keep up and adapt to it in both our personal and professional lives. Teachers have an especially important role to play in technological advancements, as incorporating technology in the classroom can be both a learning tool for students and a teaching tool for the instructor. Children seem to be adapting to the rapid advancements in technology better than many adults, and they actually embrace it. For this reason, incorporating technology in teaching is a great way to increase a child's interest in learning. There are numerous ways that teachers can use technology in the classroom, and many are already doing it. Some districts use interactive Smart Boards in place of traditional chalk or white boards in their classroom. These flat screen monitors are networked with the teacher's classroom computer and the school's Internet connection. Interactive lessons in math, spelling, science, and other subjects can be put on screen for students to participate in. The boards use touch screen technology and in some cases, children are given handheld remote "clickers" that act as controllers for answering questions presented on screen. Many school districts have made it easy for teachers to use technology in the classroom with supportive technology departments and funding, but others are still behind for budget reasons. In those cases, teachers can still use technology in more unconventional ways.

The U.S. Department of Education has concluded that preparing technology-proficient educators to meet the needs of 21st century learning is a critical educational challenge facing the nation. More than two thirds of the nation's teachers will be replaced by new teachers over the next decade. Therefore, it is crucial to ensure that the next generation of future teachers emerging from the nation's teacher education programs is prepared to meet this challenge (Bell, 2001). Technology's impact on teachers and their practice should be considered as important as student effects, for students move on, but teachers remain to influence many generations of students. Establishing clear expectations can help school leaders increase successful use of technology in schools. The reasons for technology implementation and possible challenges to such an effort should be made transparent to the educational community. According to Fulton (1998),

To ask if technology works is almost the equivalent of saying 'Do textbooks work?' Yes, some textbooks "work," in some conditions, with some teachers, with some students, but these same textbooks may not "work" in another educational context. Clearly, the question of technology effectiveness requires us to be clear in what results we seek, how we measure success, and how we define effectiveness. (p. 1)

Most educational researchers, especially those who have examined large numbers of studies (meta-analyses), agree that if used appropriately, technology can improve education in the effect-size range of between 0.30 and 0.40 (Kulik, 2002; Waxman, Connell, & Gray, 2002).

Schools must make certain that there is sufficient availability of technology and appropriate software, that the user of technology have linkages to important educational learning expectations, and, most of all, that teachers have the necessary skills and knowledge to effectively model and teach exemplary uses of technology. Thus, to be effective, teachers need to be highly involved by interacting and providing feedback when using technology. Research studies (Chang et al., 1998; Mann et al., 1999) indicate that technology may be most effective when it is used in

- Accessing information, especially from the Internet, and using that information to communicate findings to others by using graphs, illustrations, and animations.
- Reading and language arts, for phonological awareness, vocabulary, reading comprehension, writing, and spelling.
- Mathematics, to support mathematics curricula that focus on diagnosing and remediating, providing support for fundamental knowledge deficiencies, and for simulating and solving real problems with tools that are similar to tools that mathematicians use.
- Science, to stimulate and solve real problems, especially when scientific probes and other technology tools are used to assist with laboratory experiments.
- Social studies, to simulate events and when students are allowed to use the multimedia power to demonstrate student work.
- Health, for research and for personal, family, and community health self-assessments.
- Music, to teach musical theory and composition.
- Art, to view virtually the greatest artworks and to learn art composition and design.

Technology is very important for a diverse population of students, especially for those who do not have access to computers at home. In addition, the use of assistive technology in early childhood special education is extremely helpful for students with special needs. Technology also has proven to be an effective motivator for students with specific learning needs (such as language learning) and for accommodating learning styles. Obviously, addressing the needs of all students through technology use is a long-term and system-wide effort. School leaders, therefore, are expected to possess not only general leadership skills but also technology leadership skills. Technology leadership is a combination of strategies and techniques that are general to all leadership but require attention to some specifics of technology, especially those related to providing hardware access, updating rapidly changing technology, and recognizing that professional development and the use of technology are constantly evolving. (Valdez, 2004)

It is important that school leaders know the different type of technology in the classrooms. Many different types of technology can be used to support and enhance learning in early childhood special education. Everything from video content to laptop computing and handheld technologies (Marshall, 2002) have been used in classrooms, and now uses of technology such as podcasting are constantly emerging. Various technologies deliver different kinds of content and serve different purposes in the classroom. Technologies available in classrooms today range from simple tool-based applications (such as word processors) to online repositories of scientific data and primary historical documents, to handheld computers, closed-circuit television channels, and two-way distance-learning classrooms. Even the cell phones that many students now carry with them can be used to learn. More specifically, these technology tools include

- Cell phone
- PDA (Personal Digital Assistant)
- Personal computer
- Printer
- Scanner
- Internet
- Dial-up or high speed connection
- Email
- Instant Messaging
- Distribution list and/or Listserv
- Online discussion group
- Chat room
- Digital camera and/or video camera
- Recordable CD and/or DVD
- Direct broadcast satellite or high-speed digital cable TV
- Digital video recorder
- Other

FUTURE PERSPECTIVES

Technology in education is frequently seen as an array of tools that might prove helpful in advancing student learning. Educational technology is intended to improve education for the 21st century learner. Students today are considered "digital natives," who were born and raised in a digital environment and inherently think different because of this exposure to technology (Gu, Zhu, & Guo, 2013). Future teachers and leaders must know the benefits of incorporating technology into the early childhood classroom. As future educators and leaders, they need to know that

1. Technology can be beneficial to all the major domains of child development (e.g., language development). Computer play encourages longer, more complex speech and the development of fluency (Davidson & Wright, 1994). Children tend to narrate what they are doing as they draw pictures or move objects and characters around on the screen (Bredekamp & Rosegrant, 1994). Young children interacting at computers engage in high levels of spoken communication and cooperation, such as turn-taking and peer collaboration. Compared to more traditional activities, such as puzzle assembly or block building, the computer allows clients more social interaction and different types of interaction.

2. Technology enhances social and emotional development. When properly used, computers and software can serve as catalysts for social interaction and conversations related to children's work (Clements & Nastasi, 1993). A classroom set up to encourage interaction and the appropriate use of the technology will increase, not impair, language and literacy development.

3. Technology fosters cognitive development. Computers allow representation and actions not possible in the physical world. For example, children can manipulate variables such as gravity or speed, and discover the resulting effects (Clements, 1999, Seng, 1998). Compared to children in a similar classroom without computer experience, 3 and 4 year olds who used computers with supporting activities had significantly greater gains in verbal and nonverbal skills, problem-solving abstraction, and conceptual skills (Haugland, 1992).

4. Technology allows students to learn, communicate, and share their knowledge and understanding in a wide variety of ways. Computers are intrinsically motivating for young children and contribute to cognitive and social development (NAEYC, 1996). Technology offers additional ways to learn and to demonstrate learning. For some children who have unique learning styles, computers can reveal hidden strengths. At the computer, children can approach learning from a variety of perspectives and follow various paths to a goal (Clements, 1999). Computers and other forms of technology support literacy and encourage speaking, reading, writing, and listening through formal and informal language opportunities. Technology can provide children with ways to express themselves, offer support for young learners, and encourage reading and writing.

5.   Technology provides ways for children to express themselves. Young students can present or represent their learning in ways that make sense to them using tools such as digital cameras, scanners, and computer software to show information, create pictures, build graphs, and share ideas. Children make up stories as they play and frequently tell stories about the pictures they create. Technology offers a variety of ways for children to weave together words and pictures to tell their stories, then display them on the screen or print them.

6.   Technology offers support for young learners. Writing and revising can be difficult as children struggle with letter formation and fine motor skills. Word processors let them focus on ideas and more easily compose and revise text. This encourages children to view writing as a process and to refine their work. Speech synthesizers read aloud the text on the screen and allow children to experience both oral and written language. Talking books use synthesized speech to read aloud a story as the child listens and follows along with highlighted words on the screen. This same technology reads back a child's own words. Because the digital voice reads exactly what was written, and not what the writer meant to say, it provides the immediate, focused feedback helpful for learning. For example, when reading aloud a series of words without capitals or ending punctuation, the voice does not stop at the end of the idea. The importance of punctuation and capitals soon becomes clear.

7.   Technology encourages reading and writing. Seeing text on the screen encourages students to read their own and others' writing as they work at the computer. Research confirms that common sense tells us that the more time children spend reading, the better readers they become. Technology in its many forms increases the options available for children to explore, create, and communicate and provides additional ways to interact with and experience literacy. Classroom printers allow children to write for and reach a larger audience, and email allows children to correspond with distant pen pals electronically. Both provide motivation for children to write well because they know that others will read their work.

8.   Technology can be integrated with literacy. Technology fosters the use of a really great website for children to explore the alphabet, reading, writing, and phonics, to mention a few.

9.   Technology can be integrated with math. Children can construct tangram puzzles or patterns online. These can be printed and displayed in portfolios or learning logs with explanations of how they solve the challenge. As children organize thoughts to express them clearly, their metacognition develops more fully. Teachers can build a graph with objects, such as shoes or candy wrappers, then transfer the information into a graphing program. Having both the physical objects and the two-dimensional graph demonstrates that graphing is a way to show and see information

mathematically. Research shows that using manipulatives and computers *jointly* promotes more in-depth thinking and sophistication in problem solving than using either one alone.

10. Technology can be implemented effectively. Children reap the greatest benefits from technology when (a) the lesson or project is directly connected to the curriculum, (b) the technology allows for active learning, with students making decisions, (c) the software is interactive or discovery based, (d) the lesson or project is open-ended and allows learners to proceed at their own pace, (e) technology is applied to real problems with a real-life connection, and (f) the setting is designed to allow children to interact while working at the computer. Screen time (including TV, computer, video games, etc.) should be limited to a maximum of 1 to 2 hours per day. Vigorous physical activities and play should be encouraged.

CONCLUSION

Used appropriately, technology can be a positive factor in a child's learning process. The use of computers and other technology must be thoughtfully planned to provide for children's learning needs. Teachers and leaders should develop policy about computer usage. And teachers and parents should stay with children and provide guidance when they use the computer. They should let the children be in control, however, and most importantly, they should not let the computer serve as a babysitter. Overall, the use of technology in education has had a positive impact on students, educators, and leaders, as well as the educational system. Effective technologies use many evidence-based strategies (e.g., adaptive content, frequent testing, and immediate feedback), as do effective teachers (Ross, Morrison, & Lowther, 2010). It is important for teachers and leaders to embrace technology to meet the needs of their digital students (Hicks, 2011).

REFERENCES

Bell. L. (Ed.) (2001). Preparing tomorrow's teachers to use technology: Perspectives of the leaders of twelve national education associations. *Contemporary Issues in Technology and Teacher Education* [online serial] (4), www.citejounal.org/vol1/iss4

Bredekamp, S., & Rosegrant, T. (1994). Learning and teaching with technology. In J. I. Wright & D. D. Shade (Eds.), *Young children: Active learners in a technological age* (pp. 31–49). Washington, DC: National Association for the Education of Young Children.

Bowe, F. G. (2000). *Universal design in education: Teaching non-traditional students.* Westport, CT: Bergen & Garvey.

Byrom, E., & Bingham, M. (2001). *Factors influencing the effective use of technology for teaching and learning: Lessons learned from SEIR*TEC Intensive Site Schools* (2nd ed.). Greensboro, NC: SERVE.

Chang, H., Henriques, A., Honey, M., Light, D., Moeller, B., & Ross, N. (1998, April 1). The Union City story: Education reform and technology students' performance on standardized tests. New York, NY: *Center for Children and Technology*. Retrieved June 25, 2004, from http://www2.ede.org/CCT/admin/publications/report/us_story98.pdf

Clements, D. H. (1999). Young children and technology. In *Dialogue on early childhood science, mathematics, and technology education: First experiences in science, mathematics, and technology.* Washington, DC: American Association for the Advancement of Science. Retrieved November 20, 2000, from http://www.project2061.org/publications/earlychild/online/experience/clements.htm?txtRef=&txtURIOld=%2Fnewsinfo%2Fearlychild%2Fexperience%2Fclements%2Ehtm

Clements, D. H., & Nastasi, B. K. (1993). Electronic media and early childhood education. In B. Spodek (Ed.), *Handbook of research on the education of young children* (pp. 251–275). New York, NY: Macmillan.

Clements, D. H., & Sarama, J. (2003). Strip mining for gold: Research and policy in educational technology—A response to *Fool's Gold. Educational Technology Review, 11*(1), 7–69. Retrieved June 25, 2004, from http://www.aace.org/pubs/etr/issue4/clements2.pdf

Craft, A. (2012). Childhood in a digital age: Creative challenges for educational futures. *London Review of Education, 10*(2), 173–190.

Davidson, J., & Wright, J. I. (1994). The potential of the micro-computer in the early childhood classroom. In J. I. Wright & D. D. Shade (Eds.), *Young children: Active learners in a technological age* (pp. 77–91). Washington, DC: National Association for the Education of Young Children.

Donohue, C. (2003). *Technology in early childhood education: An exchange trend report.* Redmond, WA: Child Care Information Exchange.

Gu, X., Zhu, Y., & Guo, X (2013). Meeting the "digital natives": Understanding the acceptance of technology in classrooms. *Educational Technology & Society, 16*(1), 392–402.

Haugland, S. W. (1992). The effect of computer software on preschool children's development gains. *Journal of Computing in Childhood Education, 3*(1), 15–30.

Hicks, S. D. (2011). Technology in today's classroom: Are you a tech-savvy teacher? *The Clearing House, 84*(5), 188–191.

Kulik, J. (2002, November). *School mathematics and science programs benefit from instructional technology* (InfoBrief). Washington, DC: National Science Foundation.

Mann, D., Shakeshaft, C., Becker, J., & Kottkamp, R. (1999). *West Virginia story: Achievement gains from a statewide comprehensive instructional technology program.* Santa Monica, CA: Milken Family Foundation.

Marshall, J. M. (2002). *Learning with technology: Evidence that technology can, and does support learning.* San Diego, CA: Cable in the Classroom.

McHale, T. (2005, September). Portrait of a digital native: Are digital-age students fundamentally different from the rest of us? *Technology & Learning, 26*(2), 33–34.

National Association for the Education of Young Children (NAEYC). (1996). *Technology and young children—ages 3–8* [Position statement]. Washington, DC: Author.

Partnership for 21st Century Skills. (2005). *Road to 21st century learning: A policymakers guide to 21st century skills.* Washington, DC: Author.

Prensky, M. (2001, October). Digital natives, digital immigrants. *On the Horizon, 9*(5), 1–6.

Rose, D. H., & Meyer, A. (2002). *Teaching every student in the digital age: Universal design for learning.* Alexandria, VA: ASCD.

Ross, S., Morrison, G., & Lowther, D. (2010). Educational technology research past and present: Balancing rigor and relevance to impact learning. *Contemporary Educational Technology, 1*(1).

Seng, S. (1998, November). *Enhanced learning computers and early childhood education.* Paper presented at the Educational Research Association Conference, Singapore. (ERIC Document Reproduction Service No. ED 431-524)

Valdez, G. (2004). *Critical issue: Technology leadership: Enhancing positive educational change.* Naperville, IL: North Central Regional Educational Laboratory.

Valdez, G., McNabb, M., Foertsch, M., Anderson, M., Hawkes, M., & Raack, L. (2000). *Computer-based technology and learning: Evolving uses and expectations.* Naperville, IL: North Central Regional Educational Laboratory.

Waxman, H. C., Connell, M. L., & Gray, J. (2002). *A quantitative synthesis of recent research on the effects of teaching and learning with technology on student outcomes.* Naperville, IL: North Central Regional Educational Laboratory.

Wenglinsky, H. (1998). *Does it compute? The relationship between educational technology and student achievement in mathematics.* Princeton, NJ: Educational Testing Service.

CHAPTER 12

TEACHING AT A DISTANCE

Perspectives on the Growth and Impact of Electronic Learning in Special Education Teacher Preparation

Kelly Heckaman, Anthony Scheffler, and Patti Campbell

As we reflect on the growth and impact of electronic learning in special education teacher preparation, we should first take a general look at the evolution of distance education. Electronic learning in distance education goes back much further than one might realize (Osborne, 2012). In 1922, for example, Pennsylvania State College was the first college to use the radio to broadcast courses, and 12 years later, the University of Iowa became the first university to use television as a teaching tool. In 1963, the Federal Communications Commission (FCC) created the Instructional Fixed Service (ITFS), which provided 20 television channels to universities for instructional use (see Osborne, 2012). Satellite television appeared in the late 1970s and early 1980s, providing live, two-way communication, which universities used to teach courses not only to college students, but also to high school students in rural areas (Barker, 1986). The use of computers as instructional tools also became popular in the 1970s and 1980s with the advent of computer-based instruction (CBI) (Kulik & Kulik, 1991). CBI, also known as computer-assisted instruction (CAI), is traditionally used for drill

Critical Issues in Preparing Effective Early Childhood Special Education Teachers for the 21st Century Classroom: Interdisciplinary Perspectives, pages 155–164.
Copyright © 2016 by Information Age Publishing

and practice by students (e.g., Hasselbring, Goin, & Bransford, 1988), but has also been used in teacher preparation. For example, Semmel (1972) developed the Computer-Assisted Teacher Training System (CATTS) to provide objective, reliable feedback to teacher candidates using an observation coding system that categorized and operationalized teaching behaviors. Trained observers, watching in an adjacent room, would record teacher candidate behavior in a classroom where a television monitor was linked to a computer. The CATTS system allowed for repeated practice teaching with instant feedback (Semmel, 1972).

While computer technology was advancing with faster and faster processors, the concomitant availability of dedicated T1 lines and fibers optic lines, along with more sophisticated routers, increased the speed with which audio and video could be transferred. Computers soon became an instrument for delivery of electronic learning. In the late 1990s, universities began delivering coursework in teacher preparation programs through desktop video conferencing. Teacher candidates would gather in computer labs at designated public school sites for their desktop video class, during which the university instructor taught the class and interacted with the students through live video, usually from an office on the university campus. Compressed video also became a popular method for distance learning during this time, allowing students in remote locations to connect to the class instructor as well as to each other through audio and video links. A typical compressed video classroom contained a projector and screen, along with video cameras and a computer teaching station, which allowed the instructor to project computer applications, websites, and documents, and to switch between remote sites' cameras. Both desktop video conferencing and compressed video allowed students in remote locations to participate in their classes from a local classroom site, thus reducing the time and cost required to travel to campus. These technologies posed some challenges, however, as class handouts or other materials either needed to be mailed ahead of time or faxed to the class sites, and transmission speeds often were unstable. For example, the first author of this chapter, who taught classes in undergraduate and graduate special education teacher preparation programs through desktop videoconferencing and compressed video, recalls many occasions on which students would politely interrupt and say, "Dr. Heckaman, you are frozen on the screen." In these instances, the audio capability might still be functioning properly, but the ability to provide video projection to specific sites had been lost. Likewise, a remote site might suddenly disappear, having lost the connection all together.

The 1990s hosted the rapid growth of technology-mediated communication and the explosion of the World Wide Web. A Web-based e-learning system, WebCT, was released in 1997 (Osborn, 2012). The ability to offer asynchronous online courses, as well as full degree and certification programs, increased dramatically when WebCT and the course management systems, also referred to as learning management systems (LMS), that followed (e.g., Blackboard, Desire-2Learn) were licensed to colleges and universities. These dedicated systems provided an organized delivery platform for faculty to use in developing and teaching courses online, without requiring faculty to have technical knowledge of Web design. Many colleges and universities, particularly those with rural catchment areas, recognized the potential of online course delivery, and online enrollments have steadily increased at a rate higher than the overall enrollment rates in higher education (Allen & Seaman, 2014). In 2011, more than 75% of colleges and universities in the United States offered online courses (Parker, Lenhart, & Moore, 2011); and in 2013, some 7.1 million students had enrolled in at least one online course (Allen & Seaman, 2014). Recognizing, valuing, and expanding this trend in teacher preparation are major thrusts of this chapter.

DRIVING FORCES FOR ELECTRONIC LEARNING

While electronic learning in teacher preparation programs continues to grow, one might wonder what is driving this movement. As early adopters of distance education technologies, we have experienced the transformation of distance learning over the past 25 years, and we have identified several driving forces that have influenced the growth of electronic learning for course and program delivery in special education teacher preparation. These driving forces include (a) the rapid development of technology; (b) the economics of electronic learning, including consumer demands; and (c) societal pressures. None of these "drivers" or forces has been solely responsible for the rapid growth and advancements in electronic learning, however, all of these drivers have exerted pressure on colleges and universities to jump onto the distance education "bandwagon." We discuss these driving forces and identify future trends that will likely impact continued growth and change in electronic learning.

Advancements in Technology

The rapid rate in which technology has advanced and has become accessible is conceivably the most important driver in the growth of distance education. One-way, lecture-based class presentations through satellite TV were replaced when two-way, audio and video transmission allowed multipoint, interactive classes through desktop videoconferencing and compressed video. Wide-ranging Internet access, combined with the affordability of home computers and the availability of electronic learning management systems (e.g., Blackboard, Desire2Learn), made it feasible for colleges and universities to offer asynchronous, Web-based courses. In the early years of online learning, however, it was not uncommon to hear special education faculty voice "qualifications" regarding the type of courses that could be put online. For example, lecture-based courses typically were viewed as being appropriate to be put online, while methods courses often were not viewed as suitable. These viewpoints changed however with the proliferation of hardware (e.g., webcams, wireless headsets), software (e.g., Adobe Flash), digital tools (e.g., Wimba, Google Drive, wikis), and multimedia websites and streaming video. These tools and materials provided special education teacher preparation programs with a rich array of resources to develop interactive online courses and conduct remote supervision of their teacher candidates, thus lifting many restrictions to what can be done online.

Advancements in technology applications have also increased the variety of instructional tools that faculty can use in online special education teacher preparation programs. Virtual classrooms and simulations allow teacher candidates to practice instructional and behavior management decision-making skills before applying these skills to real students. These simulations can be structured to systematically vary along a number of dimensions (e.g., age, diversity, frequency of behavioral challenges) to represent different classroom scenarios. Remote supervision of candidates in their classrooms also has become more sophisticated. For example, several studies have reported successful use of webcams, Skype, and Bluetooth Bug-in-Ear technology to provide immediate e-coaching and performance feedback to teacher candidates while they were teaching in remote classroom locations (Hager, Baird, & Spriggs, 2012; Rock, Gregg et al., 2009; Rock, Schumacher et al., 2014; Scheeler, McKinnon, & Stout, 2012). Similarly, Face-Time and Google Hangouts allow for real-time interactions between faculty and teacher candidates who are on separate campuses. Accessibility to online learning also has expanded, with apps that provide teacher candidates and faculty "anytime anywhere" access to their classes using their mobile devices. All of these technological advancements have facilitated the growth of special education certification programs as well as complete degree programs being offered online.

Economics of Electronic Learning

The economics of distance learning involve not only the cost of operation and delivery but also supply and demand factors. In special education teacher preparation, for example, the demand for special educators historically has been greater than the supply of qualified teachers. In the 2003 report on the supply and demand for special education teachers from the Center on Personnel Studies in Special Education, it was indicated that "the shortage of special education teachers is chronic and long term and will get worse" (McLeskey, Tyler, & Flippin, 2003, p. 27). McLesky et al. (2003) further noted that the special education teacher shortage is widespread across geographic regions, with 98% of U.S. school districts reporting shortages. Rural school districts, which accounted for 57% of the regular school districts in the United States during the 2010–2011 school year (National Center for Education Statistics, 2013), experience particular challenges in attracting and retaining qualified special education teachers. Geographic barriers have posed challenges to teacher candidates as well as to teacher preparation programs. For example, prior to the availability of distance education programs, it was not uncommon for teacher candidates from remote areas to spend more time driving to and from the nearest university to attend class than the time they actually spent in class. Additionally, the time, expense, and loss of faculty productivity was significant when university faculty had to travel to distant sites to provide on-site field supervision to teacher candidates (Hager et al., 2012; Ludlow & Brannan, 2010).

The shortage of special education teachers in rural areas, combined with the high cost to rural teacher candidates seeking their teaching credentials and to universities to provide quality preparation programs to their consumers in remote regions, was a major driving force in advancing distance education programs. As early as the 1980s, the U.S. Department of Education's Office of Special Education Programs (OSEP) set priorities through its discretionary personnel preparation grant program for proposals that would address the shortage of special education teachers, particularly in rural areas. The University of Utah, the University of Kentucky, and West Virginia University were on the forefront in developing distance education programs to meet the need for special education teachers in their rural states (Glomb, Lignugaris/Kraft, & Menlove, 2009; Hager, 2010; Ludlow & Brannan, 2010; Ludlow & Duff, 2009). Meanwhile, simultaneous advancements in technology prompted special education teacher preparation programs to quickly move to electronic course delivery in order to reach larger numbers of teacher candidates. Indeed, Rule and Salzberg (2009) noted that, "as geographical obstacles have disappeared, access to special education teacher preparation has become a reality for nearly any student who has a computer and high-speed internet access" (p. 3).

The continuing demands by school districts for qualified special education teachers, who remain in short supply, have been joined by another demand: the demand by special education teacher candidates for convenient and accessible coursework. Electronic learning is no longer seen as a necessity only for teacher candidates who live in rural areas; it is often the preferred delivery mode regardless of geographic location due to the "any time, any place" advantages that electronic learning provides. In our Master of Arts in Teaching initial certification programs in special education, we serve primarily nontraditional students who often have busy lives on top of their teaching responsibilities, with extracurricular activities as well as family and community obligations demanding their time and attention. For many of these students, driving to a university and attending a 3-hour evening class several nights a week would be difficult, if not impossible. They want the convenience of doing their weekly course assignments on the days and times it best fits into their schedule.

Societal Pressures

Another driving force that has contributed to the growth of electronic learning in special education teacher preparation involves societal pressures to develop teachers who can function in a technology-based world. The U.S. Department of Education's *National Education Technology Plan* (2010) clearly outlined recommendations for developing teachers who are skilled in online instruction and who also can connect and collaborate professionally with other educators through online learning communities. Accrediting bodies such as the Council for the Accreditation of Educator Preparation (CAEP) also emphasize the incorporation of technology and digital learning in teacher preparation. Additionally, the Interstate Teacher and Assessment and Support Consortium (InTASC) Standards outline guidelines for teacher preparation programs that include providing their candidates with electronic access to other professionals. Special education teacher preparation programs can assist teacher candidates in meeting these recommendations and guidelines by modeling appropriate online pedagogy and by providing candidates with the tools and options available for online collaboration and professional support.

FUTURE TRENDS—A LOOK AHEAD

The pervasive availability and rapidly increasing sophistication of a broad range of computer driven technologies, shifts in the global economy, challenges to traditional higher education, and universally available content, are driving innovation in the design and delivery of educational programs at an unprecedented pace (Barber, Donnelly, & Rizvi, 2013). In all of its manifestations, online learning and its associated technologies are at the core of many of the innovations and trends that are reshaping how special education teachers are prepared. An awareness of current trends in the use of online teaching technologies provides a window into how technology and its applications will impact the preparation of special educators in the future.

Current online technologies are likely to continue to evolve into a more specialized focus that emphasizes quality assurance, cost containment, efficiency of delivery, and time to completion. These trends will manifest operationally as derivations and extensions of current practices and as key elements of future disruptive programming models (Smithers, 2014). For example, where online coursework or programs are not already in place, hybrid classes will become more prevalent, combining an enriched online presence that includes synchronous and asynchronous communications, with traditional in-classroom meetings. Additionally, peer-to-peer online interactions with external professionals will more frequently be integrated into special education teacher preparation programs, which will capitalize on the advantages of the flipped classroom model by incorporating a growing number of online resources and capabilities into tailored online experiences.

As tablet computer and cell phone technologies advance, the use of these devices to accommodate mobile learners is progressing from a convenience to an expectation (Johnson et al., 2013). Both the hardware and software are growing in sophistication as costs are dropping, making mobile computing more functional and affordable. Special educators will be challenged as they make both primary and supplemental programming available in formats that accommodate on-the-go learners who engage with program content episodically. Perhaps the greatest challenge for special education teacher preparation faculty is not simply the mastery of individual technologies or the translation of traditional delivery into new online delivery formats using these technologies, but rather it is the creative integration of technologies. Technologies must effectively engage individual learners in ways that accommodate their circumstances and reduce their time to program completion, all while enhancing the quality and depth of their learning experiences. However, providing this type of integration online is particularly challenging. One of the more promising advancements in this regard and one that capitalizes on the popularity of mobile devices is the use of digital games or "gamification" (Johnson et al., 2013). Digital gaming has advanced to the point where it can provide virtual, authentic contexts and use simulations that adapt not only to the profile and actions of the learner, but also to the expectations of the instructor. In addition, users (students) can formulate and test problem solutions both individually and while partnering with or competing against other learners. Although not currently a common practice, the use of online gamification is projected to become more prevalent in 2 to 3 years and in fact, one university has already successfully "gamified" a technical degree program (Barber et al., 2013). The challenge for special education teacher preparation faculty is translating the dialogue that characterizes most traditional teaching into a more dynamic, Socratic approach that allows teacher candidates to propose, explore, and test solutions in an authentic context. While special education faculty likely will not be expected to learn how to program learning games, they will provide the content, help define the context, and actively direct and shape teacher candidate responses based on an analysis of their gaming behaviors. One of the strengths of gaming is the ability of candidates to not only learn and apply knowledge while involved in goal-oriented activities but also to engage problem-solving situations individually and collaboratively with other teacher candidates who may be physically distant and culturally different.

Increasingly, students are being required to combine work and study and thus are receptive to programs that are designed to accommodate working students (Barber et al., 2013). In addition, there is popular expectation among students, parents, and governmental agencies that time to completion of a course of study or degree needs to be expedited (see Complete College America, http://completecollege.org/). Competency-based education (CBE) is a model of teacher preparation that empowers the learner and potentially speeds time to program completion by deemphasizing place and time requirements and instead, emphasizes measured skills acquisition. So, rather than being required to complete a specific number of courses or college credit hours, teacher candidates would be required to demonstrate competence in specific knowledge and skills, and could proceed at their own pace through the identified competencies. The success of CBE is largely dependent upon the ability of instructional and support team members to communicate effectively and engage in shared decision-making around a common goal that advances and expedites student success. The promotion of the CBE model by the federal government and its recent endorsement of non-credit-unit-based federal financial aid have further advanced interest in CBE models. For example, the rise of several highly publicized online competency-based program providers, including the Flexible Option at the University of Wisconsin Extension, Southern New Hampshire University's College for America, and Western Governors University, provide evidence of the growing interest in CBE. The efficiency of CBE and its outcomes-focused approach increases the likelihood that the competency-based model will continue to gain in popularity among students and will be advocated by political proponents. As a result, pressure to adapt the CBE model or similar approaches is expected to increase. In special education teacher preparation programs, a shift to a CBE model would impact not only how special education programs are delivered, but to some degree, the focus of these programs.

As more colleges and universities offer online CBE as an alternative to traditional credit-hour programs, the resulting competitive pressure may force traditional online program providers to streamline their programs and accelerate possible completion through the use of online directed learning, sophisticated assessments, and predictive analytic technologies to determine candidates' progress. The concern expressed by some is that the use of these strategies may diminish the role of faculty, to the detriment of program quality. In fact, proponents of online, self-paced programming such as competency-based programs believe the function of faculty members is simply repurposed. In the CBE model, faculty members function as learning facilitators and academic coaches, as opposed to the "conveyor of knowledge." Traditional faculty responsibilities in CBE are thus unbundled and distributed among a group of skilled professionals, each playing a distinct but complementary role in the education of the teacher candidate (Howell, Williams, & Lindsay, 2003). This arrangement frees the faculty to focus on individual candidate needs while allowing candidates to take more responsibility for their own learning. The use of online technologies is also maximized to ensure that candidates are progressing appropriately through the program. In many ways, a CBE model is similar to the way we approach special education service delivery (i.e., we focus on individual student progress through the curriculum, while providing assistance and remediation when student performance data indicates it is needed).

Finally, as we look ahead to the future, the facility with which special educators learn to access complex datasets and use the information to make evidenced-based program and customized pedagogical adaptations that efficiently advance learning outcomes will, in time, become an expectation. Predictive analytics, particularly at the course or competency level, may eventually provide the most informed rationale yet for pedagogical decisions (Long & Siemens, 2011). How faculty who prepare special educators will acquire this skill is not as clear at the present time as is the fact that such skills will eventually be considered essential.

CONCLUSION

The potential of online learning to accommodate a wide range of student circumstances, accelerate learning, and lower educational costs, although widely acknowledged, has yet to be fully realized. However, many of the same pressures that have defined the direction of online learning and have accelerated its implementation thus far will intensify. There is a growing expectation that learning must be relevant and exciting (Marx, 2014), and the resulting innovations and inevitable disruptions certainly will continue to shape and inform how special education teacher preparation faculty understand and use online technologies to teach, how these educators are trained to teach, and how effective their efforts will be.

As it appears, it is unlikely that the pace of growth in the use of online technologies or the disruptive influence of online technologies will slow in the near future. To maximize the potential of these current and emerging technologies, P–12 special educators will have to be aware of the available teaching technologies and able to demonstrate their effective use by creatively integrating these technologies into their teaching. To do so will require university faculty to more effectively model the instructional use of these online technologies and to actively teach the associated best practices. As Rule and Salzberg (2009) concluded, "No longer asking if distance education is feasible, new faculty hires accept, indeed should probably expect, that teaching at a distance is part of their role statement" (p. 3).

REFERENCES

Allen, I. E., & Seaman, J. (2014). 2013—Grade change: Tracking online education in the United States. *Online Learning Consortium.* Retrieved from http://sloanconsortium.org/publications/survey/grade-change-2013

Barber, M., Donnelly, K., & Rizvi, S. (2013, March 11). An avalanche is coming: Higher education and the revolution ahead. *IPPR.* Retrieved from http://www.ippr.org/publication/55/10432/an-avalanche-is-coming-higher-education-and-the-revolution-ahead

Barker, B. O. (1986). *Live via satellite: Interactive distant learning in America's rural schools.* Paper presented at the annual Colorado Rural and Small Schools Conference, Fort Collins, CO. Retrieved from ERIC database (ED 272 340).

Glomb, N., Lignugaris/Kraft, B., & Menlove, R. R. (2009). The USU mild/moderate distance degree and licensure program: Where we've been and where we're going. *Rural Special Education Quarterly, 28*(3), 18–22.

Hager, K. D. (2010). Web conferencing with distant alternate certificate student teachers. *Rural Special Education Quarterly, 30*(1), 49–55.

Hager, K. D., Baird, C. M., & Spriggs, A. D. (2012). Remote teacher observation at the University of Kentucky. *Rural Special Education Quarterly, 31*(4), 3–8.

Hasselbring, T. S., Goin, L., & Bransford, J. D. (1988). Developing math automaticity in learning handicapped children: The role of computerized drill and practice. *Focus on Exceptional Children, 20*(6), 1–7.

Howell, S. L., Williams, P. B., & Lindsay, N. K. (2003). Thirty-two trends affecting distance education: An informed foundation for strategic planning. Online *Journal of Distance Learning Administration, 6*(3). Retrieved from http://www.westga.edu/~distance/ojdla/fall63/howell63.html.

Johnson, L., Adams Becker, S., Cummins, M., Estrada, V., Freeman, A., & Ludgate, H. (2013). *NMC Horizon Report: 2013 higher education edition.* Austin, TX: New Media Consortium.

Kulik, C. L., & Kulik, J. A. (1991). Effectiveness of computer-based instruction: An updated analysis. *Computers in Human Behavior, 7*(1), 75–94.

Long, P., & Siemens, G. (2011, September 12). Penetrating the fog: Analytics in learning and education. *EDUCAUSEreview online.* Retrieved from http://www.educause.edu/ero/article/penetrating-fog-analytics-learning-and-education

Ludlow, B. L., & Brannan, S. A. (2010). Distance education program preparing personnel for rural areas: Current practices, emerging trends, and future directions. *Rural Special Education Quarterly, 29*(3), 4–15.

Ludlow, B. L., & Duff, M. C. (2009). Evolution of distance education at West Virginia University: Past accomplishments, present activities, and future plans. *Rural Special Education Quarterly, 28*(3), 9–17.

Marx, G. (2014). *21 trends for the 21st century: Out of the trenches and into the future.* Bethesda, MD: Education Week.

McLeskey, J., Tyler, N., & Flippin, S. (2003). *The supply of and demand for special education teachers: A review of research regarding the nature of chronic shortage of special education.* Gainesville, FL: Center on Personnel Studies in Special Education.

National Center for Education Statistics. (2013, May). The status of rural education. *Institute of Education Sciences.* Retrieved from http://nces.ed.gov/programs/coe/indicator_tla.asp

Osborne, C. (2012, April 1). The history of distance learning [Infographic]. *ZDNet.* Retrieved from http://www.zdnet.com/blog/igeneration/the-history-of-distance-learning-infographic/15791

Parker, K., Lenhart, A., & Moore, K. (2011, August 28). The digital revolution and higher education: College presidents, public differ on value of online learning. *Pew Research Center.* Retrieved from http://pewsocialtrends.org/files/2011/08/online-learning.pdf

Rock, M. L., Gregg, M., Thead, B. K., Acker, S. E., , Gable, R. A., & Zigmond, N. (2009). Can you hear me now? Evaluation of an online wireless technology to provide real-time feedback to special education teachers-in-training. *Teacher Education and Special Education, 32*(1), 64–82.

Rock, M. L., Schumacher, R. E., Gregg, M., Howard, P. W., Gable, R. A., & Zigmond, N. (2014). How are they now? Longer term effects of eCoaching through online Bug-in-Ear technology. *Teacher Education and Special Education, 37*(2), 161–181.

Rule, S., & Salzberg, C. L. (2009). Introduction to special topical issue on perspectives on distance education in special education—From test tube baby to freshman: Distance education grows up. *Rural Special Education Quarterly, 28*(3), 3–4.

Scheeler, M. C., McKinnon, K., & Stout, J. (2012). Effects of immediate feedback delivered via webcam and Bug-in-Ear technology on preservice teacher performance. *Teacher Education and Special Education, 35*(1), 77–90.

Semmel, M. I. (1972). Toward the development of a computer-assisted teacher training system (CATTS). *International Review of Education, 18*(1), 561–568.

Smithers, M. (2014, January 21). Higher education technology predictions for 2014. *Mark Smithers.* Retrieved from http://www.masmithers.com/2014/01/21/higher-education-technology-predictions-for-2014/

U.S. Department of Education. (2010). National education technology plan. *Office of Educational Technology.* Retrieved from http://www.ed.gov/technology/netp-2010

CHAPTER 13

CLINICAL AND FIELD-BASED TEACHER PREPARATION PEDAGOGY AND PROFESSIONAL DEVELOPMENT OF TEACHER EDUCATORS

Jessica Graves, Carolyn Gish, Karla Hull, and Jamie Bird

Darling-Hammond (2006) asserted that effective models of teacher education must include "extensive and intensely supervised clinical work—tightly integrated with coursework—that allows candidates to learn from expert practice in schools that serve diverse students" (p. 8). This is consistent with recommendations from the National Council on the Accreditation of Teacher Education (NCATE) Blue Ribbon Panel Report on Clinical Preparation and Partnerships for Improved Student Learning (2010). The Blue Ribbon Panel Report calls for redesigned teacher preparation programs focused on an integration of subject-matter preparation, theory, and pedagogy linked directly to applications in the field. The recommendations clearly call for an emphasis on redesigned field experiences. Thus, to prepare excellent teachers capable of having a positive impact on student learning, it is critical that practice must be placed at the center of teaching prepa-

Critical Issues in Preparing Effective Early Childhood Special Education Teachers for the 21st Century Classroom: Interdisciplinary Perspectives, pages 165–176.
Copyright © 2016 by Information Age Publishing
165

ration. Although most teacher educators would agree that extensive, intensively supervised teaching practice integrated with coursework is critical to the development of an effective future teacher, the implications for most teacher education programs include the need for transformative change in field experience, clinical models, curriculum, faculty roles, and partnerships with school systems.

In an effort to guide teacher education programs toward a clinically based focus, the Blue Ribbon Panel Report (NCATE, 2010) set forth design principles including recommendations that P–12 student learning is the focus; clinical preparation is integrated throughout every facet of teacher education in a dynamic way; a candidate's progress and elements of a preparation program are continuously judged on the basis of data; programs prepare teachers who are expert in content and how to teach it and are also innovators, collaborators, and problem-solvers; candidates learn in an interactive professional community; clinical educators and coaches are rigorously selected and prepared and drawn from both higher education and the P–12 sector; and specific sites are designated and funded to support embedded clinical preparation. With the goals in mind, in 2010, teacher educators, administrators, mentor teachers/school partners, and clinical supervisors in the early childhood special education department at a regional university (i.e., Valdosta State University, Valdosta, Georgia) came together to begin transforming their traditionally structured teacher education program. A description of this indulging journey follows, including links to the principles described above. Although university-based teacher preparation programs vary widely, the key findings from their experience should provide guidance for working toward a more integrated, clinically based model.

TRANSFORMATIONAL INITIATIVES

The first three design principles from the Blue Ribbon Panel Report (NCATE, 2010) and Darling-Hammond's (2006) recommendation to create intensively supervised, extensive field experiences provided a foundation for evaluating the teacher preparation program. Focus forums with mentor teachers, principals, supervisors, and faculty revealed a belief that preservice teachers needed much more time in the field to experience the progress P–5 students were making on their learning outcomes and to witness the need to occasionally re-present material to all or some students ensuring they mastered the outcomes. Faculty met over the course of 8 months to design a more intensive, integrated field experience/ clinical practice based on candidate surveys, mentor teacher and principal surveys, focus forums, and a review of research. In thinking about addressing issues and transforming the program, they asked the following questions:

1. *What would the program look like if P–5 student learning were the primary focus? (Blue Ribbon Panel Principle # 1).* To effectively transform the program, they decided to flip the focus by integrating course content more effectively with intensively supervised field experiences. It was not

as simple as adding more field experience hours or more supervised observations; it would require a dramatic program transformation. Changes in the sequence and content of curriculum, in pedagogical strategies, in the nature of the collaboration with schools and mentor teachers, and in teaching schedules and faculty roles would be necessary to effectively create a clinical practice model program.

2. *What would the program look like if clinical preparation was integrated throughout every facet of our program in a dynamic way (Blue Ribbon Panel Principle # 2 and Darling-Hammond, 2006).* Learning and reflection on field experiences had to be integrated into course content. In many teacher preparation programs, reflections and discussions about field experiences occur between the preservice teacher and the supervisor as well as in a field experience seminar. But rarely do courses take full advantage of field experiences by scaffolding course content with relevant issues that arise daily in field experiences. As such, many classes required a redesign to be able to take advantage of "in the moment" learning that was occurring in the field.

   Many courses required preservice teachers to do an "assignment" from the class in their field experience, but it was often the case that the assignment was not aligned with the actual activities in P–5 classrooms and thus became an "add-on" that had to be accommodated by the mentor teacher, disrupting the flow of classroom. Additionally, the practice of course content structured primarily around topics in a textbook was limiting the ability to take full advantage of the authentic experiences being provided to candidates. It was challenging to predict or even sequence the types of authentic learning topics preservice teachers were experiencing in a semester. Learning opportunities could not simply be contained with predefined "lectures"; there had to be a blend of planned critical content, and space for embedding critical learning that arose from authentic experiences in the schools.

3. *What would the program look like if a candidate's progress and elements of the preparation program were continuously judged on the basis of data?* The program had an interesting dilemma: suffering from collecting too much data on preservice teachers and not prioritizing or refining assessments that were actually providing evidence of change in knowledge, skills, and performance over time. Faculty came to understand that "less" data may be better and were challenged to identify key assessments that would authentically provide data on preservice teacher progress. In 2010, the program participated in a pilot of the Teacher Performance Assessment (TPA) that has since become the edTPA. This nationally validated performance assessment is being considered for use as a requirement for initial certification in many states. Results from the pilot convinced faculty that the process was extremely beneficial for pre-

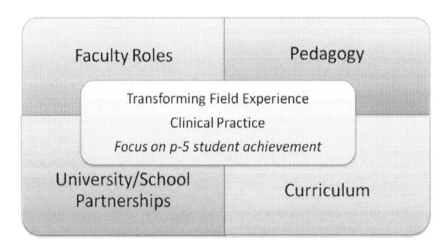

FIGURE 13.1. Transforming field experience clinical practice. This figure illustrates the interconnected influences of the field experience transformation. Each of these components influenced the development of the field experience

service students, with many students commenting they felt more confident in doing job interviews as a result of the TPA process requiring them to describe and defend their teaching decisions. The process of embedding edTPA tasks into our courses has begun, and it is anticipated that candidate growth in the program will be captured through this process. The power of a deeper assessment of teaching and learning performance provided by the edTPA framework is informing curriculum, pedagogy, and field-experience requirements.

REDESIGNING FIELD EXPERIENCES

A focus on the design of field experiences became the first target of the transformation. There were several attributes to address in the redesign of field experiences. Preservice teachers needed to spend more time in schools, they needed to have multiple, full-day experiences before their clinical practice, and they needed frequent formative feedback. The redesigned model provided three full semesters of field experience in which preservice teachers spend 2 full days a week in P–5 classrooms. Then they have a culminating semester where they are in schools full time for the entire semester doing their student teaching clinical experience.

Results of focus forums and surveys from school partners indicated mentor teachers and principals needed to be able to plan on having preservice teacher support for more than 2 days a week. To accommodate this request, the program put two preservice teachers in a classroom, enabling the mentor teacher to have preservice teachers in the classroom for 4 days of the week. Additionally, this enabled the possibility of instituting a peer mentorship and collaboration between the two preservice teachers assigned to one class. The model involved having a faculty member/university supervisor in the elementary school building full time, once a week, available to teachers as well as preservice students. The goal was to have two preservice teachers in one classroom and to have two faculty/university supervisors assigned to one school, ensuring a full-day on-site presence for 2 days per week. Faculty load was reduced to a 3/3, meaning they spent one full day in schools and taught two classes that met two times a week. This allowed them to have 2 full days a week for teaching preparation and scholarship activities.

RETHINKING CURRICULUM AND PEDAGOGY

The content of our curriculum had been redesigned multiple times over the years as faculty attempted to integrate current research into coursework and align with accrediting agency standards. The most recent redesign included offering three sequential courses in assessment, three sequential courses in classroom management, and three sequential courses in instructional strategies. The curriculum also included three sequential literacy courses and three sequential math courses every semester. The goal was to ensure that assessment, classroom management, and instructional strategies were a part of the content explored every semester. Stand-alone methods courses were eliminated in this redesign, replaced by the integration of coursework with field experiences to enable more practice in instructional strategies, assessment methods, and classroom management strategies. Science and social studies content occur in the semester before beginning the professional program.

Placing P–5 student learning at the center of the curriculum and having preservice students in schools for 2 full days a week beginning with their first semester in the professional program required earlier connections with school partners to identify key student learning assessments they were using and ensure some of the simple assessments were taught to preservice students prior to or concurrent with their first field experience. Faculty wanted to provide multiple opportunities to practice a variety of methods of assessing student learning and to enable growth in preservice students as they progressed through the program. Although the curriculum included three assessment courses with various foci, they were not specifically linked to field experience and clinical practice, thus the program was not making the best use of opportunities to provide repeated practice on key assessments. The goal of the redesign was to coordinate assessment course content with the types of assessments being done in schools or the data that schools were collecting. In this way, preservice students would have the ability to learn a variety of assessments and practice them in schools. To make needed changes in curriculum and pedagogy, certain transformational efforts must be used. These efforts are discussed in the following sections.

Exploring Flipping

Moving away from textbooks as the way to structure a course and using them as a resource to inform discussion topics generated from field experiences and observations is a necessary change that keeps the focus on the "apprenticeship" nature of extensive field experiences. Since the 1990s, there have been ongoing discussions urging teachers to move from lecturing as a pedagogical model to coaching/facilitating learning as a pedagogical model (Mazur, 1997). Recently, the term "flipped classroom" has been used to describe a pedagogical approach that moves the lecture component of a class to an out-of-class assignment with prerecorded short videos and readings, with in-class time used for applications, linkages to field experiences, and deeper learning experiences facilitated by the instructor. This is a strong model for most coursework in teacher preparation programs and ensures the integration of content and practice.

Miller (2014) identified five best practices targeting essential components of a successful flipped classroom pedagogical model, including the need to know engaging models, technology, reflection, and time/place. Putting content online, assigning reading or the watching of a recorded lecture will not ensure that preservice students come to the class prepared to actively engage with the pre-assigned content. This pedagogy requires a *"need to know"* component linked to the assigned prepreparation activities. There are pedagogical models such as project-based learning, game-based learning, and Understanding by Design that inherently create a *"need to know"* since in-class activities are *engaging* and require the use of content obtained in pre-assigned activities. *Technology* is a key component of a flipped classroom. Ideally, a flipped classroom will include short targeted videos and related readings. However, as with any pre-assigned content, it is essential to build in *reflective* activities assisting preservice students in thinking about what they have learned online and how it applies to their field experiences. Finally, structuring courses to include watching some of the very short videos in class and practicing how to get the most out of those videos will assist in ensuring learning. Linking the learning to in-class activities enabling thoughtful application of the information to actual field experiences is the goal of our redesigned curriculum.

Similarly, some faculty flipped the topics/questions of postobservation meetings or debriefings beginning the conversation with "What evidence do you have that your students learned the material you presented in your lesson?" This question is designed to guide the discussion about individual students and how they approached the learning task and how the preservice student differentiated instruction to ensure all of the students learned. This was designed to keep student learning at the center of the discussion. This intentional debriefing question signaled to preservice students that this was a critical piece of effective teaching. In the past, our preservice teachers typically began debriefing sessions by describing their own actions or behaviors rather than focusing on evidence of student learning. Although this may be a developmental process, the questions faculty ask can guide preservice students to always think first about student learning and learning outcomes they are seeking to teach. Although "flipping the classroom" is considered a pedagogical approach, it also impacts the curriculum content. The need to prioritize course content and focus on the most critical knowledge may mean that previous efforts to "expose" students to a wide range of information is replaced with a more targeted approach to the content. If a program uses an effective evaluative strategy, it becomes easy over the course of several semesters to determine content that should be emphasized and content that may not need to be covered in a particular course.

Peer Collaboration and Consultation

In the Fall 2013, a peer-support strategy was piloted. Preservice students identified someone within their assigned field experience group to become an official "field experience partner." As partners, students were responsible for offering support to one another in keeping up with assignments, meeting times, and planning/ evaluating their lessons. Faculty experienced results similar to those reported by Dee (2012), finding preservice students' anxiety level decreased and seeing them demonstrate more confidence during their placement. Several researchers have identified the important role that collaborative and consultative peer practices can have on reducing the cognitive load of learners and broadening their knowledge and views as a result of gaining insights from multiple viewpoints (Holt, 1994; Kang, 1995; Kirschner, Paas, & Kirschner, 2009; Trimbur, 1989). Preservice teachers who are engaged in a collaborative learning community including peers, mentors, and supervisors are more likely to have a more educative field experience (Bullough, Mayes, & Patterson, 2002) that includes rich reflective discussions about teaching and increases in practical knowledge (Bullough et al., 2002; Eick & Dias, 2005).

School and University Partnerships

The Blue Ribbon Panel Report (NCATE, 2010) included recommendations to prepare teachers who are expert in content and how to teach it, and teachers who are innovators, collaborators, and problem-solvers. They recommend the development of programs where teacher candidates learn in an interactive professional community. The ability to transform field experiences and clinical practice is directly linked to collaboration with school partners and transforming the nature of that collaboration. Although the university had long-standing relationships with multiple schools, this model required significant input from school partners and was built in collaboration with them. Logistically, partners were very willing to provide a room for university supervisors to use while they spent the day in the school. This room served as a space for debriefing preservice students and was a functional, but also a symbolic statement that the nature of the school/university partnership was changing.

A tremendous challenge for university supervisors/faculty was to build trust and establish relationships with mentor teachers in order for the supervisory experience to be worthwhile and beneficial for all. Inadvertently, the program was seeking to develop professional learning communities (du Plessis & Muzaffar, 2010) where all members were both contributing in meaningful ways and also growing and learning through interactions with more expert others. This trust building occurred one mentor teacher at a time, acknowledging the uniqueness of teacher partners and their comfort/discomfort level regarding having another adult in the classroom. As university supervisors/faculty became more available in schools and also began supporting mentor teachers by teaching a small group of students, or co-teaching or modeling a lesson, or problem-solving a classroom or student issue, it became clear that a professional learning community was emerging. An equally important role for university supervisors/faculty was to genuinely ask for advice, resources, and assistance of mentor teachers acknowledging the wealth of knowledge they had about the classroom, curriculum, families, and the school. Faculty/supervisors no longer drop in to observe a student, spend a few minutes connecting with the teacher, and leaving. Instead, school partners can count on having someone from the university present daily, supporting each other's work.

This year, a new preservice teacher observation instrument is being developed; one that directly aligns with the Teacher Keys Effective System (TKES) used statewide to provide formative assessment and evaluation of certified teachers. Functionally, this means mentor teachers are very familiar with the observation instrument because it is so similar to the one principals use to support professional development. Symbolically, it signals an alignment with goals of partner schools. Importantly, one aspect of the TKES instrument identifies mentorship as a leadership quality that factors into the classroom teacher's evaluation under the professionalism category. It is likely this will lead to increased interest in becoming a mentor.

The Advisory Council for the program consists of faculty, students, alumnae, and community stakeholders. It is also being transformed into an active work group. For example, the topic of mentorship was discussed at an Advisory Council meeting, and it was suggested that the program establish a teacher preparation resource teacher (TPRT) from mentors at each partnering school. This TPRT could respond to questions from mentor teachers and may also be utilized in redelivering information about practicum goals and procedures. The idea of creating and posting a training webinar for participating mentors was recommended; and it is at the top of the priority list as an attainable, worthwhile, and cost-effective goal.

CRITICAL FACULTY AND SUPERVISOR ROLES

Turning a program "upside down" is a process that will evolve differently for every program that undertakes it. Even when faculty, supervisors, and school partners agree that the new clinical model is the right direction to move in, it cannot be assumed that everyone fully understands the philosophy and goals of the new field model designed to provide a more authentic, meaningful field experience for pre-service teachers and teacher candidates in clinical practice. It should be assumed that everyone will have some discomfort as they learn new roles and strategies for supervision and time management. Understanding the paradigm shift required of university faculty members and university supervisors is a critical element to successfully moving toward a clinically based teacher preparation model. The transformative field experience model described in this chapter was based on several initial assumptions.

Assumption 1

This assumption is: *University faculty love teaching and would enjoy being actively involved in a P–5 classroom as a way of staying current and of being able to provide more frequent feedback to teacher candidates.* In most university-based teacher preparation programs, faculty members have a range of P–12 teaching experiences; but those experiences might have occurred 5, 10, or 15 years ago. It is one skill to stop in for an hour observation using an observation instrument and focusing on one preservice teacher for an extended period of time. It is a completely different skill to spend the whole day in one school, stopping in to many classrooms to do formative assessments on multiple preservice candidates. These "walk through" observations are common in schools but have not been the primary style of formative feedback in most traditional teacher preparation programs. There are differences in the focus of formative assessments, differences in supervisor comfort level in the school, differences in the energy level it takes to stay all day in the school, and differences in time management requirements. Many faculty members were used to following an observation template, however "in the moment" feedback was not a skill they were comfortable with. Next steps include faculty development in this area.

Assumption 2

This assumption is: *University faculty would co-teach with preservice candidates and/or mentor teachers to model teaching and classroom management strategies.* Some faculty members were able to go into a school and "fit in," making themselves available to teachers and teacher candidates for consulting and openly communicating that they were learning from their mentor teachers as well. This requires diplomacy skills, but more importantly, an open mind, heart, and the willingness to "not know" something but to learn. As positive relationships and trust were built, some faculty were allowed and/or invited to co-teach with a student or model a teaching strategy or co-teach with the mentor teacher. However, some faculty did not feel comfortable in this role, and some mentor teachers were not ready to partner in this way.

It was clear that faculty and university supervisors would be more willing to assume an active role in schools if they were comfortable in the school setting. University supervisors with some type of prior positive connection to assigned schools had an advantage when developing active partnership relationships. With this fact in mind, the director of placement assigned supervisors, whenever possible, to schools where they already had positive relationships. The director placed supervisors at a school for a series of semesters in order to develop a continuation of supervisor/school relationships. Honoring familiarity with partnering schools is not an absolute, but it certainly increases the likelihood of a deeper partnership. The seven consecutive hours spent in an assigned school provided opportunities for faculty to accomplish many essential matters, ranging from maintenance of required paperwork to building working relationships with the mentor teachers and holding small debriefing sessions with students. One of the challenges for faculty was structuring time so their assigned preservice students in the school received continuous feedback and support. The weekly guide in Table 13.1 is an example of a tool developed to support faculty and university supervisors in cre-

TABLE 13.1. Weekly Guideline for Practicum Supervision

Week	Suggested Procedures for Supervision of Practicum Students
1	Meeting with teacher candidates to review expectations/collect paperwork/meet with mentor teachers as a group. (This is a good time to give each mentor teacher a copy of the practicum handbook that correlates with the course number of their practicum student.)
2	"Walk through" all practicum classrooms/model a lesson for groups of practicum students using a mentor teacher's classroom and lesson plan/debriefing with all students
3	Visit 7 students' classrooms/debriefing with all students
4	Visit 7 students' classrooms/debriefing with all students
5	Mentor Teacher Conference Week—Allow mentor teachers to sign up for conference with supervisor. (Having a mentor/supervisor meeting during the middle of the field experience will allow an early opportunity to address and correct any unpleasant issues that surface. These meetings can be brief and informal.)
6	Observations—4 student slots/suggest that observations be held before 1:00/conference with practicum students from 2:00 until . . .
7	Observations—4 student slots/suggest that observations be held before 1:00/conference with practicum students from 2:00 until . . .
8	Observations—4 student slots/suggest that observations be held before 1:00/conference with practicum students from 2:00 until . . .
9	Observations—2 students slots/make up day for observations
10	Conference Week with Practicum Students/review videotaped lessons Check paperwork for packet (preliminary)

*This schedule is designed for a practicum supervision placement from 8:00 to 3:00 with 14 practicum students assigned. The items listed are suggestions for a supervisor to use to stay on track with monitoring, coaching, and observing. You may have additional or alternate ways to involve yourself in the support given to the teacher candidates

ating a schedule. It is based on one university supervisor assigned to support 14 field experience students in one school.

Apparently, with preservice students in the schools all day, the last hour of the day —2:15–3:15—is designated as group debriefing. This is a time to share ideas, discuss instructional strategies, troubleshoot behavior management issues, clarify expectations for practicum assignments, along with a wide range of questions and concerns that may come up during the semester. Debriefing meetings have become an essential part of the supervision delivery for the full-day practicum field model.

CONCLUSION

Effectively moving to a clinically based teacher preparation program requires transformation of every aspect of the program. It requires continuous improvement efforts to refine the model and adjust curriculum, pedagogy, faculty roles, and university/school partnerships. Initial feedback indicates that preservice students who have experienced this new model enter their final clinical teaching semester with a higher level of confidence and efficacy and an improved ability to manage classrooms demands. Principals have noticed the difference in the partnership and in preservice student's ability to add value to a mentor's classroom, resulting in a desire to continue the partnership. They have also begun to identify the very best mentor teachers in the building to support preservice students. Mentor teachers are increasingly pleased with the support provided by the university supervisor and the initiative and skills of the preservice students, making them more likely to request a preservice teacher placement for multiple semesters. Preservice students are clear about the value they place on this extended time in the P–5 classroom and how it enhances their understanding of course content. In the words of Dr. Lucy Greene, a long-standing adjunct supervisor at Valdosta State University's Department of Early Childhood and Special Education,

> The young candidates in my charge have presented themselves well and have done everything requested of them. I have been met by excited mentor teachers who are very pleased to have our candidates working in the various classrooms. Even the Principals have praised the work already being done by these students. I am delighted to be working with them. I will try hard to give them a bit of "polish" this semester, but your basic preparation is paying big dividends for them, their students and the reputation of your program. I look forward to seeing their progress. (L. Greene, personal communication, January 24, 2014)

REFERENCES

Bullough, R. V., Jr., Mayes, C. T., Patterson, R. S. (2002). Wanted: A prophetic pedagogy: A response to our critics. *Curriculum Inquiry, 32*(3), 341–347.

Darling-Hammond, L. (2006). Constructing 21st-century teacher education. *Journal of Teacher Education, 57*(1), 1–15.

Dee, A. L. (2012). Collaborative clinical practice: An alternate field experience. *Issues in Teacher Education, 21*(2), 147–163.

du Plessis, J., & Muzaffar, I. (2010). Professional learning communities in the teachers' college: A resource for teacher educators. *USAID*. Retrieved from http://files.eric.ed.gov/fulltext/ED524465.pdf

Eick, C., & Dias, M. (2005). Building the authority of experience in communities of practice: The development of preservice teachers' practical knowledge through coteaching in inquiry classrooms. *Science Education, 89*(3), 470–491.

Holt, M. (1994). Dewey and the "cult of efficiency": Competing ideologies in collaborative pedagogies of the 1920s. *Journal of Advanced Composition, 14*(1), 73–92.

Kang, H. (1995). Meeting the needs of linguistically diverse students through collaboration. *The Educational Forum, 59*(3), 319–326.

Kirschner, F., Paas, F., & Kirschner, P. A. (2009). A cognitive load approach to collaborative learning: United brains for complex tasks. *Educational Psychology Review, 21*, 31–42.

Mazur, E. (1997). *Peer instruction: A user's manual.* Upper Saddle River, NJ: Prentice Hall.

Miller, A. (2014, November 18). 5 tips for flipping your PBL classroom. *Edutopia.* Retrieved from http://www.edutopia.org/blog/5-tips-flipping-pbl-classroom-andrew-miller

National Council on the Accreditation of Teacher Education (NCATE). (2010, November). *Transforming teacher education through clinical practice: A national strategy to prepare effective teachers: Report of the Blue Ribbon Panel on clinical preparation and partnerships for improved student learning.* Retrieved from http://www.ncate.org/LinkClick.aspx?fileticket=zzeiB1OoqPk%3D&tabid=715

Trimbur, J. (1989). Consensus and difference in collaborative learning. *College English, 51*(6), 602–616.

CHAPTER 14

FORGING EVIDENCE-BASED INQUIRY AND TEACHING IN TEACHER EDUCATION

Alicja Rieger, Ewa McGrail, and J. Patrick McGrail

The Teacher Leader Model Standards by the Teacher Leadership Exploratory Consortium (TLEC, 2011), together form a theoretical model to guide the preparation of effective teacher leaders for the needs of the 21st century student. They acknowledge the need for preparing teachers who can model and apply systematic inquiry as an essential element of their ongoing learning and professional development. This is important in all disciplines, including early childhood special education programs. Unfortunately, in light of the most recent report on educational research by Knight et al. (2012), derogative epithets such as "flawed," "lacking rigor and relevance," "missing conclusive evidence," or "less advanced than the mainstream research" (p. 5) are often leveled at educational research in general and research on teaching in particular. Within this identity crisis in teacher educational research, the call for preparing teacher practitioners who are skilled both in evidence-based teaching and evidence-based inquiry takes on a new urgency (Knight et al., 2012; Roblin & Margalef, 2013). In this chapter, we focus on modern educational research, advocate various models of teacher education research that can promote rigorous and systematic evidence-based inquiry in teacher edu-

Critical Issues in Preparing Effective Early Childhood Special Education Teachers for the 21st Century Classroom: Interdisciplinary Perspectives, pages 177–190.
Copyright © 2016 by Information Age Publishing

cation, and present suggestions from multiple disciplines on how to prepare a new generation of teacher educational researchers.

The call to prepare effective teachers and engage them in rigorous evidence-based practice and research is not a new idea in the field of teacher education preparation. In fact, Imig and Imig (2005) closely examined the historical, *Learned Report* on teacher preparation from 1920, *The Professional Preparation of Teachers for American Public Schools*, and found that this report boldly called for "the transformation of teacher education into a professional, evidence-based clinical preparation program" (p. 60). We believe such a recommendation, although almost 95 years old, is still as relevant as ever. A facially similar concept is at the core of the *Teacher Leader Model Standards* (TLEC, 2011), a theoretical model to guide the preparation of effective teacher leaders for the needs of the 21st century student. TLEC acknowledged the need for preparing teachers who can model and apply systematic inquiry as an essential element of teacher ongoing learning and professional development.

Interestingly, TLEC's goals resonate with those established by the *NCATE Blue Ribbon Panel on Clinical Preparation and Partnerships for Improved Student Learning* (NCATE, 2010), which made teacher education clinically based experiences a focal point of guiding principles and recommendations directed to teacher preparation programs, districts, teacher unions, and policymakers. Unfortunately, according to the most recent report on educational research by Knight et al. (2012), existing research has not achieved desired goals. Some educational researchers, then, have labored under the perception created by other social scientists that their own research is not "real."

CONCERNS ABOUT QUALITY AND RELEVANCE OF EDUCATIONAL RESEARCH

Educational observers, including laypersons, policymakers, and social scientists in other disciplines, have found educational research to be a target-rich environment for criticism. Biesta (2007), relying on overwhelmingly critical national reports about educational research, cited "serious doubts about the quality and relevance of educational research," which he found lacking answers to the questions posed by the government putatively to advance educational policy. Biesta found that it "did not provide educational professionals with clear guidance for their work, that it was fragmented, noncumulative, and methodologically flawed, and that it was tendentious and politically motivated" (pp. 1–2). Hargreaves (1997) went as far as to accuse "teachers-as-researchers and their supervisors" as not having "generated the cumulative body of knowledge" that is evidence based (p. 412). Such criticisms are no doubt the result of comparing research in education to that conducted for other social sciences. However, it is our contention that education poses unique challenges to researchers in the social sciences for several key reasons. The first is that children, logically the primary subjects and participants for much research, change and grow irregularly in ways that will not be replicated again in their lives. It is only in their futures that they will stabilize into adults, with professions, jobs, fixed aspirations, steady incomes, and the likelihood of geographical stasis. As children, they frustrate prediction, which, while problematic for researchers, enables them ultimately to become diverse and robust individuals. Second, children start at different places, learn at different speeds, learn different kinds of subject matter with greater or less proclivity, and express enthusiasm for differing kinds of knowledge. Their learning behavior, both as individuals and as members of a cohort, is untidy and irregular. Third, the potential population from which samples should representatively be drawn numbers in the tens of millions. Fourth, despite initiatives such as No Child Left Behind (U.S. Department of Education, 2001), U.S. states have traditionally borne the heavy lifting of educating their populations, and they do this with greater and lesser budgets, differing political objectives, and with highly variable success. And fifth, the large cities within these states provide yet another layer of complexity to consider as they organize their school children in yet other ways.

Educational research must contend with the aforementioned complexities, and they provide layers of bureaucracy that uniquely affect school children in the United States. This is why calls for the cumulativity of research in education miss the point; the people involved in educating children and the children themselves resist being put into easy rubrics. Even if the education in, say, Alabama were to be exactly like that in Massachusetts or Wisconsin, the children themselves would differ culturally, economically, and politically. Critics of educational research are right to point out methodological oversights and errors if and when they occur. However, they have rarely stopped there. As paradigms of what constitutes preferred research wax and wane, what has been demanded of educational research has also changed, methodologically and epistemologically. The difficulty, in our view, with universal, federal policy-based calls for educational research of a quantifiable and generalizable nature is that they seek a "single bullet" theory of learning that has yet to be discovered. As paradigms have risen and fallen, and as researchers have struggled to understand human cognition and the ways that it is scaffolded, elaborated upon, and improved, no one method has emerged as to how best to teach and how best to cause another to learn.

Following World War II, psychological processes, some of which had external origins, were thought to most strongly impinge on learning behavior; this was termed the "constructivist approach" (Lincoln, Lynham, & Guba, 2011). The first of several long-standing contentious issues then arose. What is the true and central purpose of teaching? Is it the imparting of certain knowledge that society deems fit and sufficient for everyone to possess and use? Or is it to support and expand the act of learning itself? Shuell (1986) noted that changes in how we view learning, whether it is primarily a "what-" based approach or a "how-" based approach, affect policy in subtle and gross ways. Starting in the 1960s, norm-referenced views in learning by students have been supplanted by criterion-referenced views (see Shuell, 1986). It is now much more important that all students know some of the same things than different students know different things, depending on taste and talent. Hence, we have standards and common cores. Following behaviorist, constructivist (and then perhaps postmodernist) theories of teaching and learning, in recent years, a new thread has been strengthened, which is sometimes called the neurobiological (Duke & Mallate, 2011). Its researchers attempt to find the physical bases for behavior based on advances in neuronal studies and brain imaging. If regularities can be observed in the brain as it deals with inputs, it should be possible to maximize the efficacy of those inputs if they are connected with learning. The neurobiological approach is generally located much more firmly than psychology in the natural sciences and is generally carried out by practitioners of "pure science." Today, the critics of educational research tout the natural sciences as possessing the "gold standard" in terms of appropriateness of method and methodological rigor. It is not surprising that they should feel this way; for the past century, science and scientists have enjoyed a lofty status as the harbingers of truth, or at least as much of truth as can reliably be gotten. As Mershon and Schlossman (2008) pointed out,

> Establishing a scientific basis for educational practice mattered because science—or, to be precise, certain popular conceptions of it—occupied an exalted place in American culture. . . Science was commonly understood in positivistic, inductive, instrumental terms that stressed fact gathering and the generation of useful knowledge. Its findings ostensibly constituted objective truths, not personal interpretations, and therein lay their power. (p. 310)

As early 20th century, progressives such as Dewey began to stress the importance of a compulsory education for children as school populations exploded, particularly in the cities (Mershon & Schlossman, 2008). It became necessary to hire professional full-time administrators and specialists to assist them in the implementation of progressive policies. Powerful superintendents of schools and elected school boards were formed. To assist them, after World War II, educational sociologists, political scientists, and others were soon involved in the study of education. Despite this, an empirical basis for "best practices" in American education remained elusive. "Equally important, however, was what educational research did not achieve. . . The establishment of a scientific basis for public education proved to be more abrasive and elusive than its advocates had expected" (Mershon & Schlossman, 2008, p. 333). Some 70 years later, a new challenge has emerged. While most university researchers are comfortable with plurality in their approaches to studying education, the view from policymakers is considerably different. As Feuer, Towne, and Shavelson (2002) noted at the dawn of NCLB,

> Academic scientists are usually startled to find the arcana of their craft inserted in law; but surprise turns to anxiety when the law appears to instruct them on methodology and to tie public funding of research to specific modes of inquiry. The combined force of [NCLB] and the impending OERI reauthorization has rekindled old debates over the nature of educational research and has spurred scientists in many

domains to reexamine the nature of scientific inquiry in a democracy: For many, the key question is whether legislators or scientists should ultimately decide issues of research method. (p. 5)

Feuer et al. (2002) did not overtly prescribe a set of methodological conditions themselves, but stated that a culture of scientific inquiry is desirable and ought to be fostered through the following aims:

Pose significant questions that can be investigated empirically; Link research to relevant theory; Use methods that permit direct investigation of the questions; Provide a coherent and explicit chain of reasoning; Yield findings that replicate and generalize across studies; and [D]isclose research data and methods to enable and encourage professional scrutiny and critique. (p. 7)

Feuer et al. later concluded that "when properly applied, quantitative and qualitative research tools can both be employed rigorously and together often can support stronger scientific inferences than when either is employed in isolation" (p. 8).

One pressing concern of some researchers in the educational research community is conducting qualitative research that emphatically denies any "truths" that might be discovered in their research. As Bridges (1999) observed, the "truth" of educational findings are "denied in favour of, for example, some kind of theory of political dominance or multiple subjectivities," which he termed likely was a "postmodernist" stance (p. 598). Theoretical positioning of this sort has probably not aided the public relations of relevant research, as far as policymakers are concerned. They might ask, "Where are the tangible, graspable implications of such research? Why on earth was it conducted if its conclusions cannot ever be proposed as 'true'?" And, as policymakers would be only too willing to add, "Why was it paid for with taxpayer funds?" Educational research has also not been helped by a deep and pervasive balkanization of methodology. Perhaps firmer than even the choice of study subject is the choice a researcher makes as to *how* to study that subject. In other words, methodology has come to trump subject matter in pursuit of research. Innovative methodologists of one stripe or the other are now sought out by researchers to help with subject areas outside their area of specialty, notwithstanding their lack of familiarity with the area of research. Not only do researchers feel they have to choose from the Coke-or-Pepsi-like binarity of the qual/quant divide, they are often discouraged by colleagues from ever doing the *other* kind of research. This is dangerous!

CRITICISM OF THE LOW STATUS OF THE EDUCATION PROFESSION

A further problem, and one somewhat further afield, is that of the social status of teachers and its effect on educational research. What concerns many, and is perhaps a problem in American society at-large, is that the profession of teaching has maintained a low status relative to other professions like medicine and law (Hargreaves et al. 2006). This is by itself a cause for concern, although all of its causes are outside the scope of this chapter. Nevertheless, such a deficient status may have indirectly affected the quality of educational research. Scott (2010) argued that "the low quality of education faculty and the schools in which they work leads in turn to a low performance by their graduates and thus the low status of the teaching profession" (p. 326). Drawing upon the work of Labaree (1997), Scott (2010) pointed out that the origin of this low education status is related to the rise of market forces and a market-based philosophy regarding various professions. Such an emphasis on market forces has had some unforeseen consequences. One has been that it may have led to deficient teacher education programs. As the Baby Boom Generation was born and grew up, this particularly large age cohort required large numbers of teachers to educate it. That is, "For teacher preparation programs, the need to educate a large volume of teachers cheaply led to, in Labaree's (1997) words, 'a thinly educated faculty, academically weak students, and a foreshortened and unchallenging curriculum'" (p. 232). Thus, "By choosing to meet the demand for teachers, the institution gave up any claim it might once have had for elite status. By becoming socially useful, it lost social respect" (p, 232). The market-based context that was implied meant that schools of education should shift away from their primary "role of educating teachers" and "introduce more programs of general education to attract the larger number of students" (p. 327). This has, according to Scott, consequently reduced their functions to nothing more than "training workers to fit the existing job market (social efficiency)" (p. 327) and to become a "low-status cash cow . . . scarcely likely to increase its prestige in the university setting" (p. 328).

Not surprisingly, the high demand for teachers led to lowered entry standards for applicants and teaching becoming "for many, something to do if other more desirable options were out of reach" (Scott, 2010, p. 329). Callejo Pérez (2008), agreed that this criticism "is a direct assault on how we educate teachers; calling for an efficient corporate solution to the 'production of high quality teachers'" (p. 19). The much-vaunted efficiency of the corporate model has led political figures, who have for many decades controlled education through elected school boards, to solicit solutions and methodologies from the worlds of business and commerce. Callejo Pérez (2008) further argued that "the major problem with teacher education policy today is that too much decision-making takes place in Congress and in the boardroom of major corporations instead of in schools and schools of education" (p. 20). This is not to say that actual deficiencies have not been observed in the teacher education curriculum. The unique situatedness of the education of young people requires a broad understanding of research and data collection approaches and techniques (Duke & Mallate, 2011). Capraro and Thompson (2008), in their review of research methodology requirements within schools and colleges of education at the 21 top-10-ranked universities across the country, pointed out that approximately 72% of doctoral programs required at least one quantitative course, 42% required at least one qualitative course, with a mean number of required research-based courses of 2.6. However, none of these programs required any mixed-methodology coursework, which is a mainstay of educational research. According to Capraro and Thompson, a lack of sufficient training in all appropriate educational research methodologies is a recipe for disaster, especially since "such requirements operationalize visions about the meaning of educational research and the functions that educational researchers should be able to perform" (p. 247).

DEBATE OVER WHAT COUNTS AS EDUCATIONAL RESEARCH

Along with the criticism of and concerns about the quality and relevance of educational research, the question of what counts as a high quality educational research has been a highly debated topic for a long time within educational, research, and professional communities (Horn, 2004; Hostetler, 2005). Historically, a gulf of misunderstanding has formed between the two competing and oppositional paradigms of quantitative and qualitative research, known in the subject literature as "the great divide" (Horn, 2004, p. 199) and as opposing forces in "the grand narrative of social inquiry" (Cladindin & Connelly, 2000, p. xxv). Within this context, high quality research has come to be divided along methodological lines, as these two research paradigms markedly differ in the way they define, perform, and interpret research. The divide exists as well in what their practitioners view the purpose of research to be, the nature and generalizability of educational knowledge, and consequently, the basis for teacher education practice, policy, and decision making (Lincoln et al., 2011).

A bias toward one of these research traditions emerged when the No Child Left Behind Act (U.S. Department of Education, 2001) contributed a mandated federal definition of educational research. It was defined as

> scientifically based research . . . that involves the application of rigorous, systematic, and objective procedures to obtain reliable and valid knowledge relevant to education activities and programs . . . and is evaluated using experimental or quasi-experimental designs in which individuals, entities, programs, or activities are assigned to different conditions and with appropriate controls to evaluate the effects of the condition of interest, with a preference for random-assignment experiments, or other designs to the extent that those designs contain within-condition or across-condition controls.

The above defined scientifically based research narrowly defines educational research to promote knowledge from only one type of methodology, that is, empirical and statistical research (Horn, 2004). The difficulties emerge when problem, issues, and testable variables have to be narrowly and carefully defined in order to be quantified and counted. As Horn (2004) pointed out, a lot of "richness" in definitions and states of affairs is lost in such narrowly delimited variables. Such narrowly defined research also disempowers teachers in disparate areas of knowledge production because it limits their participation to "their role of technicians who implement the policies of others" (Horn, 2004, p. 203), while the top-down "experts" who are not connected to a given school's daily realities are the empowered deciders and policymakers. But there are other serious implications for scholars and research practitioners. Horn (2004) argued, "If only research compatible with the NCLB legislation is used in policy making, then only quantitative researchers will be credible participants in the determination of educational policy" (p. 203). Horn warned that "by de-emphasizing all sources of knowledge except that of the quantitative/objectivist view, our ability to deal with the contextual complexity of education would become limited" (p. 204).

WHAT RESEARCH IS SCIENTIFIC?

Duke and Martin (2011) noted the use of terms like "scientific," and "scientifically-based" formed an irrelevant distinction since they propose that "all research is scientific" (p. 12). Instead, they seek to answer the question of what research is *not*. According to Duke and Martin,

> one common misconception that we encounter is the notion that if something is written by a researcher, it automatically counts as research. . . Similarly, just because a researcher is presenting a set of practices does not mean that those practices are research-tested or research-based. (p. 12)

They further added,

> We use research-tested to mean that one or more research studies tested the impact of that particular practice, approach, or product. In contrast, we use research-based to mean that the particular practice, approach, or product has not been tested in a research study but has been designed to be consistent with research findings. (pp. 12–13)

Duke and Martin (2011) propose the following questions for determining if a given course of action is truly research-tested:

> What exactly did the research test? For the research-tested claim to be valid, it needs to be applied to a practice, approach, or product that is highly similar to or the same as what was originally tested. What exactly did the research find? Just because something was research-tested does not mean that the test/research found it to be effective. Did the research test the practice, approach, or product against something else? Simply trying out something provides limited information. If the practice, approach, or product is not tested against something, then it is difficult to infer whether any impact that we observe would have been seen even without that practice, approach, or product. . . To what exactly was the practice, approach, or product compared? When there is a comparison, you need to ask what it is. (p. 17)

Duke and Martin's (2011) approach is a call toward parsimony and care, but we note that studies that meet every one of their benchmarks of being "research-tested" rather than being merely "research-based" would be few indeed. Instead, in the real world, we often must muddle along with tantalizing findings from studies of schools, teachers, and subjects (students) that are very like, but not exactly the same as the ones in our own purview. In the meantime, teachers whose long experience, strong anecdotal memories of successful practices, and commitment to the success of students who are right in front of them find themselves devalued. These are the practitioners who are in the trenches during the trend toward government standardization of educational research and feel its impact most directly on their educational practice. As an example, Michelle, who was a secondary English Language Arts teacher for 15 years reported that

> for the first half of my career. I enjoyed a great deal of autonomy and [I] felt generally respected as a professional, as an intellectual, and as a practitioner who had a voice in education reform. During the last half of my career. I felt increasingly marginalised and stifled (Hulburt & Knotts, 2012, p. 96)

In fact, she further argued that

> the last few years of my career were plagued by a long list of acronyms, new hires (including a Director of Research and Assessment), fads, and anything else that could be attributed to "scientifically valid research." Rigour and relevance, benchmarks, best practices, scientifically-driven . . . these were the catchphrases that marked my final years in the secondary classroom. (Hulburt & Knotts, 2012, p. 96)

RECONCEPTUALIZING TEACHER EDUCATION RESEARCH

Several reconceptualized models of educational research have been articulated in the literature to address the criticism and concerns about quality and relevance of educational research. For instance, building upon Kincheloe (2003) and Freire (1970/1998), Price-Dennis (2010) advocated for a "praxis-oriented" approach to teacher research (p. 273). That is, teacher research should be "committed to alleviating oppressive conditions for all people" (p. 273). Grounded in critical theory (Freire, 1970/1998), such an approach urges the teacher-researcher to engage in the continuous critique and questioning of current school practices that may result in the inequitable distribution of learning opportunities. This teacher research may then be perceived as "a political act" (Price-Dennis, 2010, p. 273) by which schools are conceptualized as sociopolitical and economic learning environments that are meant to be disrupted and transformed into more democratic and just educational systems for all students. Price-Dennis (2010) argued that

> Teacher research begins with the assumption that responsive teaching is not formulaic, [nor] does it follow a script or blueprint. . . .Working in concert with other anti-oppressive measures, it [critical teacher research] encourages political agency, advocacy, and commitment to the transformation of our education system. (p. 275)

Earlier, Callejo Pérez (2008) argued that "ultimately good research is political. And good researchers understand that their work is political (whether within their own field or in the public domain)" (p. 22). He proposed that the conceptualization of education research at its core should be the politics of "reclaiming the language of research" (p. 22). That is, researchers should examine the research rhetoric for such absolute language as "research-based," or "research-driven," used in a context of a quantitative research because "these ostentatious statements assume the infallibility research has assumed as unquestioned if it follows a methodology" (p. 22). Callejo Pérez further argued that with overreliance on statistics, quantitative research "serve[s] to limit rather than expand knowledge by placing limits of what the research is searching" (p. 24), as is evident in the narrowly defined and federally mandated definition of research that was provided above.

Capraro and Thompson (2008) advocated for the better alignment between research methodology requirements at doctoral-level programs and the type of educational scholarship that is deemed desirable in a given discipline. Within this context, they called for a mixed-methods requirement for teacher training in doctoral programs, and they consider a mixed-methodology framework to be the direction in which the field of educational research should move in the future. They also envisioned reconceptualized models of educational research as ones that move away from a primarily focus on methodological and technical issues (i.e., the acquisition of techniques for collecting and analyzing data) to thoughtful reflection and critical data analysis of current research theory and practice. In their view, "good methodology instruction focuses primarily on reasoning and thoughtfulness rather than on technical issues" (p. 251). Such methodological requirements should be then "expressions of what students must do (e.g., present research at annual meetings, publish refereed journal articles, submit funding proposals) rather than expectations of what students know or which courses they should take" (p. 251).

Ball and Forzani (2007) recognized the need for examining more systematically the interplay between teaching and learning. That is, they regarded the instructional dynamic inside education as the basis for framing research questions, conducting educational research, and thus building an education discipline and specialized body of knowledge that is distinguished from other domains of research. They claimed that such a body of knowledge would be able to contribute to solving challenging problems in education and noted that

> Until education researchers turn their attention to problems that exist primarily inside education and until they develop systematically a body of specialized knowledge, other scholars will propose solutions. Because such solutions typically are not based on explanatory analysis of the dynamics of education, the education problems that confront society are likely to remain unsolved. (p. 530)

More specifically, Ball and Forzani (2007) proposed that for educational research to be *educational*, it has to "investigate questions about the instructional dynamic at play in problems directly related to schooling and the formal educational process" (p. 532). Earlier, Nuthall (2004) suggested "an explanatory theory for research on teaching that can be directly and transparently linked to classroom realities" (p. 273). This kind of research "must provide continuous, detailed data on the experience of individual students, in-depth analysis of the changes that take place in the students' knowledge, beliefs, and skills, and ways of identifying the real-time interactive relationships between these two different kinds of data " (p. 273). For Nuthall, the methodological preferences is not as issue because "it matters not what research 'paradigms' are used, so long as they provide the kind of data that it is essential for this purpose" (p. 295). However, he claimed that for the research data to be effective, valid, and based on explanatory theory, it had to meet the following six criteria:

1. Independent in-depth assessment of what students learn.
2. Complete, continuous data on individual student experience.
3. Complete, continuous data on classroom activities.
4. Analysis based on the continuous connections among classroom activities, student experiences, and learning processes.
5. [The avoidance of] the aggregation of data.
6. Explanatory theory must be directly and transparently connected to relevant evidence. (pp. 296–297)

Hulburt and Knotts (2012) concluded that,

as a consequence of its seeking reproducible and predictable results, it [scientifically based research] diminishes the role of practitioners to "technicians" rather than professionals, as it seeks to "teacher-proof" the profession with an emphasis on scientifically proven "best practices" purported to work in all contexts. (p. 95)

Teacher practitioners and researchers within the era of the educational research standardization both reported feeling marginalized, alienated, and powerless. According to Hurlburt and Knotts (2012), instead of alienating and marginalizing teacher educators, educational research should deal with "the lived experiences of practitioners" (p. 95). That is, teacher educators' personal narratives and experiences should be at the center of teacher inquiry. Furthermore, they embraced the idea of educational research as a "context-specific" process rather than one best "solution for all schools for all times" (Hulburt & Knotts, 2012, p. 100). Such research would be highly individualized, relevant, and most importantly, verified in the classroom environment and thus directly applicable to their daily teaching practice. This is because "the question of whether it works or not would then be tested in the classroom" (Hulburt & Knotts, 2012, p. 99). They refer to this very pragmatic approach to educational research as "an inquiry stance" (Hulburt & Knotts, 2012, p. 101). If these reconceptions of educational research are to be realized, they need to go along with creating "new cultures of evidence or inquiry in institutions" of higher education themselves "so that using evidence and assessment data become central to the way decisions about local policy and practice are made" (Beare, Marshall, Torgerson, Tracz, & Chiero, 2012, p. 160). In addition, educational research communities and governmental organizations, especially, have to broaden their perspectives about educational research agenda to acknowledge the interplay between research, policy, and practice. Biesta (2007) argued that "we must expand our views about the interrelations among research, policy, and practice to keep in view education as a thoroughly moral and political practice that requires continuous democratic contestation and deliberation" (p. 1). Thus, the reconceptualized research should undergo "a double transformation of both educational research and practice" in order to inform both policy and practice (p. 2); and it should, at the same time, move beyond the "what works" in education agenda (Kvernbekk, 2011) and "'the gold standard' of randomized controlled field trials" that "have become the preferred—if not prescribed—methodology for educational research" (Biesta, 2007, p. 3). Educational research must become less abstracted and more "real." That reality is how real teachers who are there to teach can teach real students who want to learn.

CONCLUSION

In this chapter, we argue that purely quantitative approaches to educational research are both unprofitable and disempowering to teachers. They are unprofitable because tens of millions of children across 50 states cannot be quantitatively lumped together in ways that will produce valid hypotheses or a grand theory about how U.S. children learn. No Child Left Behind has called not just for quantifiable results, but those based on experiments with control groups. Experimenting on large numbers of children is not feasible. Generalizing from small sets to the tens of millions of children in the United States will inevitably lead to error and misapplied results. Moreover, the process of quantification requires that multifaceted real-world events in the ordinary lives of schoolchildren would have to be operationalized and reduced to numericized results, eliminating the rich data that can only be captured by qualitative methods such as case studies and participant observation.

Clearly, a "top-down" quantitative approach, sanctioned by distant researchers without familiarity or a stake in the affairs of a given school, disempowers local teachers and teacher educators who seek to grasp the problems that are unique to their respective city, state, or school system. In this vein, teachers, who are the professionals closest to students, are marginalized or ignored when they raise reasonable objections or suggest amending the courses of action sought by distant policymakers. Moreover, we cannot ignore that business people, often with a stake in the financial outcome of a given course of action, whether that be educational software, an Internet platform, or hardware, regularly lobby politicians to implement "reforms" that will improve their own bottom line. They are assisted in this by well-meaning (and well-heeled) but misguided "reformers" who have become enchanted with the efficiencies and relentless improvements that market forces purportedly provide. It is seemingly unimportant to them that schools do not produce products—they produce students. These students are citizens who will one day take their place as stakeholders with a voice in the polity and economy of our nation. If we, by design, ignore their most salient characteristics, we do them a disservice and disempower them as well.

REFERENCES

Ball, D. L., & Forzani, F. M. (2007). What makes education research "educational?" *Educational Researcher, 36*(9), 529–540.

Beare, P., Marshall, J., Torgerson, C., Tracz, S., & Chiero, R. (2012). Toward a culture of evidence: Factors affecting survey assessment of teacher preparation. *Teacher Education Quarterly, 39*(1), 159–173.

Biesta, G. (2007). Why "what works" won't work: Evidence-based practice and the democratic deficit in educational research. *Educational Theory, 57*(1), 1–22.

Bridges, D. (1999). Educational research: Pursuit of truth or flight into fancy? *British Educational Research Journal, 25*(5), 597–616.

Callejo Pérez, D. M. (2008). Teacher education and research: Imagining teacher education between past and future. *American Educational History Journal, 35*(1), 19–40.

Capraro, R. M., & Thompson, B. (2008). The educational researcher defined: What will future researchers be trained to do? *The Journal of Educational Research, 101*(4), 247–253, 256.

Clandinin, D. J., & Connelly, F. M. (2000). *Narrative inquiry: Experience and story in qualitative research.* San Francisco, CA: Jossey-Bass.

Duke, N., & Mallate, M. (2011). *Literacy research methodologies* (2nd ed.). New York, NY: Guilford.

Duke, N. K., & Martin, N. M. (2011). 10 things every literacy educator should know about research. *The Reading Teacher, 65*(1), 9–22.

Feuer, M., J., Towne, L., & Shavelson, R. J. (2002). Scientific culture and educational research. *Educational Researcher, 31*(8), 4–14.

Freire, P. (1970/1998). *Pedagogy of the oppressed.* New York, NY: Herder and Herder.

Hargreaves, D. H. (1997). In defence of research for evidence-based teaching: A rejoinder to Martyn Hammersley. *British Educational Research Journal, 23*(4), 405–419.

Hargreaves, L., Cunningham, M., Everton, T., Hansen, A., Hopper, B., McIntyre, D., . . . Wilson, L. (2006). The status of teachers and the teaching profession: Views from inside and outside the profession: Interim findings from the Teacher Status Project. Research Report #755. *Department for Education and Skills.* Cambridge, UK: University of Cambridge. Retrieved from http://webarchive.nationalarchives.gov.uk/20130401151715/https://www.education.gov.uk/publications/eOrderingDownload/RR755.pdf

Horn, R. A., Jr. (2004). The new federal definition of educational research: Implications for educators. *The Teacher Educator, 39*(3), 196–211.

Hostetler, K. (2005). What is "good" education research? *Educational Researcher, 34*(6), 16-21.

Hulburt, K. J., & Knotts, M. (2012). Making the turn: Fostering an inquiry stance in teacher education. *English Teaching, 11*(2), 94–112.

Imig, D., & Imig, S. (2005, September/October). The learned report on teacher education. *Change, 37*(5), 58–62, 64–66.

Kincheloe, J. (2003). *Teachers as researchers: Qualitative inquiry as a path to empowerment* (2nd ed.). New York, NY: Palmer.

Knight, S. L., Lloyd, G. M., Arbaugh, F., Edmondson, J., Nolan, J., McDonald, S. P., & Whitney, A. E. (2012). Getting our own house in order: From brick makers to builders. *Journal of Teacher Education, 63*(1), 5–9.

Kvernbekk, T. (2011). The concept of evidence in evidence-based practice. *Educational Theory, 61*(5), 515–532.

Labaree, D. (1997). *How to succeed in school without really studying: The credentials race in American education.* New Haven, CT: Yale University Press.

Lincoln, Y. S., Lynham, S. A., & Guba, E. G. (2011). Paradigmatic controversies, contradictions,and emerging confluence, revisited. In N. K. Denzin & Y. S. Lincoln (Eds.), *The Sage handbook of qualitative research* (4th ed., pp. 97–129). Thousand Oaks, CA: Sage.

Mershon, S., & Schlossman, S. (2008). Education, science, and the politics of knowledge: The American Educational Research Association, 1915–1940. *American Journal of Education, 114*(3), 307–340.

National Council for Accreditation of Teacher Education (NCATE). (2010). *Transforming teacher education through clinical practice: A national strategy to prepare effective teachers. Report of the Blue Ribbon Panel on Clinical Preparation and Partnerships for Improved Student Learning.* Retrieved from http://www.ncate.org/Link-Click.aspx?fileticket=zzeiB1OoqPk%3D&tabid=715

Nuthall, G. (2004). Relating classroom teaching to student learning: A critical analysis of why research has failed to bridge the theory-practice gap. *Harvard Educational Review, 74*(3), 273–306.

Price-Dennis, D. (2010). Teacher research as a political act. *Childhood Education, 86*(4), 273–275.

Roblin, N. P., & Margalef, L. (2013). Learning from dilemmas: Teacher professional development through collaborative action and reflection. *Teachers and Teaching: Theory and Practice, 19*(1), 18–32. doi:10.1080/13540602.2013.744196

Scott, C. (2010). The status of education and its consequences for educational research: An anthropological exploration. *Australian Journal of Education, 54*(3), 325–340.

Shuell, T. (1986). Individual differences: Changing conceptions in research and practice. *American Journal of Education, 94*(3), 356–377.

Teacher Leadership Exploratory Consortium (TLEC). (2011). The standards. *Teacher Leader Model Standards.* Retrieved September 30, 2012, from http://www.teacherleaderstandards.org

U.S. Department of Education. (2001). *No Child Left Behind Act. Public Law print of PL 1 07-110 (Title IX, Sec. 9101, para 37).* Washington, DC: U.S. Department of Education. Retrieved from http://www2.ed.gov/policy/elsec/leg/esea02/pg107.html

CHAPTER 15

MOVING FORWARD

Coalescence of General Education, Special Education, and Teacher Education Programs Into Collaborative Partnerships in Education

Satasha Green, Cheryl A. Utley,
Florah Luseno, Festus E. Obiakor, and Alicja Rieger

Federal regulations, such as the Individuals with Disabilities Education Improvement Act (2004) and No Child Left Behind (2001) highlight the importance of teacher preparation programs. These programs are challenged to produce general and special education teachers who (a) know strategies for working collaboratively with their peers and families of students in designing and implementing strategies for student success; (b) reflect on their own feelings and biases concerning students with special and diverse learning needs and their families; (c) know how to treat each child with fairness and equality while striving to meet his/her needs; and (d) appreciate the cultural norms of the school and community and demonstrate respect for students with special and diverse learning needs and their families in the manner in which they communicate and behave (Harvey, Yssel, Bauserman, & Merbler, 2010; McLeskey & Billinsley, 2008). One of the issues teacher education programs currently face pertains to preparing and graduating enough general and special education teachers who have the necessary skills and

Critical Issues in Preparing Effective Early Childhood Special Education Teachers for the 21st Century Classroom: Interdisciplinary Perspectives, pages 191–206.
Copyright © 2016 by Information Age Publishing

knowledge needed in working with students with disabilities. This is especially critical in an environment where school districts, state and local educational agencies are held accountable for improving students' learning and developmental outcomes and their successful transition to postsecondary educational and workforce settings (Murnane & Steele, 2007; Spooner, Algozzine, Wood, & Hicks, 2010).

It is important to identify the variables that account for teacher shortages, especially if teacher preparation programs are to determine what they need to focus on in training highly qualified educators who are well prepared to work with all students. According to McLeskey and Billingsley (2008), lack of funding, poor administrative support, insufficient time needed for preparing are problems that impede quality teacher preparation. When these poorly prepared teachers go to public schools, they are faced with problems of outdated school buildings, lack of resources and technology needed for instructional purposes, poor support received from school administrators as they work with students with diverse learners with diverse cultural needs. In addition, they face high rates of discipline and behavioral problems and unsupportive parents. All of these problems culminate to problems of teacher's retention (National Comprehensive Center for Teacher Quality, 2008). Drame and Pugach (2010) also noted that the increase in the number of students identified as individuals with disabilities, combined with a reduction in the number of candidates graduating from special education teacher education programs, also accounted for the current personnel shortages school districts are experiencing. These shortages, thus, play a significant role in the increase of unqualified teachers school districts hire to work in their classrooms as they strive to meet regulations specified under P.L. 108-446 (Individuals with Disabilities Education Improvement Act – I.D.E.A 2004), and P.L. 107-110 (No Child Left Behind Act of 2001). Similarly, Sindelar, Brownell, and Billingsley (2010) indicated that variables such as age, race, gender, and personal factors influence teacher attrition, as younger teachers, compared to older teachers, leave the field of teaching. They also indicated that more White female teachers working in urban schools are more likely to leave their positions, as compared to African American or Hispanic teachers. Other personal factors such as retirement, family obligations, or work opportunities outside of teaching also play a role in teacher attrition.

Given these issues, the purpose of this chapter is to discuss the interplay between general education, special education, and teacher preparation programs in building collaborative partnerships in education.

CURRENT TRENDS IN THE PERSONNEL SUPPLY AND DEMAND FOR GENERAL AND SPECIAL EDUCATION

According to Boe (2006), ideally, a balance should be achieved between the demand for teachers (evident by the number of created teaching positions and their funding) and the supply of available teachers who are qualified and certified to teach. In reality, a chronic demand-supply imbalance has been extensively documented and reflects shortages in general education and special education teachers (Boe, 2006; McLeskey, Tyler, & Flippin, 2003). More specifically, using 15 years of the Data Analysis System of the Office of Special Education Programs (U.S. Department of Education for the years 1987/1988 through 2002/2003), Boe (2006) reported that "despite the steady growth in demand for highly qualified special education teachers the shortage of fully certified teachers for students aged 6–21 years by 2002/2003 was 13.4 %" (p. 144). This indicates that "the field of special education has been unable to keep up with the long-term increasing demand for fully certified teachers" (p. 144). The shortage of highly qualified special education teachers has been reported across all disability categories with the greatest shortages of teachers in urban and high-poverty school districts (McLeskey, Tyler, & Flippin, 2004). Similarly, a 10.5 % chronic shortage of fully certified general education teachers for K–12 students has been noted based on 1999/2000 SASS data (Boe & Cook, 2006).

Unfortunately, the most recent data provided by *Preparing and Credentialing the Nation's Teachers: The Secretary's Ninth Report on Teacher Quality* (U.S. Department of Education, 2013) indicated that teacher shortages did not dissipate in the 2009–2010 academic year; 49 states still reported special education as the most common shortage area. Such reporting is expected to continue since "employment of special education teachers is projected to grow 6 percent from 2012 to 2022, slower than the average for all occupations" (The United States Department of Labor, Bureau of Labor Statistics, 2012–2013, pp. 2014-2015).

The shortages of both qualified general education and special education teachers from culturally, linguistically, and racially diverse backgrounds have been even more severe (Rosenberg & Sindelar, 2005). Kozleski, Mainzer, Deshler, Coleman, and Rodriguez-Walling (2000) reported that only 14% of the teaching force in special education and 14% of those in the teacher education pipeline have been identified as coming from historically culturally and linguistically diverse (CLD) groups. Comparably in the context of general education, the most recent data from the National Center for Education Statistics indicate that "eighty-three percent of full-time teachers were White" while only "7 percent were Black, 7 percent were Hispanic, and 1 percent were Asian in 2007–08" (Aud et al., 2012, p. 50). It is noteworthy that teacher shortages in both general education and special education CLD teachers have been reported to be more prominent in poor urban schools and remote rural areas (Rosenberg & Sindelar, 2005). Clearly, this overwhelming nondiverse teaching force serves a student population that is becoming increasingly diverse:

> From fall 2000 through fall 2010, the number of White students enrolled in prekindergarten through 12th grade in U.S. public schools decreased from 28.9 million to 25.9 million, and their share of enrollment decreased from 61 to 52 percent. In contrast, Hispanic public school enrollment during this period increased from 7.7 to 11.4 million students, and the percentage of public school students who were Hispanic increased from 16 to 23 percent. (Aud et al., 2013, p. 52)

With chronic shortages in highly qualified as well as culturally, racially, and linguistically competent teachers in general education and special education, it may seem a perplexing task to engage in a scholarly dialogue about what teacher preparation might look like in the future. Yet this is a necessary undertaking! Research on student academic achievement and teacher effectiveness has suggested that teachers are one of the most important contributing factors in student learning and academic growth (Brownell, Sindelar, Kiely, & Danielson, 2010). When school districts hire teachers who are inadequately trained and who lack expertise, school districts only increase the number of ineffective and ill-prepared teachers and intensify teacher attrition (Berry, Petrin, Gravelle, & Farmer, 2011). The data on teacher qualifications reported by the *Status and Trends in the Education of Racial and Ethnic Groups* (NCES 2010-015) (Aud, Fox, & KewalRamani, 2010) revealed that

> Twelve percent of teachers whose main assignment was secondary mathematics had neither a major nor a certification in the subject. This percentage was higher than the percentage of English teachers or science teachers that had neither qualification (8 and 4 percent, respectively). For schools with at least half White enrollment, 8 percent of mathematics teachers had neither qualification, which was lower than the overall rate and the rate for schools with at least half Black enrollment (25 percent). (p. 49)

Reduced representation by teachers who come from CLD backgrounds in both general education and special education will only further contribute to the already existing overrepresentation and disproportionality among CLD, especially African American male students (Ford, 2012; Obiakor & Utley, 1997; Utley & Obiakor, 2001). Without proper exposure and training in multicultural issues and color blindness "teachers can and do make unwarranted referrals because they often lack behavior management skills in general and culturally responsive management skills in particular" (Ford, 2012, p. 402).

To produce an adequate supply of suitable and qualified teachers, the fields of general and special education should analyze more closely the teacher preparation program enrollment data and the pipelines to general and special education to better understand how to recruit more candidates into both general and special education programs, especially those who will contribute to a CLD teacher force. According to the most current available data from *Preparing and Credentialing the Nation's Teachers: The Secretary's Ninth Report on Teacher Quality* (U.S. Department of Education, 2013) out of a total of 728,310 students who were enrolled in teacher preparation programs in 2009–2010,

> Seventy-four percent of individuals enrolled in teacher preparation programs were female and 25 percent were male. Sixty-eight percent of individuals enrolled in teacher preparation programs in AY 2009–10 identified as white, 11 percent identified as Hispanic or Latino, and 9 percent identified as black or African American. (p. xiv)

These data suggest that many young individuals, especially males and CLD persons, still do not choose teaching as their career option. It is clear that teacher education programs in collaboration with federal and state legislatures should make among their future goals the promotion of better recruitment strategies that will make teaching as a career more appealing, especially to those persons who will increase cultural, racial, and linguistic diversity among teachers.

Ford (2012) noted that the 2004 report by the National Collaborative on Diversity in the Teaching Force can serve as a foundational resource and a good initial point for engaging in a dialogue about how to solve issues associated with teacher shortages. Some of the approaches recommended by this task force include appointing a teacher candidate to the position of the teacher of record after his/her initial 6 months of training. This will permit the teacher candidate to be employed while completing his/her teacher preparation program. Providing financial incentives in the forms of grants, scholarships, and loan forgiveness initiatives might make teacher training more affordable and attractive to students. Given that "approximately 20% of the current teacher work-force began their education in community colleges" (National Collaborative on Diversity in the Teaching Force, 2004, p. 7), engaging in community college outreach and precollegiate programs that would allow teacher candidates to pursue their associate degree and then bachelors degree may prove fruitful.

Rosenberg and Sindelar (2005) argued that the future goals for reducing teacher shortages should include alternative route programs. Some of these programs have been successful in recruiting prospective teachers, particularly in urban school districts with a high concentration of CLD teachers. Rosenberg and Sindelar suggested a review of Shen's (2000) study that reported that alternative programs have been shaped in ways that attracted more diverse pools of teacher candidates for teaching in schools with CLD students.

Unfortunately, no one seems to know how effective the alternative routes have been in reducing chronic teacher shortages. For instance, Darling-Hammond's (2000) national study of teacher standards reported that not only do "the students of these [alternatively certified] teachers learn less than those taught by traditionally prepared teachers" but

> evaluations of truncated alternative certification programs have found that about 60% of individuals who enter teaching through such programs leave the profession by their third year, as compared to about 30% of traditionally trained teachers and only about 10 to 15% of teachers prepared in extended, five-year teacher education programs. (p. 17)

Overall, however, the future of general and special education requires more systematic research into teacher effectiveness and what factors contribute to not only quality and quantity, but also contribute to the diversity of individuals pursuing general and special education careers.

EMBODIMENTS OF TRADITIONAL
TEACHER PREPARATION PROGRAMS

The No Child Left Behind Act (NCLB, 2001) has focused unprecedented national attention on the importance of ensuring adequate academic progress by all students. The NCLB Act explicitly recognizes that one of the key requirements for achieving this goal is that all teachers be adequately qualified. Title I of NCLB (Section 1112) requires each state to ensure "that low-income students and minority students are not taught at higher rates than other students by unqualified, out-of-field or inexperienced teachers." Darling-Hammond and Post (2000) noted that "the difference in teacher quality may represent the single most important school resource differential between minority and white children and that it explains at least as much of the variance in student achievement as socioeconomic status" (p. 128). Therefore, school reforms in teacher preparation must be aimed at improving teacher quality by raising standards for certification and licensure, accountability, student outcomes, and for the accreditation of teacher preparation programs to have improved practices for future teachers.

The National Council on Teacher Quality (2013) conducted a Teacher Prep Review on 1,130 institutions of higher education that prepare 99% of the nation's traditionally trained new teachers. The Review noted that the vast majority of teacher education programs—housed in universities and colleges across the United States—were not sufficiently preparing future teachers to manage their own classrooms. Programs that earned three- or four-star ratings required coursework and clinical practice to better prepare their teacher graduates to handle classroom responsibilities than they would have been without such preparation. Based on a four-star rating system, the Review reported the following findings: (a) Less than 10% of rated programs earned three stars or more. Only four programs, all secondary, earned four stars: Lipscomb and Vanderbilt, both in Tennessee; Ohio State University; and Furman University in South Carolina. Only one institution, Ohio State, earned more than three stars for both an elementary (3½ stars) and a secondary (4 stars) program; (b) Just over a quarter of programs restricted admissions to students in the top half of their class, compared with the highest-performing countries, which limit entry to the top third; (c) Fewer than one in nine elementary programs and just over one third of high school programs are preparing candidates in content at the level necessary to teach the new Common Core State Standards now being implemented in classrooms in 45 states and the District of Columbia; (d) Three out of four elementary teacher preparation programs still were not teaching the methods of reading instruction that could substantially lower the number of children who never become proficient readers, from 30% to under 10%; (e) Some 7% of programs ensured that their student teachers will have uniformly strong experiences, such as only allowing them to be placed in classrooms taught by teachers who are themselves effective, not just willing volunteers; and (f) Of the 59 rated special education programs, the undergraduate program at the University of Central Florida received a three-star rating in special education. In conclusion, the evaluators of teacher preparation programs noted that

> through an exhaustive and unprecedented examination of how these schools operate, the Review finds they [teacher preparation programs] have become an industry of mediocrity, churning out first-year teachers with classroom management skills and content knowledge inadequate to thrive in classrooms with ever-increasing ethnic and socioeconomic student diversity. (p. 1)

Critics of the teacher education reform movement have stated that efforts to improve the quality of teachers in high-poverty, low-performing schools have been largely uneven and unfocused (National Partnership for Teaching At-Risk Schools, 2005). Hollins (2010) noted that in many instances, new standards have been incorporated into preservice teacher preparation programs with few changes in course content and practices in field experiences. These new standards and the mandated conceptual framework for program design have not resulted in coherence, consistency, and continuity in program content and practices across courses and field experiences in teacher preparation programs. Similar criticisms continue to be charged of traditional urban teacher education programs because universities have not prepared highquality teachers for urban schools and continue to prepare teachers who have little desire to teach where they are most needed; and administrators from these urban school districts lament the quality of recruits that they hire (American Federation of Teachers, 2012). In other words, traditional teacher preparation programs have failed to produce the level of quality demanded by the urban educational environment (Koh, 2007; Neville, Sherman, & Cohen, 2005). Researchers such as Zeichner (2003) and Lankford, Loeb and Wyckoff (2002) noted that there is a substantial "cultural divide" between urban teachers and their students as a result of their disparate upbringings. Most of these traditional teacher preparation programs reflect demographics that reveal about 80% to 93% of teacher candidates, depending on the region of the country, identify as White middle-class females (Cochran-Smith, 2004; Leonard & Evans, 2008). Few teachers in urban schools have received adequate training by the time they enter the profession; they are often ill-prepared to cope with students from CLD backgrounds. These deficiencies make it difficult for teachers to teach effectively in urban or rural schools.

Conflicting evidence exists as to how effective teacher education programs have been in preparing future teachers for current demographic changes (Boyd, Grossman, Lankford, Loeb, & Wyckoff, 2006; Humphrey, Wechsler, & Hough, 2005). Researchers have documented that there is more variation within current traditional, university-based and alternative pathway programs (whether university based or not) than between them (Evans & Leonard, 2013). For many traditional, university-based programs, there are challenges, such as (a) difficulty in consistently attracting high academic achievers and CLD teacher candidates; (b) too few opportunities for prospective teachers to be taught by exemplary classroom teachers; (c) failure to target district needs in subjects such as math, science, and special education, as well as the need for English Language Learners (ELLs) teachers; (d) limited resources and structures to provide induction support for their graduates in a systematic way once they begin teaching; and (e) lack of accountability for the effectiveness of their graduates (National Commission on Teaching and America's Future, 2003). Traditional teacher education programs are designed to grant teacher licensure after completion of a bachelor's degree with a program of study in early childhood, elementary education, and so on. Traditional programs are rigorous and require completion of a major or minor in the content and anywhere from 200 to 800 student contact hours (e.g., practica and student teaching) at the undergraduate level, or 18 months to 2 years of intensive study at the graduate level with student teaching.

Rochkind, Ott, Immerwahr, Doble, and Johnson (2007) focused their attention on the challenges intertwined with alternate pathways to certification. These challenges include (a) an abbreviated curriculum that leaves too few opportunities to learn how to teach diverse learners; (b) insufficient clinical experiences prior to becoming the teacher of record; (c) too few opportunities to learn content and how to teach it simultaneously; and (d) an overemphasis on preparing teachers for a singular context (e.g., a particular district) or a limited, prescriptive curriculum. In essence, quality teacher preparation programs are not about place (university-based or alternative institutions) but about embodying the characteristics of effective teacher development (Berry et al., 2008). Furthermore, regardless of entry level, almost all traditional education programs require teacher candidates to pass *Praxis* examinations prior to admission to candidacy in a teacher education program. Darling-Hammond and Post (2000), along with a number of other researchers (e.g., Ingersoll, 1999), have argued that *Praxis* tests do not predict teacher effectiveness and are not valid measures of teacher preparation. What matters most is teacher expertise in his/her subject matter, in-depth knowledge about teaching and learning, and knowledge about strengths and capabilities of students.

MOVING FORWARD WITH INNOVATIVE TEACHER PREPARATION PROGRAMS

Colleges and Schools of Education must move forward to provide innovative teacher preparation programming and practices that would prepare their teacher candidates to effectively teach *all* students. There has been a notable shift in U.S. public schools demographics in the last decade—this has brought to the forefront the need for innovative education teacher preparation programs (Green, 2013). Research indicates the importance for preservice teachers to be prepared to deal with the increasing diverse population of students found in today's classrooms (Villegas & Lucas, 2002). Innovative teacher preparation programs that incorporate multicultural education are needed to insure that educators and service providers provide culturally relevant support systems so their CLD students can succeed academically (Green, 2010). In order to do so, teacher education faculty must begin to move away from the traditional Eurocentric model of teacher preparation and challenge and educate themselves on culturally responsive practices. It is absolutely necessary for them to convey to their preservice teachers the knowledge and skills needed to be successful when teaching in urban, suburban, and rural schools (Green, 2013). Teacher education faculty must begin to deconstruct their prior experiences from their own teacher preparation programs to impact how they prepare the next generation of teachers.

There are visible cultural divides between teachers in classrooms and the students they teach (Lankford et al., 2002; Zeichner, 2003). Overwhelmingly, teachers are White, middle class, and female (Cochran-Smith, 2004; Leonard & Evans, 2008), while public classrooms are made up of students from racially, ethnically, culturally, and linguistically diverse backgrounds representing various socioeconomic classes and ability levels (Green, Edwards, & Lynch, in press). Therefore, an examination is needed of the cultural divide between teachers and their students on three different levels: (a) preservice teachers and students in K–12 settings, (b) faculty and preservice teachers, and (c) faculty and students in K–12 settings. There must be continuous inquiry into how effectively we can prepare preservice teachers to successfully teach in urban 21st century classrooms when faculty themselves do not promote and utilize culturally responsive practices that recognize and support CLD students' unique learning needs. According to Fuller (1992), based on a study of 19 Mid-West Holmes Group teacher preparation programs, only 56% of these institutions required their elementary education students to take an urban education course. The study also revealed that multicultural content in most programs lacked continuity and was individual-professor dependent (Obiakor & Green, 2011). These trends in teacher education preparation found in Fuller's study in 1992 still apply to how preservice teachers are prepared today. Continuing "business as usual" in teacher preparation will only continue to widen the gap between teachers and the learners they teach (Sleeter, 2001).

To move forward with innovative models of teacher preparation, teacher education faculty must begin to understand that culture, language, attitudes, and belief systems are significant parts of educating the whole student (Wayman & Lynch, 1991). For these reasons, faculty must address cultural consciousness so that they can begin to reflect and assess their own values, biases, and stereotypes that they bring into teacher preparation (Obiakor & Green, 2011). Faculty in teacher education who acquire these attitudes and behaviors will allow themselves to move toward a culturally responsive instructional approach in their courses that meet the academic needs of *all* students. Subsequently, both faculty and preservice teachers alike will come to see multiculturalism and human diversity as assets to their knowledge and skillsets and learn to embrace differences among cultures and languages.

Teacher preparation programs must be restructured to equip preservice teachers for 21st century classrooms. Institutions of higher education must become innovative in how they deliver teacher preparation and most importantly what is delivered to preservice teachers in those programs. Approximately 50% of alternative programs are operated by colleges and universities, and they often closely resemble teacher preparation programs in terms of required professional coursework and in clinical experiences (Duncan, 2009a). Many teachers in alternative teacher preparation programs actually are less prepared than teachers who were trained in traditional models of teacher preparation and leave the field within 3 years (60%) compared to 30% of their peers (Darling-Hammond, 2000). Increasing the number of highly qualified educators while at the same time ensuring teachers are culturally competent requires innovative and new ways of recruiting, training, retaining, and supporting preservice teachers. The current models of teacher preparation traditionally focus on coursework provided by colleges and universities that are many times dictated by state and federal mandates as it relates to certification and licensure requirements as well as field and clinical experiences often over one semester (16 weeks) placing preservice teachers in K–12 urban classrooms. When we examine this traditional model of teacher preparation, at its center and core of programming are the university requirements (e.g., coursework), the university students (e.g., our preservice teachers), and other constituent groups (e.g., state education department; see Figure 15.1). This traditional model of teacher preparation does not take into account the unique needs of CLD

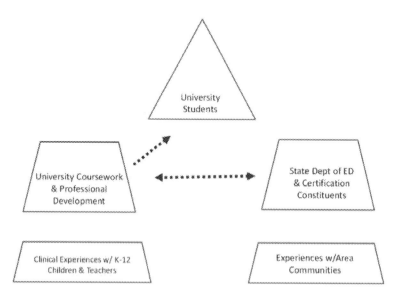

FIGURE 15.1. Traditional model of teacher preparation. This model presents how teacher preparation programs traditionally provide preparation of preservice teachers centered around the university, the university students, and other constituent groups (*Culturally Responsive Teaching in Higher Education*, Green, n.d.).

students in all settings. Preservice teachers need firsthand experiences in urban schools and an understanding of the communities from which their students come (William & Obiakor, 2009).

Innovative teacher preparation programs are evidence based, current, and consistent with 21st century learning that provides students with content mastery. Preservice teachers must experience rigorous and extensive clinical experiences and practices within their programs in local schools. These new teachers must be prepared for the realities of a new kind of classroom. Innovative teacher preparation programs must comprise good teaching, best practices, and multicultural education that focus on improving student learner outcomes. Innovative models of teacher preparation (see Figure 15.2) must provide preservice teachers with a variety of experiences in schools and opportunities to engage in the surrounding community to help develop a better understanding of their students' communities and life outside of the school building. Therefore, a collaborative model of teacher preparation is needed to ensure that preservice teachers are receiving relevant and rigorous clinical and field experiences that involve all stakeholders (e.g., university, K–12 schools, community, and parents). A collaborative model of teacher preparation requires that in its center of programming are its university

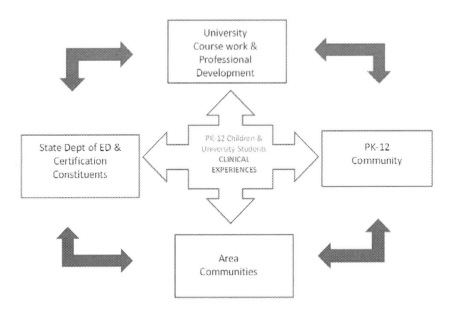

Figure 15.2. Collaborative teacher preparation. The collaborative model presents how teacher preparation programs should provide preparation of preservice teachers centered around the university students and K–12 students with collaboration and communication with all stakeholders. *(Culturally Responsive Teaching in Higher Education, Green, n.d.).*

students (preservice teachers), however, just as important and fundamental to the success of teacher preparation is our K–12 students. While these two groups are imperative in effective teacher training, universities, area constituent groups, and the local community must be engaged in the training of preservice teachers. Any true education transformation requires sustaining partnerships with Colleges and Schools of Education, the K–12 community, state education departments, our university students, and most importantly, our K–12 students.

CONCLUSION

In this chapter, we have discussed the interplay between general education, special education, and teacher preparation programs in the education of *all* students. We believe in innovative and futuristic teacher preparation that builds on collaboration and communication amongst all stakeholders; the goal is to equip preservice teachers for the realities of *all* students and classrooms. Collaborative models of teacher preparation operate outside of the traditional model and can help to produce highly qualified teachers in today's schools. In addition, teacher education programs must be evidence based in preparing teachers for 21st century classrooms (Duncan, 2009a). They must have a robust and extensive clinical component in schools that parallels the coursework being taught in the university courses to support them in classroom management and student learning outcomes (Duncan, 2009a). Clinical and field experiences must have the following principles embedded in all levels of the preparation

1. Weaving education theory and classroom practice tightly together in a year-long residency model of highly relevant teacher education.
2. Focusing on resident learning alongside an experienced, trained, and well-compensated mentor.
3. Preparing candidates in cohorts to cultivate a professional learning community, foster collaboration, and promote school change.
4. Building effective partnerships with community-based organizations.
5. Serving school districts by attending to both their teacher shortages, curricular goals, and instructional approaches.
6. Supporting residents for multiple years once they are hired as teachers of record.
7. Establishing incentives and supporting differentiated career goals to retain residents and reward accomplished and experienced teachers.

Finally, we are convinced that teacher preparation programs must innovate or they will perish. In order to transform teacher preparation programming, true culturally responsive and clinically based collaborative models must be instituted. If K–12 students remain at the core of teacher preparation programs, and if studies of academic content and pedagogy paired with significant rigorous and well-structured clinical experiences remain at the heart of preservice programs, then we owe it to our future generations to redesign and restructure how we do business in general education and special education.

REFERENCES

American Federation of Teachers Teacher Preparation Task Force. (2012). *Raising the bar: Aligning and elevating teacher preparation and the teaching profession.* Washington, DC: Author.

Aud, S., Fox, M., & KewalRamani, A. (2010, July). Status and trends in the education of racial and ethnic groups (NCES 2010-015). *National Center for Education Statistics.* Washington, DC: U.S. Government Printing Office. Retrieved from http://nces.ed.gov/pubs2010/2010015.pdf

Aud, S., Hussar, W., Johnson, F., Kena, G., Roth, E., Manning, E., Wang, X., & Zhang, J. (2012). The condition of education 2012 (NCES 2012-045). *National Center for Education Statistics.* Washington, DC: U.S. Government Printing Office. Retrieved from http://nces.ed.gov/pubs2012/2012045.pdf

Aud, S., Wilkinson-Flicker, S., Kristapovich, P., Rathbun, A., Wang, X., & Zhang, J. (2013). The condition of education 2013 (NCES 2013-037). *National Center for Education Statistics.* Washington, DC: U.S. Government Printing Office. Retrieved from http://nces.ed.gov/pubs2013/2013037.pdf

Berry, A. B., Montgomery, D., Curtis, R., Hernandez, M., Wurtzel, J., & Snyder, J. (2008). *Creating and sustaining urban teacher residencies: A new way to recruit, prepare, and retain effective teachers in high-needs districts.* Washington, DC: Aspen Institute.

Berry, A. B., Petrin, R. A., Gravelle, M. L., & Farmer, T. W. (2011). Issues in special education teacher recruitment, retention, and professional development: Considerations in supporting rural teachers. *Rural Special Education Quarterly, 30*(4), 3–11.

Boe, E. E. (2006). Long-term trends in the national demand, supply, and shortage of special education teachers. *The Journal of Special Education, 40*(3), 138–150.

Boe, E. E., & Cook, L. H. (2006). The chronic and increasing shortage of fully-certified teachers in special and general education. *Exceptional Children, 72*(4), 443–460.

Boyd, D., Grossman, P., Lankford, H., Loeb, S., & Wyckoff, J. (2006). How changes in entry requirements alter the teacher workforce and affect student achievement. *Education Finance and Policy, 1*(2), 176–216. Retrieved from http://cepa.stanford.edu/content/how-changes-entry-requirements-alter-teacher-workforce-and-affect-student-achievement

Brownell, M. T., Sindelar, P. T., Kiely, M. T., & Danielson, L. C. (2010). Special education teacher quality and preparation: Exposing foundations, constructing a new model. *Exceptional Children, 76*(3), 357–377.

Cochran-Smith, M. (2004). *Walking the road: Race, diversity, and social justice in teacher education.* New York, NY: Teacher College Press.

Darling-Hammond, L. (2000). Solving the dilemmas of teacher supply, demand, and standards: How we can ensure a competent, caring, and qualified teacher for every child. Evaluative report. *National Commission on Teaching & America's Future.* Retrieved from http://nctaf.org/wp-content/uploads/2012/01/supply-demand-standards.pdf

Darling-Hammond, L., & Post, L. (2000). Inequality in teaching and schooling: Supporting high-quality teaching and leadership in low-income schools. In R. D. Kahlenberg

(Ed.), *A Notion at risk: Preserving public education as an engine for social mobility* (pp. 128–167). Washington, DC: Century Foundation.

Drame, E., & Pugach, M. (2010). A HOUSSE built on quicksand? Exploring the teacher quality conundrum for secondary special education teachers. *Teacher Education and Special Education, 33*,(1), 55–69.

Duncan, A. (2009a, October 22). Teacher preparation: Reforming the uncertain profession. Remarks of Secretary Arne Duncan at Teachers College, Columbia University. *U.S. Department of Education.* Retrieved from http://www.ed.gov/news/speeches/teacher-preparation-reforming-uncertain-profession

Duncan, A. (2009b, June 14). *States will lead the way toward reform.* Retrieved from http://files.eric.ed.gov/fulltext/ED506068.pdf

Evans, B. R., & Leonard, J. (2013). Recruiting and retaining Black teachers to work in Urban Schools. *Sage, 3.* 1–12.

Ford, D. Y. (2012). Culturally different students in special education: Looking backward to move forward. *Exceptional Children, 78*(4), 391–405.

Fuller, M. L. (1992). Teacher education programs and increasing minority school populations: An educational mismatch? In C. A. Grant (Ed.), *Research and multicultural education: From the margins to the mainstream* (pp. 184–200). London, UK: Falmer.

Green, S. (n.d.). *Culturally responsive teaching in higher education.* Unpublished Article.

Green, S. L. (2010). Multicultural education: A necessary tool for general and special education. In F. E. Obiakor, J. P. Bakken, & A. F. Rotatori (Eds.), *Advances in special education: Current issues and trends in special education: Research, technology, and teacher preparation* (pp. 107–122). Bingley, UK: Emerald.

Green, S. L. (2013). What's so special about special education. In F. E. Obiakor, M. J. Mc-Collin, & R. Smith, R. (Eds.). *Special education practices: Voices of African American scholars, educators, and related professionals.* New York, NY: Nova Science.

Green, S. L., Edwards, K. M., & Lynch, D. (in press). *School diversity.* In S. McPherson & E. Blue (Eds.), *Students, environment, task and technology tools (SETT) for the digital learner.* New York, NY: Nova Science.

Harvey, M., Yssel, N., Bauserman, A., & Merbler, J. (2010). Preservice teacher preparation for inclusion: An exploration of higher education teacher-training institutions. *Remedial and Special Education, 31*(1), 24–33.

Hollins, E. R. (2010). The centrality of a theoretical perspective on learning to teach. In I. M. Saleh & M. S. Khine (Eds.), *In teaching* (pp. 1–12). New York, NY: Nova Science.

Humphrey, D.,Wechsler, M. E., & Hough, H. (2005). *Characteristics of effective alternative certification programs.* Menlo Park, CA: SRI International.

Individuals with Disabilities Education Improvement Act (IDEA) Amendments of 2004, P. L. 108-446. Individuals with Disabilities Education Improvement Act, 20, U.S.C §1400 et seq.

Ingersoll, R. M. (1999). The problem of underqualified teachers in American secondary schools. *Educational Researcher, 28*(2), 26–37.

Koh, M.-S. (2007). Practice teaching in urban schools: The effectiveness of special education preclinical experience in urban school settings. *The Scholarship of Teaching and Learning,1.* 4–10. Retrieved from http://commons.emich.edu/sotl/vol1/iss1/6

Kozleski, F., Mainzer, R. W., Deshler, D., Coleman, M. R., & Rodriguez-Walling, M. (2000). *Bright futures for exceptional learners: An agenda to achieve quality conditions for teaching and learning.* Arlington, VA: Council for Exceptional Children.

Lankford, H., Loeb, S., & Wyckoff, J. (2002). Teacher sorting and the plight of urban schools: A descriptive analysis. *Educational Evaluation and Policy Analysis, 24*(1), 73–62.

Leonard, J., & Evans, B. R. (2008). Math links: Building learning communities in urban settings. *Journal of Urban Mathematics Education, 1*(1), 60–83.

McLeskey, J., & Billingsley, B. (2008). How does the quality and stability of the teaching force influence the research to practice gap?: A perspective on the teacher shortage in special education. *Remedial and Special Education, 29*(5), 293–305.

McLeskey, J., Tyler, N., & Flippin, S. (2003). The supply of and demand for special education teachers: A review of research regarding the nature of the chronic shortage in special education. *Center on Personnel Studies in Special Education, University of Florida.* Retrieved from http://copsse.education.ufl.edu//docs/RS-1/1/RS-1.pdf

McLeskey, J., Tyler, N., & Flippin, S. (2004). The supply and demand for special education teachers: A review of research regarding the chronic shortage of special education teachers. *The Journal of Special Education, 38*(1), 5–21.

Murnane, R., & Steele, J. (2007). What is the problem: The challenge of providing effective teachers for all children. *The Future of Children, 17*(1), 15–43.

National Commission on Teaching and America's Future. (2003). *No dream denied.* Washington, DC: Author.

National Collaborative on Diversity in the Teaching Force (2004). *Assessment of diversity in America's teaching force.* Retrieved from http://www.ate1.org/pubs/uploads/diversityreport.pdf

National Comprehensive Center for Teacher Quality. (2008). *Lessons learned: New teachers talk about their jobs, challenges, and long-range plans.* Washington, DC: Author. Retrieved from http://www.publicagenda.org/files/lessons_learned_3.pdf

National Council on Teacher Quality. (2013). *Teacher prep review: A review of the nation's teacher preparation programs.* Washington, DC: Author.

National Partnership for Teaching At-Risk Schools. (2005). *Qualified teachers for at-risk schools.* Washington, DC: Author.

Neville, K. S., Sherman, R. H., & Cohen, C. E. (2005). *Preparing and training professionals: Comparing education to six other fields.* Washington, DC: The Finance Project. Retrieved from http://www.financeproject.org/Publications/preparingprofessionals.pdf

No Child Left Behind (NCLB) Act of 2001, Pub. L. No. 107-110, § 115. Stat. 1425 (2002).

Obiakor, F. E., & Green, S. L. (2011). Racial identity and teacher preparation: Impacts on teaching and learning of culturally and linguistically diverse urban students. *Myriad, 18*–22.

Obiakor, F. E., & Utley, C. A. (1997). Rethinking preservice preparation for teachers in the learning disabilities field: Workable multicultural strategies. *Learning Disabilities Research & Practice, 12*(2), 100–106.

Rochkind, J., Ott, A., Immerwahr, J. Doble, J. & Johnson, J. (2007). *Working without a net: How new teachers from three prominent alternate route programs describe their first year on the job. Lessons learned: New teachers talk about their jobs, challenges and long-range plans. Issue No. 2.* Washington, DC: National Comprehensive Center for Teaching Quality and Public Agenda.

Rosenberg, M. S., & Sindelar, P. T. (2005). The proliferation of alternative routes to certification in special education: A critical review of the literature. *The Journal of Special Education, 39*(2), 117–127.

22

Shen, J. (2003, April). *New teachers' certification status and attrition pattern: A survival analysis using R & R: 93197*. Paper presented at the annual meeting of the American Educational Research Association, Chicago, IL.

Sindelar, P., Brownell, M., & Billingsley, B. (2010). Special education teacher education research: Current status and future directions. *Teacher Education and Special Education. 33*(1), 8–24.

Sleeter, C. (2001). Preparing teachers for culturally diverse schools: Research and the overwhelming presence of whiteness. *Journal of Teacher Education, 55*(1), 25–38.

Shen, J. (2000). The impact of the alternative certification policy: Multiple perspectives. In D. J. McIntyre & D. M. Byrd (Eds.), *Research on effective models for teacher education: Association of teacher educators yearbook VIII* (pp. 235–247). Thousand Oaks, CA: Corwin Press.

Spooner, F., Algozzine, B., Wood, C., & Hicks, S. (2010). What we know and need to know about teacher education and special education. *Teacher Education and Special Education, 33*(1), 44–54.

U.S. Department of Education, Office of Postsecondary Education. (2013). *Preparing and credentialing the nation's teachers: The Secretary's ninth report on teacher quality.* Retrieved from https://title2.ed.gov/Public/TitleIIReport13.pdf

U.S. Department of Labor, Bureau of Labor Statistics. (2012). *Occupational Handbook, 2012–13.* Washington, DC: Author.

U.S. Department of Labor, Bureau of Labor Statistics. (2012–2013). *Occupational outlook handbook, 2012-13: Special education teachers.* Retrieved from http://www.bls.gov/ooh/education-training-and-library/special-education-teachers.htm

U.S. Department of Labor, Bureau of Labor Statistics. (2014). *Occupational Handbook, 2014–15.* Washington, DC: Author.

Utley, C. A., & Obiakor, F. E. (2001, March). Culturally responsive teacher preparation programming for the 21st century. In C. A. Utley & F. E. Obiakor (Eds.), *Special education, multicultural education, and school reform: Components of a quality education for students with mild disabilities* (pp. 188–207). Springfield, IL: Thomas.

Villegas, A. M., & Lucas, T. (2002). *Educating culturally responsive teachers: A coherent approach.* Albany: State University of New York Press.

Wayman, K. I. & Lynch, E. W. (1991). Home-based early childhood services: Cultural sensitivity in a family systems approach. *Topics in Early Childhood Special Education, 10*(4), 56–76.

Williams, G. L., & Obiakor, F. E. (2009). *The state of education of urban learners and possible solutions: The Milwaukee experience.* Dubuque, IA: Kendall Hunt.

Zeichner, K. M. (2003). The adequacies and inadequacies of three current strategies to recruit, prepare, and retain the best teachers for all students. *Teachers College Record, 105*(3), 490–519.